SACRED HABITAT

IBERIAN ENCOUNTER
AND EXCHANGE
475–1755 | Vol. 9

SERIES EDITORS
Erin Kathleen Rowe
Michael A. Ryan

The Pennsylvania State
University Press

ADVISORY BOARD
Paul H. Freedman
Richard Kagan
Marie Kelleher
Ricardo Padrón
Teofilo F. Ruiz
Marta V. Vicente

The Iberian Peninsula has historically been an area of the world that fostered encounters and exchanges among peoples from different societies. For centuries, Iberia acted as a nexus for the circulation of ideas, people, objects, and technology around the premodern western Mediterranean, Atlantic, and eventually the Pacific. Iberian Encounter and Exchange, 475–1755 combines a broad thematic scope with the territorial limits of the Iberian Peninsula and its global contacts. In doing so, works in this series juxtapose previously disparate areas of study and challenge scholars to rethink the role of encounter and exchange in the formation of the modern world.

OTHER TITLES IN THIS SERIES

Thomas W. Barton, Contested Treasure: Jews and Authority in the Crown of Aragon

Mercedes García-Arenal and Gerard Wiegers, eds., Polemical Encounters: Christians, Jews, and Muslims in Iberia and Beyond

Nicholas R. Jones, Staging Habla de Negros: Radical Performances of the African Diaspora in Early Modern Spain

Freddy Cristóbal Domínguez, Radicals in Exile: English Catholic Books During the Reign of Philip II

Lu Ann Homza, Village Infernos and Witches' Advocates: Witch-Hunting in Navarre, 1608–1614

Adam Franklin-Lyons, Shortage and Famine in the Late Medieval Crown of Aragon

Sarah Ifft Decker, The Fruit of Her Hands: Jewish and Christian Women's Work in Medieval Catalan Cities

Kyle C. Lincoln, A Constellation of Authority: Castilian Bishops and the Secular Church During the Reign of Alfonso VIII

SACRED HABITAT

NATURE AND CATHOLICISM IN THE
EARLY MODERN SPANISH ATLANTIC

RAN SEGEV

THE PENNSYLVANIA STATE UNIVERSITY PRESS
UNIVERSITY PARK, PENNSYLVANIA

Portions of chapter 4 were originally published in "Spatial Evidence in a New World: Fray Antonio Vázquez de Espinosa's Geography," in *Evidence in the Age of the New Sciences*, edited by James A. T. Lancaster and Richard Raiswell (Dordrecht: Springer, 2018), 209–27.

Library of Congress Cataloging-in-Publication Data

Names: Segev, Ran (Historian), author.
Title: Sacred habitat : nature and Catholicism in the early modern Spanish Atlantic / Ran Segev.
Other titles: Iberian encounter and exchange, 475–1755 ; v. 9.
Description: University Park, Pennsylvania : The Pennsylvania State University Press, [2023] | Series: Iberian encounter and exchange, 475–1755 ; vol. 9 | Includes bibliographical references and index.
Summary: "Investigates the links between religion, empire, and the study of nature across the Spanish world during a period of Iberian global expansion, showing how geographies, cosmographies, and natural history were used to advance multiple Catholic goals"— Provided by publisher.
Identifiers: LCCN 2023013035 | ISBN 9780271095349 (paperback)
Subjects: LCSH: Catholic Church—Spain—History—16th century. | Catholic Church—Spain—History—17th century. | Catholic Church—Latin America—History—16th century. | Catholic Church—Latin America—History—17th century. | Cosmography—History—16th century. | Cosmography—History—17th century. | Christianity and geography—Latin America—History—16th century. | Christianity and geography—Latin America—History—17th century. | Natural history—Religious aspects—Catholic Church—History—16th century. | Natural history—Religious aspects—Catholic Church—History—17th century. | Natural history—Latin America—History—16th century. | Natural history—Latin America—History—17th century.
Classification: LCC BX1584 .S44 2023 | DDC 282/.46—dc23/eng/20230503
LC record available at https://lccn.loc.gov/2023013035

Copyright © 2023 Ran Segev
All rights reserved
Printed in the United States of America
Published by The Pennsylvania State University Press,
University Park, PA 16802–1003

The Pennsylvania State University Press is a member of the Association of University Presses.

It is the policy of The Pennsylvania State University Press to use acid-free paper. Publications on uncoated stock satisfy the minimum requirements of American National Standard for Information Sciences—Permanence of Paper for Printed Library Material, ANSI Z39.48–1992.

To my parents, Boaz (z"l) and Yola
And to Sarah and our children, Hodaia, Aviad, and Alma

"The family is one of nature's masterpieces."
  —George Santayana

Contents

LIST OF ILLUSTRATIONS ix
PREFACE AND ACKNOWLEDGMENTS xi

1 The Ladder to God: Empire, Faith, and Knowledge in the Hispanic World 1

2 Finding God and His Church in the Fabric of Nature 27

3 Sor María's Cosmos 47

4 *Descripción* and the Art of Piety 79

5 The Origin of (American) Species 119

   Conclusion 159

NOTES 163
BIBLIOGRAPHY 183
INDEX 209

Illustrations

1. Frontispiece, Francisco Ximénez, *Quatro libros de la naturaleza*, 1615 3

2. Frontispiece, Juan de Plasencia, *Doctrina christiana en lengua española y tagala*, 1593 15

3. Solar eclipse. From Alejo Venegas, *Primera parte de las diferencias de libros que ay en el vniuerso*, 1569 18

4. The four elements and their qualities. From Ginés Rocamora y Torrano, *Sphera del universo*, 1599 33

5. Compass rose. From Rodrigo Zamorano, *Compendio del arte de navegar*, 1588 36

6. Alejo Fernández, *Virgin of the Seafarers*, ca. 1531–36 37

7. Representation of the Christian cosmos. From Martín Cortés, *Breue compendio de la sphera y de la arte de nauegar*, 1551 56

8. Twelve Franciscan "apostles" erect the sacred cross. From Diego Muñoz Camargo, *Historia de Tlaxcala* [*Descripción de la ciudad y provincia de Tlaxcala*], 1585 59

9. Classical natural philosopher measuring the earth. From Diego Valadés, *Rhetorica christiana*, 1579 63

10. Frontispiece, Abraham Ortelius, *Theatrum orbis terrarum*, 1570   65

11. "What is geography?" From translation of *Cosmography* by Petrus Apianus and Gemma Frisius, 1575   86

12. The union between compass and sword. From Bernardo de Vargas Machuca, *Milicia y descripción de las Indias*, 1599   88

13. One of the four maps in Ocaña's description of Chile. From Diego de Ocaña, *Relación del viaje de Fray Diego de Ocaña por el Nuevo Mundo*, 1599–1605   97

14. Llamas (or *vicuñas*). From Pedro de Cieza de León, *Parte primera dela chronica del Peru*, 1553   122

15. American bison. From Francisco López de Gómara, *Primera y segunda parte dela historia general de las Indias*, 1553   127

16. Lizard (iguana). From Gonzalo Fernández de Oviedo, *La historia general delas Indias*, 1535   129

17. Armadillo. From *Relación de las minas de Temazcaltepeque en Nueva España*, 1577   131

18. Thomas Aquinas. From Gregorio García, *Origen de los Indios de el Nuevo Mundo*, 1729   143

Preface and Acknowledgments

Writing in the sixteenth century, the Spanish humanist Alejo Venegas (ca. 1498–1562) recounted an illuminating tale about the hermit Saint Anthony the Abbot (251–356), who lived an ascetic life in the Egyptian desert. The story was frequently cited in Spanish texts of the time and tells of how, when the Christian monk was asked how he could live in the wilderness in solitude and without books, he explained that "the book of nature was his entire library."[1] As Venegas understood it, Saint Anthony's response captured how nature was believed to embody the true meaning of scriptural revelation, suggesting that humans could show no greater devotion to God than by carefully observing his works. Of course, Venegas's generation had a much different set of tools and concepts for observing and understanding nature from those available in Saint Anthony's time. His generation lived in a time of new scientific discoveries and colonial encounters in places around the earth where life had previously been unimaginable. Nonetheless, Venegas evoked the figure of the desert father, the patriarch of monks, linking Christian tradition to the art of observing the environment and thereby legitimating the study of nature. In doing so, he depicted the path that considers knowledge of nature to be in accord with tradition, and scientific investigation to be an expression of devotion. Those who adhered to such a course are the focus of this study, which attempts to excavate the cultural and intellectual conditions in imperial Spain that fostered such an intimate link between faith and the study of the earth.

In concentrating on a transformative era for both church history and Iberian global expansion, *Sacred Habitat* aims to analyze the religious significance given to the study of nature and to overturn long-standing biases in Spanish historiography that have led to separating science from religion and modernity from tradition. Weaving together historical narratives on the "discovery of America" with scholarship on the Catholic Reformation, Atlantic science, and environmental history, this study reevaluates the interrelated nature of Catholicism and the scholarly fields of geography, cosmography, and natural history, disciplines that gained prominence during a time of dramatic Iberian expansion. In an era of religious renewal, knowledge about nature allowed pious Catholics to reconnect with their religious traditions and apply their system of beliefs to foreign lands.

Every book reflects its author's time and place. My focus on the crystallization of early modern Catholic identities through the prism of the study of geography, fauna, and flora is no different. I have been continually fascinated by stories of how people are acclimatized to a new place. Arriving in Austin, Texas, from the holy city of Jerusalem prompted me to think of the early modern Catholic travelers who also migrated to a new world. Given the significance of space for theories of religion, I was particularly motivated to understand how, in the face of strange and foreign landscapes, religious writers found meaningful dwellings in their new environments. To be sure, there is excellent scholarship on the encounters between Europeans and native peoples (in America and elsewhere) and on how the latter were subjected to the European imagination. But what about the *spiritual conquest* of the land itself? How was the land incorporated into the Euro-Christian episteme?

Now, in hindsight, it is clear that my departure from *terra sancta* influenced my curiosity. In Jerusalem, where religious myths have long colored every square inch of land and stone, there might seem to be a less urgent need to sacralize space. For better and worse, it has been done quite thoroughly. As a famous Israeli song from the late 1980s bluntly puts it, "all the places are holy; chances to build a dream are slim." This was not the case for the religiously minded authors I have chosen to study, who found themselves in places where they could build dreams. These European believers were faced with the task of sacralizing new worlds in a Christian key. How did they go about this in the absence of a long-standing local Christian history? What tools did they employ to make foreign landscapes meaningful?

My previous studies in geography have helped me to be mindful of the propensity of scientific disciplines, now and in the past, to present themselves as arbiters of objective, ultimate truth. In the context of geography, this self-representation and its concomitant agenda have clear benefits for the creation of social knowledge, and specifically for the formation of collective identities. With this in mind, I began to discern the symbolic and spiritual aspects of making knowledge, rather than investigating its practical use. This perspective on early modern science soon led me to ecological thinking, specifically with regard to the fundamental relationship between Christianity and the environment. Whereas historians of the colonial period have shown how the empirical study of nature could bring food to the table, or promote a new medicine using unknown therapeutic plants and herbs, I was intrigued by the ways in which knowledge of nature came to sanction religious tradition. For example, while seventeenth-century natural historians in the Spanish colonies had obviously studied flora and fauna for pragmatic reasons, such as nutrition and medicine, some also engaged in discussions about the biblical flood and Noahide animals, which illustrate a very different motive behind the study of the natural environment, a motive that from our own modern standpoint appears far less practical. But this observation misses the point. In sacralizing space through the study of nature, early modern agents not only incorporated new territories into Christendom and made homes for themselves in new locations; they also safeguarded their religious tradition back home. This is an untold story of the Catholic Reformation, one that places at its center the interconnectedness of religion, empire, and the study of the earth.

Over the years that have passed since I began this project, and across the many places I have visited and called home, I have had the privilege of meeting and learning from a number of individuals without whom the research and writing of this book would never have been possible. I owe a profound debt of gratitude to Jorge Cañizares-Esguerra, who was my supervisor during graduate school at the University of Texas at Austin. Jorge supported me when this book was first conceived and has continued to be a source of regular help and encouragement. Mil gracias, Jorge, for your guidance, advice, and unfailing generosity throughout the years! I would also like to express my deepest thanks to María Portuondo, Neil Kamil, Virginia Garrard, Alison Frazier, and James Sidbury, who helped me develop ideas that would eventually find their way into this book. They were generous with their wisdom and insight, but also with their kindness and patience. I am also extremely thankful for the friendship of the brilliant and supportive individuals whom I met while in Austin, including María José Afandor-Llach, Benjamin Breen, Karin Sánchez Manríquez, Hadi Hosainy, and Lior Sternfeld. I would like to thank the UT History Department for its generous support, which allowed me to take the first steps in this journey.

This book would not have been possible without the help of the librarians and staff at the University of Texas at Austin, especially the Nettie Lee Benson Latin American Collection; the Memorial Library at the University of Wisconsin–Madison; the John Carter Brown Library at Brown University; the Huntington Library in San Marino, California; the Newberry Library in Chicago; Archivo Histórico Nacional in Madrid; the Biblioteca Nacional de España in Madrid; the Archivo General de Indias in Seville; the Beinecke Rare Book and Manuscript Library at Yale University; and the Max Planck Institute for the History of Science in Berlin. In particular, I would like to thank Melissa Grafe, librarian for medical history at Yale, for taking extra time to introduce a then novice graduate student to the many resources available in my field; and Neil Safier and the friendly staff at the JCB Library for all their assistance while I worked there. Ken Ward was especially helpful and guided me through the library's wonderful Latin American collection. During my residence at the John Carter Brown Library, I was also lucky to find myself surrounded by bright and enthusiastic people who were more than happy to share their wisdom and insights: Jason Dyck, César Manrique, Pepa Hernández, Daniel Webb, João Pedro Gomes, Arianne Urus, Amaruc Lucas Hernández, Miguel Martínez, and Ana Hontanilla made my stay enjoyable and intellectually rewarding.

During my research at the Huntington Library, I was fortunate to get to know Bob (may he rest in peace) and Bonnie Boyd, the kindest and most generous people one can meet so far away from home. Their openness and generosity touched me deeply and reminded me of the many profound ways in which we touch one another's lives. I would also like to thank Jürgen Renn and Matteo Valleriani for their hospitality during my stay at the Max Planck Institute for the History of Science in Berlin, and Esther Chen, the head of the library, for all her assistance. I am deeply indebted to Mario Berner, who saved my laptop, including all my files and resources, after a coffee-related accident on one of my clumsier mornings (herzlichen Dank an dich und die IT-Abteilung!).

I am indebted to all the friends and colleagues at Tel Aviv University who have been a tremendous source of encouragement and support: Yosef Schwartz, Rivka Feldhay, Aviad Kleinberg, José Brunner, Leo Corry, Naama Cohen-Hanegbi, Oded Rabinovitch, Ido Yavetz, Shlomo Dov Rosen, and Manar Makhoul. This project especially benefited from my participation in the Migrating Knowledge research group directed by Rivka Feldhay at the Minerva Humanities Center.

I'm extremely thankful to Tamar Herzog, John Tortorice, and Giuseppe Veltri for their crucial and generous support at various stages of my academic path. Special thanks go to Jan Szeminski, who was the first to introduce me to the colonial history of Spanish America. His passion for history and critical thinking has inspired me to revisit colonial history in my own critical terms. I would also like to recognize the invaluable assistance of the following friends and colleagues for kindly sharing thoughtful comments and suggestions at various stages of this project: Alvaro Llosa Sanz, Yoav Meyrav, Beatriz Carolina Peña, Matthew Cosby, Jessica Boon, Dani Schrire, Dana Loyd, Lior Flum, Paul Worden, Francisco Molinero Rodriguez, Jamie Cohen-Cole, James Lancaster, Richard Raiswell, Daniel Davies, and Florence Hsia. Daniel Hershenzon kindly introduced me to Erin Rowe and encouraged me to send my book manuscript to the Iberian Encounter and Exchange, 475–1755 series. Daniel was very generous with his advice and help. I am grateful to Penn State University Press for accepting my manuscript. I warmly wish to thank Erin Rowe and Michael Ryan, the series editors, for their enthusiastic support of this project and for contributing to its fruition. Penn State's acquisitions editor, Eleanor Goodman, has been exceptionally helpful during the production of the book and I am indebted to her and everyone at the Press for helping make this book possible. Finally, I would also like to thank Suzanne Wolk for her meticulous editorial work and the two anonymous reviewers for their insights and suggestions.

The following institutions provided research funding that allowed me to work in truly exceptional intellectual environments: the Huntington Library, the John Carter Brown Library, the Newberry Library, and the Max Planck Institute for the History of Science, Berlin. I am also grateful to the Cohn Institute for the History and Philosophy of Science and Ideas and to the Zvi Yavetz School of Historical Studies, both at Tel Aviv University, which generously supported me, and also to the Dan David Foundation for awarding me a prize for postdoctoral researchers in the history of science.

The book is dedicated to my family, whose enduring love and support have been the ground beneath my feet throughout the years. My parents, Boaz (z"l) and Yola, taught me the most valuable lessons in life and always stood by me. My sister, Osnat, has encouraged me to pursue my dreams ever since I was a child. My father, sister, and I shared a passion for literature and books, without which I would never have dreamed of setting off on the long and convoluted journey of writing my own book. My father was my earliest intellectual companion and biggest fan, and I wish that he had had a chance to read these lines; his absence fills these pages. This book would not have been possible without my wife and our children. Sarah read the manuscript numerous times, at different stages, and each time astounded me with her critical insights. More than this, Sarah always kept me grounded, helped me see the forest for the trees, and has been supportive in so many other ways. Time-consuming projects like writing a book take us away from our loved ones. Our children, Hodaia, Aviad, and Alma, without ever being conscious of it, motivated me to finish writing so that I could finally begin to compensate them for all the time we lost. They, and Sarah, are the light that fills my world.

Hamburg, 2022

I

THE LADDER TO GOD
Empire, Faith, and Knowledge in the Hispanic World

There isn't a ladder more appropriate and clearer for us mortals to climb and ascend in order to see God than through his works.
—Cardinal Roberto Bellarmino, *Escala espiritual*, 1619

Catholicism and New Worlds of Knowledge

The frontispiece of Francisco Ximénez's *Quatro libros de la naturaleza* (Mexico City, 1615) evokes the instructive relationship between scientific learning and church teachings during an era of colonial expansion and scientific growth (fig. 1). The frontispiece—the only image in this book—depicts a monk wearing a Dominican robe with a circular halo around his head, perhaps a depiction of Dominic de Guzmán, who founded the Order of Preachers in the thirteenth century, or, even more likely, of Saint Thomas Aquinas.[1] In his right hand, the saintly figure holds a quill, and in his left, a small church edifice on top of what appears to be a book. The quill and the placement of the church atop a book, rather than on the ground, point to the artist's understanding of the true foundations of the Roman Catholic Church. Wisdom and knowledge, symbolized by the book, were the groundwork that underpinned the church and gave it stability in the face of the significant turbulence of the preceding years. But Francisco Ximénez, a Dominican friar who worked at the Hospital de la Santa Cruz at Huaxtepec, did not write a religious or theological treatise. His *Quatro libros* instead described the flora, fauna, and minerals in Mexico, on the basis of the biological and pharmacological discoveries of Dr. Francisco Hernández (ca. 1515–1587), the Spanish court physician who conducted the first scientific expedition in the Americas. Instructed by King Philip II to gather information on the New World's medicinal plants and herbs,[2] Hernández returned to Spain after years of intensive research in Mexico (1571–77), having identified more than three thousand plants and hundreds of bird and animal species; he brought back with him many biological specimens and some two thousand paintings of the natural world in America.[3] Ximénez edited and published Hernández's writings, contributing information that Ximénez had personally gained while at the hospital at Huaxtepec, a place known for its tradition of Aztec herbal medicine.

The particular role played by the Dominicans and their academic mission is addressed below. For now, the illustration of a monk carrying a quill and a book at the beginning of a therapeutic survey of the New World's natural bounty provides a telling example of the mutual relationship between religion and scientific activities in the Spanish realms. Ximénez, like the figure in his book's illustration, participated in a multigenerational, uninterrupted process of amassing knowledge and broadcasting it—in this case, via the publication of biological findings in America. Knowledge in this sense was restricted neither to scripture and its commentaries nor to the words and deeds of the apostles, saints, and church doctors but included natural facts derived from observing "the book of nature." The expanding colonial frontiers offered new source material, which was avidly integrated into Hispanic religious outlooks. As the Dominican Gregorio García, whom we will meet again in chapter 5, put it, "Not everyone who goes to the West Indies goes in search of gold and silver; there are those who search for the treasure of science and the understanding of all that has been found in the New World."[4]

The sixteenth and seventeenth centuries saw rapid developments in science, characterized by the emergence of new disciplines and ways of knowing. It was during this era that scientific knowledge became increasingly based on mathematical and empirical methods rather than on ancient texts and learning. New instruments like the telescope and microscope allowed humans to stretch the boundaries of their perceptions of the world around them. New worlds opened up, new information was gathered, and natural philosophers, as the fledgling scientists called themselves, boasted that their

Fig. 1. Francisco Ximénez, *Quatro libros de la naturaleza y virtudes de las plantas y animales que estan receuidos en el uso de la medicina en la Nueva España* (Mexico City: Casa de la Viuda de Diego Lopez Davalos, 1615), frontispiece. Courtesy of the John Carter Brown Library, Brown University, Providence, RI.

generation had far outstripped the collective learning of esteemed ancient civilizations such as the Romans and Greeks.[5] Iberian geographical discoveries played no small part in the contemporary generation's perception of its own superiority in redefining the state of the art. Writing at the close of the seventeenth century, Juan Bautista Juanini, an Italian physician who resided in Spain, connected the discovery of new worlds to recent discoveries in medicine and the human body: "Just as this machine of the Great World . . . discovers new provinces and mighty rivers every day, so new parts and new humors and movements are discovered in man, who is a small and condensed world: Just as the ancients were ignorant of the New World of America and other lands and islands that have been discovered after their times, so too the Founders of Medicine did not achieve many things that have been discovered in the human body over the course of time."[6]

As this book shows, the expansion of scientific data, methods, and disciplines did not escape the attention of religiously minded writers who searched for confirmation of the truth of their church in the particularities of nature. Not all of them wrote in the language of "science" per se; instead, some writers incorporated new teachings into catechisms, orations, spiritual guides, and other kinds of religious texts. For Juan Rodríguez de León, a member of the cathedral chapter of Puebla, Mexico, for instance, the advancement of learning presented a genuine opportunity to spread faith across the Spanish Empire and beyond. In his *El predicador de las gentes* (1638), Juan Rodríguez contended that the ideal preacher was best served by a strong grasp of the scholarship of the day. He therefore divided the chapters of his book according to scientific disciplines, including astronomy, geography, cosmography, navigation, medicine, and surgery, providing definitions for each field along with its themes and topics. The pursuit of tradition vindicated new spheres of scholarship that were smoothly assimilated into Catholic doctrine and piety.

Confessing Science

Over the course of the second half of the twentieth century, a paradigm shift in the field of the history and philosophy of science placed greater emphasis on cultural and social elements in knowledge creation.[7] This revision has allowed for integrating new themes and previously excluded geographies into the narrative of modern science, especially by focusing on the local contexts in which the knowledge in question has been produced. As a result, the relationship between science and empire has become a prominent topic in scholarship, and studying this relationship has shed new light on the processes of both nation building and knowledge production.[8]

As part of this trend, historians have reevaluated the achievements of Iberian natural sciences after many years of neglect, noting in particular the decisive role of Atlantic (and, later, Pacific) maritime expansion.[9] By studying diverse scientific activities across Spain and its colonies, this historical school has focused on the ways in which royal bureaucratic institutions shaped innovative empirical practices on the eve of the Scientific Revolution.[10] As scholars have noted, in order to benefit from its new territorial possessions, the Spanish Crown established administrative institutions, such as the Casa de la Contratación in Seville (the House of Trade, established in 1503) and the Consejo de las Indias (the Council of the Indies, in 1524), which were responsible for overseeing Spain's colonial objectives in the Americas and the Philippines. For instance, cosmographers at the Casa—the royal institute that was responsible for the administration and regulation of the import of goods and peoples between the Indies and Spain—were responsible for developing techniques and technologies for sailing, for training pilots, and for the vast enterprise of collecting cosmographical information.[11] Such bureaucratic developments had tremendous repercussions for the process of gathering information over vast areas. New tools and methods for inspecting and verifying natural facts were devised by the Spanish administration, setting out the conditions for an unprecedented, large-scale scientific enterprise that cooperated with indigenous populations and with the many European officials, merchants, missionaries, emigrants, travelers, and experts on nature who traversed the unfamiliar territories. The global exchange of information and specimens and the very institutionalization of empirical observations would ultimately shape scientific practices in diverse scholarly fields, including natural history, medicine, geography, cartography, and navigation. The new science envisioned by Francis Bacon was thus preceded by legislation and regulations founded on Iberian experience from across the oceans.[12]

The effects of Habsburg imperial policies and mercantile global networks on the development of natural sciences are well known today, and it is accepted that cosmography, geography, and natural history played a vital role in the transformation of early modern societies because of their immediate application to pragmatic politics and commercial interests.[13] Nevertheless, less is known about the impact of Spain's empirical pursuits on the constitution of new Catholic knowledge. The present study seeks to address this lacuna and to explore how the proliferation of "raw" natural data, following

Spain's Atlantic expansion, interacted with yet another crucial dimension of Iberian society and culture: Catholicism.

Sacred Habitat examines the significance of the knowledge of nature for religion during a period of territorial expansion and religious renewal. It analyzes the ways in which new bodies of knowledge were imaginatively integrated into Catholic identities, contributing to the propagation of Catholic visions and expressions of faith. My larger objective is to consider how the flow of information from around the world affected religion, as Christianity redrew its borders both territorially and spiritually. The book therefore contributes both to the cultural history of knowledge and to the study of early modern religion by investigating the intersection between the two in the expanding Hispanic world.

To this end, I focus on fields that investigate the earth, including geography, cosmography, and natural history, which gained the utmost importance as Europeans navigated new oceans and lands. Studies by María Portuondo and Ricardo Padrón have already demonstrated how the disciplines of geography and cosmography had a profound influence on evolving Spanish perceptions of nation and empire.[14] *Sacred Habitat* offers a new perspective by examining the particular Catholic integration of new cosmographical information into a traditional theological framework. As earth sciences increased in their significance and utility in early modern society, religiously minded writers and reformers embraced new methods and data in order to connect nature to centuries-old church tradition. As we shall see, at a time when religious confessions competed over the meaning of God's word, observing nature opened new ways to conceptualize and transmit religious ideologies in the Hispanic world.

Spain's leading role in the European voyages of exploration and, in particular, the "discovery" of the New World in the Western Hemisphere holds an important place in this book. Scholars have studied European intellectual responses to "new worlds" through a variety of scientific questions, with an increasing awareness that the world outside Europe not only functioned as a source of data to be absorbed but also served as a site of knowledge, in which new epistemologies shaped a wide range of discourses and scholarships.[15] More recently, Peter Mancall has applied this framework to environmental history, arguing for a shift in ecological sensibilities in the Atlantic world over the course of the long sixteenth century.[16] I share Mancall's interest in the intersection of nature and culture. Yet, rather than point to a paradigmatic shift from a premodern, godly explanation for natural phenomena to a newer, "naturalistic" mode of reasoning, I am interested in continuities no less than in the changes that took place as Catholic writers grappled with an unknown ecology.

The religious view enshrined in Genesis 1 and held by most early modern Christians conceived the existence of the world only in relation to the creation of humankind. Accordingly, as a sacred habitat, the entire earth necessarily had to contain all the essential physical and spiritual arrangements to facilitate humanity's well-being. The European discovery of a fourth part of the world, unknown to ancient and church authorities, introduced Europeans to new flora, fauna, geographies, and anthropological facts that presented a series of challenges to naturalists, geographers, and theologians alike. Following the discovery of America, the Jesuit scholar Juan Eusebio Nieremberg (1595–1658) remarked that "nature has never been so clear as it is today," and his generation's exposure to nature's configurations, patterns, and diversity challenged older theories and understandings more than ever before.[17] This not only necessitated absorbing ecological findings in America into Christian consciousness but also involved the subordination of new scholarship and empirical findings in order to support religious claims.

As scholar of religion Guy Stroumsa has argued, early modern writers made a sustained effort to integrate the newly discovered civilizations into the model of *Heilsgeschichte* (history of salvation), which revealed the manifestation of the divine in human history.[18] *Geographia sacra* (sacred geography) was harnessed to a similar end, in order to incorporate the new hemisphere—not only its peoples but also its environment—into religious narratives. Although sacred geography usually refers to the study of the Holy Land, it has typically involved more than this and has employed biblical texts to connect the divine with world history and geography, including, for example, by trying to identify biblical sites (such as the Garden of Eden) on earth. In the absence of a prior tradition of *geographia sacra* in relation to the West Indies, Spanish writers turned to the study of nature to sacralize the new landscape and thereby contributed to how the West perceived and interpreted the natural world.

The arrival of the Catholic mission in the New World therefore represented a watershed not only in the history of the church but also in the development of global science. More than merely fulfilling their evangelizing duties, many missionaries cultivated an immeasurable interest in the study of native peoples and their environments and, in so doing, contributed to the spread of science. Thanks to their learning infrastructure, which included educational institutions, hospitals, and convent libraries, members of religious orders were indispensable in documenting and circulating new cosmographical, biological, and anthropological facts. For example, the Franciscan Colegio de Santa Cruz in Tlatelolco (founded in 1536) was an important center for the study of natural history and native customs. The friars at the *colegio* compiled *Libellus de Medicinalibus Indorum Herbis* (The book of medicinal herbs of the Indians) (Codex *Badianus*, 1552), the first codex of its kind, which documented the botanical knowledge and medicinal recipes of the Nahuas and described the therapeutic features of some 250 local plants.[19] From the literary production at Tlatelolco to the dissemination of materia medica and pharmaceutical knowledge, as seen in the story of the *antimalarial* "Jesuit's bark" (i.e., cinchona), missionaries' privileged position as intermediaries allowed them to collect precious information and specimens that were valuable to many research fields.[20]

Scholarly interest in Jesuit intellectual networks, in particular, has turned historians' attention to the intersection of the history of science with the history of Catholicism and colonization.[21] For instance, Andrés Prieto has shown how Catholic teachings on the teleologically ordered world provided the theological underpinnings of Jesuit descriptions of American nature.[22] Yet the importance of scientific knowledge for Jesuit spirituality was no anomaly. Rather, as we shall see, it reflected a wider tendency in the sixteenth-century Iberian religious landscape. In the context of "collective empiricism" in the Spanish Atlantic, members of the mendicant orders also played a critical role in producing and circulating reports on nature, as in the publication of *Quatro libros* by the Dominican Francisco Ximénez, discussed above.[23]

Far from being fundamentally at odds or in "conflict," as long worn out historiography once maintained, we shall see throughout this book that in the early modern period, Hispanic religion and science, broadly defined, were thought to be intimately related and complementary cultural spheres.[24] To be sure, there was a certain ambivalence within church tradition toward new data that was not originally inscribed in scripture, and the drive to know for the sake of knowing (*curiositas*) had a pejorative meaning. To mention one notable example, for Augustine of Hippo, *curiositas* represented the beginning of all sin with "lust of the eyes," which directs man to "empty longing" of the flesh. He famously included this drive in the catalogue of vices, linking it to the sin of pride and the Fall, an association that became conventional in medieval Christian thought.[25] Nonetheless, as historian Stephen Gaukroger reminds us, the emergence of modern science in Europe depended on "religion being in the driving seat." Gaukroger explains that the "legitimation and consolidation of the scientific enterprise in the early modern West derives not from any separation of religion and natural philosophy, but rather from the fact that natural philosophy could be accommodated to projects in natural theology."[26] The situation was no different in Spain, which had come "to identify its destiny with that of Catholicism" well before the Reformation era.[27]

Nonetheless, until relatively recently, and certainly in the popular imagination, the metanarrative of the history of science has portrayed Protestant Europe as the cornerstone of modernity and rationality, while Catholicism—as the simplistic representation of the Galileo affair once taught us—was seen as being bound by the chains of its traditions.[28] This negative perception was even more pervasive concerning Catholic Spain, where religion, until not long ago, was deemed responsible for policies of intolerance and inquisitional censorship. Contrary to this persistent myth, historian Henry Kamen has noted that, unlike the anxiety toward spiritual works, "scientific books written by Catholics tended to circulate freely. . . . The 1583 Quiroga Index had a negligible impact on the accessibility of scientific works, and Galileo was never put on the list of forbidden books. The most direct attacks mounted by the Inquisition were against selected works in the area of astrology and alchemy, sciences that were deemed to carry overtones of superstition."[29] Yet, despite the fact that modern historians have repeatedly pointed out that the Holy Office rarely censured scientific books or persecuted the supporters of new scientific ideas in the way that has often been presented, this perception of Hispanic religion and science still haunts us (at least outside of a cadre of specialists). The Black Legend that once marginalized Ibero-American sciences has also overshadowed our perceptions of the relationship between Iberian Catholicism and science, presenting the two as antipodes: tradition versus modernity.[30]

The Spanish Atlantic was not only a stage for the "early Scientific Revolution";[31] it was also a key site in the Catholic world during an era of momentous religious reforms. The renewal movement, which historians have dubbed the Catholic Reformation, aimed at strengthening the Roman Catholic Church, and belief among its members, against the backdrop of a confessionally divided Christendom. But instead of viewing the Catholic reforms merely as a reaction to the rise of Protestantism (they are thus also known as the Counter-Reformation), historians have come to understand that the church's renewal was the continuation of earlier reforming trends and aspirations. (Obviously, from the church's perspective, the spiritual and administrative renovations were not innovations but rather a return to the true spirit of the Gospel and the teachings of the primitive church.)[32] Adding to the well-known story of the initiation of doctrinal and liturgical reforms by the Council of Trent (1545–63), recent historiography has integrated local manifestations of Catholic practices and visions from around the world, suggesting that, in effect, "the New

World converted the Old."[33] Viewing the Catholic Reformation from this global perspective, Spain and its colonial legacy deserve special consideration.

During the breakdown of Western Christendom and the ensuing European wars of religion, Habsburg Spain emerged as the leading force of the Catholic world and played a critical role in refashioning Catholicism. In fact, Spain was quick to incorporate the decrees of the Council of Trent into state law, a deed carried out by King Philip II on July 12, 1564, soon after they were approved by the pope. Notwithstanding the different interests of the papacy and the Roman Catholic states, especially given the *patronato real*[34] of the Iberian kingdoms over New World possessions, the Spanish monarchy perceived itself as the guardian of Counter-Reformation orthodoxy at home and its exporter overseas. While other Catholic countries feverishly fought Lutheran and other forms of "heresy," imperial Spain placed itself on the front line of this battle in Europe and elsewhere in the world, willing to take on the political and financial burdens in order to secure what it perceived as the future of Christendom.

The religious climate of early sixteenth-century Spain and Spanish humanism both played a determining role in the genesis of Catholic renewal. Even before the unfolding sessions of the Council of Trent equipped the church with a clear vision and a defined body of doctrine that inspired the renewal process, major reforms were carried out in Spain under the leadership of Cardinal Francisco Jiménez de Cisneros (1436–1517).[35] As an influential participant in the fifteenth-century Observant movements, Cisneros's educational and institutional reforms, which aimed to return to a stricter and more pristine mode of Christian living, provided a model of action for the reformers at Trent, helping to make Spanish delegates at the Council influential during the sessions.[36] Furthermore, Iberian Catholicism inspired the establishment of new religious orders and renewal movements that gave rise to many of the defining characteristics of early modern Catholicism. As the birthplace of Ignacio de Loyola and the Jesuits and of Teresa de Ávila (1515–1582) and Juan de la Cruz (1542–1591) and their Discalced Carmelite reforms, Spain provided the foundations for a theological reorientation that "prized the cultivation of interior religious life."[37] This religious background was not without importance to the history of knowledge in the Spanish realms, especially given the wide participation of friars and overseas missionaries in emerging global intellectual networks.[38]

Nonetheless, with the exception of the Jesuit Order, this connection between observing nature and Iberian religious outlooks remains largely unexplored territory in Spanish and colonial Latin American historiographies, especially when compared to the far greater attention given to the topic among scholars of the early modern Protestant world. Early on, historiography on Protestant Europe recognized the place of religion in the foundation of modern science. Already in the 1930s, the sociologist Robert Merton pointed to the importance of English Puritans, famously arguing for an "intrinsic compatibility" between ascetic Protestantism and science (including what he referred to as "anti-traditionalism") that led to "the happy marriage of these two movements."[39] This perception of Protestants' prominent role in the rise of science continues, for instance, in Peter Harrison's influential thesis, according to which Protestant scriptural literalism paved the way for modern science by eliminating "endless" allegorical references and allowing for a new classification of the natural world.[40] With the current historiographical revision of the place of Spain in the constitution of empirical science, the need to rethink the perceived binaries between tradition and modernity becomes clearer. This book, I hope, contributes to a much-needed reappraisal of the relationships among Iberian Catholicism, imperialism, and early science.

In what follows, we will consider the theological postures in Iberian Catholicism that granted primacy to empirical evidence in constructing arguments for God's existence and divine attributes by focusing on how they deployed the metaphor of "the book of nature." The Iberian tradition of natural theology, from the Catalan Ramón (also Raimundo) Sabunde to later theologians such as the Dominican Luis de Granada, stimulated the exploration of the physical world as a gateway to God, in the process shaping a particular, *experiential* way of approaching nature that became fundamental to Catholic natural philosophy.[41]

God's Three Books

Others, in order to find God, will read a book. Well, as a matter of fact there is a certain great big book, the book of created nature. Look carefully at it top and bottom, observe it, read it. God did not make letters of ink for you to recognize him in; he set before your eyes all these things he has made. Why look for a louder voice? Heaven and earth cries out to you, "God made me."
—Augustine of Hippo, Sermon 68.6

Como el arca se invento para guardar en ella las cosas del cuerpo, así en el libro se conserva el tesoro del conocimiento que pertenece al entendimiento.
—Alejo Venegas

The sixteenth and seventeenth centuries witnessed a remarkable florescence of devotional, mystical, and ascetic literature in Spain, which was produced and disseminated under the watchful gaze of the church.[42] Ideas concerning the relationships between God and creation and between the church and humankind were formed and crystalized by engaging with and further developing earlier Catholic teachings. With its rich Sufi and Kabbalistic traditions, the Iberian Peninsula was a particularly fertile ground for the intriguing blend of mystical ideas that were to emerge. Iberian authors had encouraged religious enthusiasm, often emphasizing the personal religious quest and subjective interpretation rather than strict adherence to scholastic tradition.[43] Spanish authors like Miguel Godínez (1591–1644), a Jesuit missionary to New Spain, made repeated references to mystical thought as an alternative way of knowing, different from that of Scholasticism. Godínez distinguished between the scholastic theology that represented "perfection of understanding" and the "science" of mystical theology, which is the "perfection of will"; scholastic theology, he wrote, "removes ignorance and rectifies discourses in order to know the Divine truths; mystical theology [*mystica*] removes the defects, and rectifies affections to unite the soul with God by supernatural means."[44]

While Spanish mysticism is often associated with ascetic methods of introspection and detachment from the material world—Teresa de Ávila's *Las moradas del castillo interior* (*Interior Castle*) and Juan de la Cruz's *Subida al monte Carmelo* (*Ascent to Mount Carmel*) are among the finest examples of such literature—another aspect of the aspiration for union with the divine emphasized contemplating creation.[45] The connection between the rise of science and natural theology, the branch of theology that attempts to acquire knowledge about God and the divine from unrevealed sources (i.e., sources other than scripture and religious experience), has been explored extensively in relation to the Protestant world.[46] But similar attitudes had been pervasive in Iberian natural philosophy and throughout the Christian world as early as the High Middle Ages.[47] As we shall see, Spanish writers developed a natural theology that prioritized the observation of nature by elevating and redefining the significance of the book of nature (also known as the "book of creatures") for Christian faith and ethics. In so doing, they instructed believers to engage the natural world directly, bridging natural theology and contemporary empirical impulses. To be sure, in the fragmented Christian world after the Lutheran Reformation, all confessional sides saw nature as a reflection of God's divine attributes. Nevertheless, on the grounds of "scripture alone," Protestants rejected church tradition. Whereas all Christian denominations, Protestant included, deployed hermeneutical techniques to "read" the physical world,[48] the central concern for natural theologians in Counter-Reformation Spain was not merely to decipher the correspondences between scripture and the book of nature but to place the church at the heart of the study of nature. The discourse on the two "books" was extended to agree with another body of knowledge, or a "third book," that comprised the accumulated teachings of the church.

There were many interpretations of the metaphor "book of nature." Although authors offered different accounts of what could be inferred from the idea of reading the universe as a text, they all were based on the notion that God's omnipotent power manifested itself in two works, the book of nature and the book of revelation (scripture).[49] God's two books were considered historical creations (in the sense that they had been created in time) that contained valuable clues for interpreting the present state of the world and its future redemption. The two books were considered overlapping and harmonious, since they had originated from the same divine source. The metaphor entailed an additional meaning that merged natural philosophy with the tenets of Christian theology: one of divine and purposeful order.[50] Like a book that is essentially composed of smaller elements that correspond to one another—chapters, paragraphs, sentences, words—so the universe is composed of a startling variety of facets that come together in one intelligible, perfect work. This concept of an intelligible "cosmic text" was powerful in an age in which nature's students sought to describe the universe by revealing its laws through scientific observation.[51] In an oft-quoted passage, the Italian Dominican Thomas Campanella (1568–1639) argued that since there are no contradictions between the two books (i.e., creation and revelation), "anyone who forbids Christians to study philosophy and the sciences also forbids them to be Christians." Campanella avowed that "anyone who fears contradiction by the facts of nature is full of bad faith."[52]

The idea that the created world was *oratio*, or a speech, that confirmed scripture and Christian teachings dates back to the early writings of the church fathers—it can be found, for instance, in Paul's letter to the Romans (1:20) and in the statement by Augustine that opened this section—yet the metaphor of the "two books" by which God revealed himself to humanity matured during the late medieval and early modern period. Iberian authors like the Catalan theologian Ramón Sabunde (ca. 1385–1436), who taught at the University of Toulouse (and served as its rector from 1428 to 1435), were significant in this development. In his *Theologia naturalis*,[53] Sabunde argued that divine revelation manifested itself through scripture and "the book of creatures": "no creature exists, save as a certain letter written by the hand of God. And out of many creatures, as out of many letters, the first book is composed, which is called the book of creatures." For the Catalan writer, nature was not only a legitimate source of revelation but also offered certain advantages over scripture: it could not be falsified or misinterpreted. God's creations were diverse signifiers brought into existence so that humans, regardless of their origins or beliefs, could understand divine truths. The knowledge that can be inferred from nature was, Sabunde argued, accessible to all, clerics and laymen alike, and did not require an intermediary: "This science teaches every man to know.... This science does not rely on any authority, neither sacred Scripture nor any doctor. On the contrary, this science confirms sacred Scripture for us."[54] Sabunde's interpretation of the book of nature as an accessible source of knowledge reinforced the image of an immediate and nearby God. However, his suggestion, in the prologue to *Theologia naturalis*, that nature could be read without the supervision of clergy would later provoke serious questions about the ramifications of Sabunde's ideas for Catholic orthodoxy. In the suspicious climate of the post-Reformation era, Sabunde's *Theologia* was placed on the Index of Prohibited Books prepared by the Council of Trent in 1559, where it remained until 1564, when only the prologue was left on the Index.

Nonetheless, Sabunde's *Theologia* and his notion of the two overlapping "books" had a profound influence in the Spanish realms, especially among Franciscans who propagated the teaching of Bonaventure (ca. 1217–1274) that creation is a mirror of its creator.[55] Franciscans were vital to the dissemination of Sabunde's *Theologia* through intermediary translations and adaptations. Such works included a Latin version, published under the protection of the Franciscan Cardinal Jiménez de Cisneros in 1500 and translated into Castilian as *Violeta del anima* (Valladolid, 1549).[56] Sabunde's writings were published in another Spanish-language edition in 1616 by a friar of the Order of Minims, Antonio Ares, who emphasized the *Spanishness* of the Catalan writer, describing him as "one of the most distinguished theologians and pious worthy men to have flourished in these Catholic kingdoms of Spain."[57] The Franciscan reform movement contributed to the focus on nature in Iberian mystical texts and spiritual guides by further developing the idea that the physical world offered insights into the mind of God.[58]

The Franciscans' involvement in the Catholic mission of Habsburg Spain helped to spread these ideas from Iberia to the four corners of the world, merging evangelical and intellectual aims into an ideal that came to define the missionary enterprise of the time (fig. 2). For instance, the Peruvian-born Franciscan Luis Jerónimo de Oré (1554–1630), who later became the bishop of La Imperial in Chile, provided patriotic and religious motivations for the study of American nature. In his multilingual catechism *Símbolo católico*

Fig. 2. The frontispiece of the first catechism printed in the Philippines depicts a Dominican saint holding a plant in his right hand and holy scripture in his left. The plant and scripture, signifying nature and revelation, affirm the universal truth of the church, as its overseas missionaries were struggling to "save" the souls of indigenous peoples. From Juan de Plasencia, *Doctrina christiana en lengua española y tagala* (Manila: S. Gabriel, de la Orden de. S. Domingo, 1593). Courtesy of the Rosenwald Collection, Rare Book and Special Collections Division of the Library of Congress, Washington, DC.

indiano (Lima, 1598), Oré argued that the book of nature was written on no more than "four pages," each of which represented a different material category: the first comprised lifeless objects such as metals and minerals; the second, plants and vegetation; the third, animals; and the fourth, human beings.[59] Christianity's encounter with pagan rituals and beliefs in the New World influenced Oré's invocation of the book of nature. He reported that the Amerindians had developed naturalistic belief systems, sacralizing "the sun, the moon, the stars, the snowcapped mountains, the volcanoes and *guacas*,"[60] which they worshipped, but he emphasized that all of these objects were merely creations of God and reflected his omnipotent powers. Oré then applied his natural theology to the place of his birth, describing the realm of Peru in chapters VIII–IX of the book. While his descriptions were very limited and superficial, this early articulation of the two-books metaphor in the context of the "spiritual conquest" of America attested to the continued legacy of spiritual ideas from Iberia in the colonial reality across the Atlantic.

By the mid-sixteenth century, the notion that observing nature led to higher truths was shared by Iberian theologians of various religious backgrounds, who attempted to develop hermeneutic techniques to decipher entities and patterns in nature. The Spanish Dominican Luis de Granada (1504–1588), to mention only one famous example, asserted that by observing nature, the human being "is re-created, grown and set free from the prison of the flesh, returning to his origin and beginning."[61] Such a return to the "origin and beginning" through the disclosure of nature's secrets alluded to a symbolic Eden, where humanity could again possess Adam's knowledge and achieve intimacy with God.[62] Granada, one of the influential natural theologians in early modern Spain, developed in his writings methods of contemplative prayer that enjoyed significant recognition in the Hispanic world—despite the initial inclusion of his influential *Libro de oración y meditación* (The book of prayer and meditation, 1554), along with other mystical and spiritual treatises, in Valdéz's Index of Prohibited Books (1559).[63] In Granada's *Introducción del símbolo de la fe* (Introduction to the symbol of the faith, 1583), a summa of Christian theology that considers the tenets of the church in the light of reason, the presence of nature in everyday life facilitated a mystical encounter with God. Granada discussed the shape of the heavens, the earth, oceans, climatic phenomena such as rain and wind, and animal species, emphasizing the abiding interdependence of creatures in the chain of being. Granada's book of nature was not only open to scholars with capacities for critical textual learning but was offered to "the eyes of all nations of the world, Greeks as well as barbarians, the learned as well as the ignorant."[64]

The theological orientation toward the book of nature was important as well for the Society of Jesus, which came to play a leading role in natural sciences in Catholic countries very soon after its establishment in 1540. Following their founder Ignacio de Loyola's readiness to embrace secular knowledge "for the greater glory of God" (*ad majorem Dei gloriam*, as their motto declares), the Jesuits came to view the study of nature as part of their corporate spirituality, and they integrated natural philosophy into their curriculum in their many colleges throughout the world. The theologian Juan Eusebio Nieremberg exemplified this tendency, writing two natural histories—one in Latin, *Historia naturae* (1635), and another in Spanish, *Curiosa y oculta filosofía* (1643)—that are often understood through the lens of Jesuit spirituality.[65] Nieremberg suggested that nature was "a copy of God" (*Nos dio una copia suya en la naturaleza*) and proclaimed God's essence through "its ingenuity, its design, its framework, its order, its correspondences."[66]

Despite these trends, at a time when the Catholic Church strove to create conformity among its members by purifying worship and beliefs, any discourse on the book of nature had to be framed cautiously. Without clerical guidance on the proper techniques of interpretation, the idea that there are two sources of revelation could undermine the whole authority of knowledge as depicted by the church for more than a millennium. After all, the church defined itself according to an "unbroken historical tradition of teaching which [was] first enshrined in Scripture and its interpretation by the Fathers of the early Church and then in the doctrinal decisions ratified by the councils of the Church in the light of reference to the whole of the Tradition."[67] This ideal picture was certainly more wishful thinking than realistic representation. Nevertheless, in the wake of urgent calls for religious renovation, the Protestant Reformation being only one example, this historical tradition of the church was challenged more than ever before. Catholic writers faced the task of incorporating the two books into their lexicon without falling victim to a "Protestant reading" that would emphasize *only* nature or scripture while eschewing the tradition and the church's mediating function.

In this context, the work of the prominent humanist Alejo Venegas de Busto (ca. 1498–1562), *De las diferencias de libros que hay en el universo* (Of the different books existing in the universe, 1540), is particularly noteworthy for providing an intriguing perspective on the history of knowledge in Catholic Spain in the wake of the Reformation.[68] In this popular work, Venegas aimed to write about all the books of the universe, maintaining that there were three copies of the original, "uncreated book," including the books of nature and revelation. It seems that the church's distrust of a binary model of God's revelations provoked Venegas to describe no fewer than four divisions of "books," three of which—natural, revealed (sacred scripture), and rational—allowed humans to approach God.

For Venegas, a "book" was an "ark of deposit" (*arca de deposito*) that guarded "essential information." He explained that, like the biblical ark, which "was invented to save corporeal objects, so [too] the book saves the treasures of knowledge that [are] part of understanding." Venegas first distinguished between the *metagrapho*, or the "translations," and the original (*libro Archetypo* or *Increado*) that only God himself could read to the last letter and syllable.[69] Venegas continued by proposing a typology of three copies (scripture, nature, and "Reason") and drew a connection between all of God's books. Along with the book of scripture, Venegas's exaltation of the book of nature was unconditional. He examined various bodies of knowledge, including Aristotelian physics, the elements and the four qualities, Ptolemaic geography

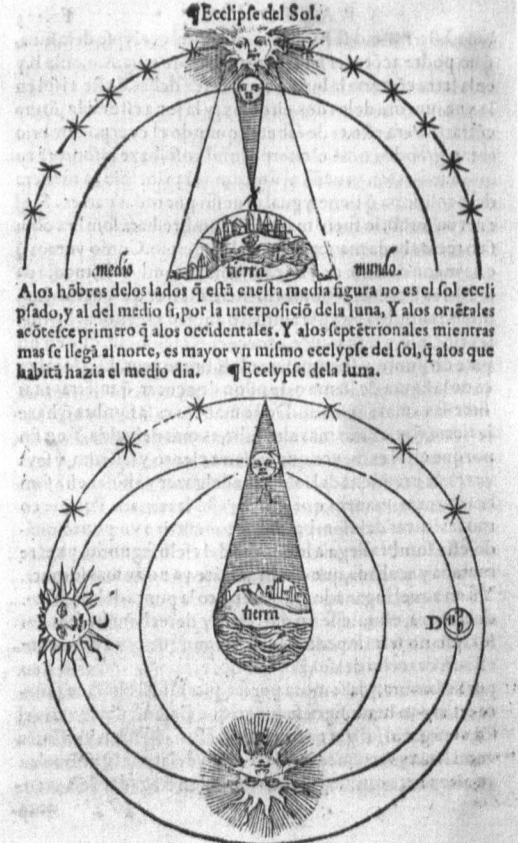

Fig. 3. Solar eclipse. From Alejo Venegas, *Primera parte de las diferencias de libros que ay en el vniuerso* (Madrid: Alonso Gomez Impressor de Corte, 1569), fol. 113v. Photo: Biblioteca Histórica de la Universidad Complutense de Madrid. BH FLL 8712.

(supplemented with a description of America), geological and climatic processes, and the celestial system, dedicating chapters to each topic, as contemporary cosmographical texts did (fig. 3). Like Sabunde before him, Venegas emphasized that "the university of created things" reflected God's divine attributes for the benefit of all of humanity: "la universidad de las criaturas es un libro tan común para todos." The book of nature, Venegas argued, had far greater importance than other writings: "the book written by the hands of God, exceeds those books that were written by the hands of men."[70]

Aware of the complications presented by the two-books metaphor (which lacked a mediator between the believer and God), Venegas offered a third book: the book of reason. In spite of what this name might suggest, by "book of reason" Venegas did not mean the human capacity to verify facts by applying logic or the capacity to deduce natural systems based on rational and analytic tools. Instead, the book of reason was nothing other than a guide for proper behavior and Christian living based on church teachings. Among its topics were the Trinity, the sacraments, saints, faith, and ethics. Venegas did not call it the book of the church or of tradition but adopted a rhetoric of rationality and enlightenment, subtly contesting the language used by Protestant reformers, who presented their movement as "the light dispelling intellectual ignorance."[71] Reason, Venegas claimed, was the mirror of the soul that discerned between good and bad. By applying reason, one comes "to the understanding of God through the understanding of one's own soul."[72] Venegas's tripartite division of interconnected books sidestepped the problematic dichotomy of two sources of knowledge (scripture and nature), establishing proper behavior and belief as a third and equally necessary path to divine revelation. This classification supported the church position that there were two legitimate and equal sources of revelation—scripture and tradition—without clearly establishing a hierarchy between the two.[73] The additional book of reason became a means of ensuring the application of Catholic "behavior and charity" to the study of nature. Natural and moral histories were inseparable, and Catholic decorum was placed at the forefront of natural studies.

The various and nuanced "instructions" for typological readings of the book of nature played an important role in establishing the significance of the study of nature in Catholic Spain. In the Spanish world, as elsewhere in Europe, the study of nature did not gain legitimacy because it was self-evidently convincing; rather, the importance of natural knowledge had first to be established within the parameters of ethics and theology.[74] Such attitudes provided scientific practice with spiritual directions and authority by elevating the observation of nature to a Christian duty. These ideas did not remain in theological classrooms in Iberia but had important ramifications for both lay and religious students of nature. The ladder to God by means of material and sensory perceptions paved the way for an empirical encounter with God's creation. The unintended consequence of this theological orientation took nature out of the shadow of revelation and placed observing it at the center of a new way of knowing.

Time, Space, and Methodology

The time frame of this book encompasses the colonial expansion of the Spanish monarchy during the sixteenth and seventeenth centuries, especially the decades from shortly before the Council of Trent to the close of the

Thirty Years' War (1648), which other historical accounts take as the core years of the Catholic Reformation. This time line allows me to juxtapose the apogee of geographical exploration under the Habsburg Crown with narratives on the so-called cultural field of the Counter-Reformation.[75] Historians of religion have studied this period by investigating the formation of distinct Catholic and Protestant confessions, paying attention to education, propaganda, and the monitoring of religious beliefs and practices.[76] To these narratives on confessionalization in Europe, this book adds a different viewpoint by examining how ecclesiastical naturalists and geographers incorporated natural data from new ecological environments into their spiritual lexicon and religious outlook. This perspective highlights the global nature of the Catholic Reformation by considering the ways in which evangelization outside Europe affected emerging Catholic awareness. I argue that the process by which new information from Spain's colonies was used to revalidate Catholic traditions and narratives shaped not only *criollo* self-consciousness and the religious life in the colonies (i.e., for missionaries themselves) but also, and critically, as we shall see in chapter 3, forms of religious consciousness that emerged in the Iberian Peninsula.[77]

The connection between Christian praxis and spirituality, on the one hand, and natural philosophy, on the other, obviously did not start in the post-Reformation period. Yet my point is not to engage in lengthy genealogies of the dialogue between religion and science. As historian Barbara Diefendorf observes, "The central preoccupation of the historian of religious practice is not to trace a characteristic form of spiritual expression back to its most distant theological and historical roots, but to explain why, among many possibilities, this particular set of ideas and behaviors came to the fore at a given time and space."[78] It is this approach that I adopt in the following pages, asking how, in a historical era that granted greater authority to empirical evidence, new modes of knowing were recruited to promote confessional ideologies and visions.

Since I aim to examine Hispanic religiosity during a peak moment of the imperial project, I have taken a rather broad geographical scope that covers both the Iberian Peninsula and the Americas, without limiting my focus to a particular territory or region. Nonetheless, I am informed by recent scholarship that has shown how European perceptions in a wide array of subjects, from nutrition and food to premodern anthropological thought, conditioned how New World knowledge was introduced into European consciousness, and how such perceptions played a vital role in colonial expansion as it underwent striking adaptations in local contexts.[79] This study explores the ways in which many groundbreaking ideas emerged and were expressed in the context of a new continent. I show, for instance, that long before Darwin revolutionized the study of biology, Spanish theologians presented remarkably modern ideas about biodiversity and variations in animal species that took into account the role of the environment in shaping life.

Sacred Habitat is based on a diverse selection of sources, including chronicles, descriptive geographies, navigation manuals and cosmographies, missionary reports, letters, and visual and cartographic imagery. I have also incorporated literary genres that are frequently ignored in the history of science, including a close examination of scholastic and devotional texts (especially in chapters 3 and 5) that were in conversation with "secular" scholarship. Historians have begun to address new agents and topics, and have gradually shifted their attention away from studying supposedly universal scientific methods and toward appreciating contingent and multiple approaches to the study of nature. This approach to science aims to analyze human engagement with nature in past societies, rather than merely pointing to major scientific breakthroughs.[80] Informed by this trend, the present study is predicated on the idea that religious sources contain vital information regarding conceptualizations of nature, and complete a larger puzzle that is crucial for understanding the knowledge that early modern societies possessed. Taking cues from the sociology of knowledge and the history of science, I have attempted to detect the multiple ways in which Catholic writers co-opted natural information and to investigate their motives. I have aimed to "situate" knowledge in these texts and to illustrate the ways in which they transmitted values, norms, and meanings that were targeted specifically to their religious communities.[81] Science in this sense was not merely a series of methods for gathering new facts but also a tool that provided a symbolic vocabulary, through which pious interlocutors could articulate and broadcast religious ideologies. The concept of "symbolic vocabulary" is drawn from anthropological research (namely, the ethnographic work of Victor Turner) and has guided my thoughts as I have attempted to grapple with the richness of "secular" writings among the Spanish clergy and monks of the period.[82] It provides coherence to the wide array of approaches by which the spectacles of nature nurtured the self-representation of religious writers.

Seen from this perspective, religion cannot be reduced to sacred beliefs and practices, institutions, or even a "single moral community," to use Durkheim's classic definition.[83] In his oft-cited *Map Is Not Territory*, scholar of religion Jonathan Z. Smith explains that "what we study when we study religion is one mode of constructing worlds of meaning, worlds within which men find themselves and in which they choose to dwell." The spatial trope is extremely significant for Smith, who understood religion as the quest, within the limits of historical experience, to "negotiate one's 'situation' so as to have 'space' in which to meaningfully dwell."[84] The power of religion to create a symbolic dwelling, a home for the believer, is the crux of *Sacred Habitat*. As presented in this book, religion is closer to an "orientation," which is how the historian of religion Charles H. Long has defined it. In Long's view, religion is an "orientation in the ultimate sense, that is, how one comes to terms with the ultimate significance of one's place in the world."[85] The significance of orientation is appropriate and revealing in the context of geography and cosmography, disciplines that aspired to provide *orientation* in a very concrete, tangible fashion. As we shall see, this analogy between the spiritual and earthly dimensions of *orientation* persisted in the writings of Catholic writers whose studies of nature took part in the process of mapping and creating a sacred dwelling and worlds of meanings.

Finally, it is important to clarify how I use the terms "science" and "knowledge," and how they differ from their use in early modern documents. For early modern Iberian writers, the term *ciencia* usually referred to knowledge of the material world and was defined and used according to an Aristotelian framework: "know the object through its cause."[86] Nonetheless, the study of nature in early modern Spain was influenced by widely disparate systems of thought, including Renaissance trends that promoted a new understanding of humans' engagement with the world. This included various Neoplatonic streams, such as Hermeticism and other occult philosophies, which shifted the focus of study to the hidden properties of nature.[87] When I write about "science" in the following pages, I refer to any systematic investigation, accumulation, or presentation of knowledge of nature that was based on observation and reflection. I use the term "information" to refer to data that was relatively "raw," and I use "knowledge" to denote that which was processed or systematically analyzed. By employing the label "empirical," I denote a variety of epistemological and methodological ideas that privileged experience and observation in creating knowledge. Of course, in early modernity there was neither a single philosophical tradition nor a set of thinkers who self-identified as "empiricists."[88]

Structure of the Book

At its core, this book identifies a post-Tridentine impulse to transmit a Catholic worldview and demonstrates how such propagandistic efforts informed writings on nature and geography. By focusing on a specific body of knowledge in each chapter—cosmography, descriptive geography (*descripción*), and zoological thinking—I show how confessional self-identification was reimagined and reconstructed by observing nature. Chapter 2 explores the projection of church doctrine and priorities onto the content and the iconography of mundane texts of cosmography, astronomy, and navigation. Following the Council of Trent, Catholic norms, values, and teachings were adopted in various cultural spheres, including literature and the arts. The chapter identifies religious themes that caught the attention of Spanish cosmographers, including discussions of church sacraments, Marian devotion, God's grace, and human free will. The focus on the religious reflections of lay savants rather than the theology of church theologians underscores the efficacy of earth literature for the propagation of faith.

Chapter 3 examines cosmographical knowledge in the Iberian Peninsula by focusing on a visionary nun, Sor María de Jesús de Ágreda, one of the celebrated advocates of the Immaculate Conception in the seventeenth century and a cloistered mystic, who famously claimed to have explored the universe through her spiritual journeys. Sor María's juvenile tract *Redondez de la tierra*, a devotional treatise on the shape of the cosmos, allows us to examine the cross-pollination between mysticism and cosmographical knowledge. The chapter begins with an analysis of the ways in which Sor María appropriated cosmographical information in order to promote Catholic ideologies. In particular, I place Sor María's method of mystical learning of the universe (what she describes as "infused science") in the context of Franciscan spirituality. The chapter continues by demonstrating how Sor María's claims to have traversed worlds were later recruited to promote Franciscan ambitions in the colonial frontier of New Mexico, emphasizing the role of cosmography as a language of communication that allowed a secluded nun to transmit a religious vision to overseas missionaries.

Chapters 4 and 5 examine the sacralization of foreign space by examining knowledge produced in Spanish America, specifically about the New World's geography (chapter 4) and the classification of animal species (chapter 5). The two chapters build upon the conceptual framework of the "invention of America," evoked by the Mexican historian Edmundo O'Gorman to describe the processes by which European assumptions and imagination came to *invent* America rather than discover it.[89] My analysis focuses on monastic writers and their particular use of the knowledge of nature as they incorporated the Western Hemisphere's unfamiliar ecological environment into recognized Catholic frameworks.

Chapter 4 analyzes geographical literature in the Spanish American colonies. Historical literature tends to present the development of geography in relation to the rise of the early modern state and European hegemonic power. The chapter adds nuance to this view by examining how religion came to shape the practice of geography, demonstrating the multiple ways in which geographical investigations supported religious ideologies. America was an unfamiliar space for Christianity, not yet sacralized by generations of Christian tradition. In a land without church history, descriptive geography became an effective tool for sacralizing a foreign land by evoking Catholic images of piety and devotion. In particular, chapter 4 introduces the reader to what I call "confessional geographers," friars affiliated with various religious orders who crafted detailed geographies of parts of America, including the Hieronymite Diego de Ocaña and the Carmelite Antonio Vázquez de Espinosa. While the friars' writings conformed to the geographical standards of their time, my analysis exposes the many religious and social sensibilities in local and global contexts, which shaped their geographic descriptions.

Chapter 5 examines the encounter of Catholic orthodoxy with new zoological information. The discovery of unknown animals troubled natural philosophers and biblical exegetes: were the native animals of America different from those in the known world? How was this possible? Catholic writers, in particular the theologians José de Acosta and Gregorio García, reckoned that in answering these questions they might aid in understanding how humans and animals were dispersed on the planet after they disembarked from Noah's ark. This chapter examines how a particular set of exegetical concerns resulted in groundbreaking ideas surrounding bio-distribution and the origin of species. Attempting to understand diversity in nature, Spanish theologians presented innovative theories on animal migration, extinction, and speciation though environmental adaptation. The chapter relates the writers' zoological thinking to broader congregational concerns, showing how zoological discoveries were employed to support theological hegemony within the church at a time when religious orders competed against one another.

Together, these four chapters show how observing nature became a cultural force that supported confessional objectives across the Spanish world. They point to a broader pattern in the intellectual life of the post-Reformation world: the appropriation of scholarly knowledge to the needs of faith. Cosmographical texts that propagated religious ideas, a cloistered nun's cosmographic visions, the writings of confessional geographers, and theological debates on biodiversity and the origin of life: all serve as case studies that demonstrate how scholarly writings and new scientific evidence were harnessed to support the transformation of Catholicism into a global religion. Placing religious texts in dialogue with ostensibly secular works reveals how imperialism and overseas evangelization affected Catholic identities in Spain and its colonies, a perspective that is critical to understanding both early modern imperialism and confessionalization. The so-called age of discovery was not merely a period of colonial expansion and the creation of new, secular ways of knowing but a time in which religious ideologies innovatively permeated and shaped new forms of scholarship. As we shall see, knowledge and faith were intrinsically bound together in a sacred habitat: the cult of the Virgin Mary and the saints, the sacraments, orthodox exegetical tradition, and the nature of political and ecclesiastical hierarchies were all woven into the very fabric of nature and could be revealed through the study of the earth.

2

FINDING GOD AND HIS CHURCH IN THE FABRIC OF NATURE

The sixteenth-century royal cosmographer of Spain, Pedro de Medina (1493–1567), was held in great esteem for his instructive textbooks on navigation and cosmography. His nautical works enjoyed a large readership, especially his *Arte de navegar* (1545), which was reprinted and translated into several European languages, including French, Italian, English, and Dutch. Medina was also an ordained priest and, in a very different kind of work, he considered the study of the earth from the perspective of his service for the Catholic Church.[1] This work, *Libro de la verdad* (1555), was widely read and was published thirteen times between 1563 and 1626. In it, Medina imagines a series of discussions between a young fictional heroine, Truth, and an affluent nobleman who is blessed with many material resources and intellectual gifts but who has forsaken God. The nobleman, captivated by the beauty of Truth, first believes that he is fortunate to possess the many honors and riches of the world. However, Truth teaches him that worldly pleasures are short-lived and shows him the way to salvation. The conversations between the two stretch over two hundred dialogues and are divided into three parts; they permitted Medina to comment on a wide variety of themes, including God's relationship to the world, the nature of humankind, the sacraments, the saints, death and the afterlife, and the experience of the soul. Most important, the conversations allowed the Spanish cosmographer to make the case for the compatibility of his scholarship with his religious beliefs, stressing, in the tradition of the church fathers, that the created world offers a path to God and divinity.

Truth asks man to "observe how admirable are God's works," including the heavens, the sun, the moon, and the stars, so that he "may come to know of the very high power and wisdom of God." "Look and consider," Truth tells the nobleman, "how all the land and water in the world is a round body, and the order and harmony within these elements." Through the character of Truth, Medina claims that God's harmonious order in the world—the diversity of animals, plants, trees, metals, and precious stones—grants humanity a greater understanding of God.[2]

Pedro de Medina's approach to the relationship between the realm of the divine and the realm of the natural world was rooted in the medieval scholastic doctrines of God's omnipresence and omnipotence.[3] This approach was promoted by Iberian natural theologians who emphasized the theological importance of nature. Similar perceptions were repeatedly expressed in scholarly writings, which also conveyed the idea that observing nature was the most profound and effective method at arriving at deeper spiritual conclusions. Indeed, such ideas were so widespread and so common in contemporary Spanish natural histories, cosmographies, and mathematical tracts that, seen together, they attest to the intimacy between faith and science in the period. Drawing on Amos Funkenstein's conceptual framework of "secular theology"—that is, how lay thinkers voiced theological ideas in seventeenth-century secular writings—this chapter highlights Catholic principles that were promulgated by Spanish writers.[4] The focus on the moral and theological reflections of lay savants, rather than on the theology of church thinkers, underscores the efficacy of the study of the earth for religious objectives.

The study of the earth's formation and arrangement was most typically (though not exclusively) conducted within the discipline of cosmography—the science that explained the earthly sphere and offered a representation of the universe. Cosmography, derived from the Greek word *kosmos*, meaning "ordered harmonious whole" or "universe," attempted to organize facts about the entire world.[5] New developments in cosmography began to emerge during the fifteenth century, as three classical literary traditions were woven together: Aristotelian natural philosophy, Ptolemaic geography, and natural histories that followed the works of Pomponio Mela and Pliny, which offered a model for incorporating earthly elements into the universal description.[6] Early modern cosmographers were more than theoreticians; as John Rennie Short reminds us, "they were also practitioners of earth measurement. Practical concerns with mapmaking, navigation, cartographic projection, and instrument-making and design were central elements in the whole project."[7] Their utility at a time of European expansion was indispensable.

As noted above, historians have drawn a connection between imperialism and cosmographical practices in Habsburg Spain, showing how scientific activity was marked by an ideological objective to build a universal Catholic monarchy.[8] In this context, cosmography emerged as a particularly sophisticated field in the Spanish realms. Because of their training and experience, Spanish cosmographers were well respected across national boundaries, and their writings were translated into every major European language.[9]

By identifying thematic fields and motifs that caught the attention of Spanish cosmographers, this chapter demonstrates how church doctrine and priorities were projected onto cosmological treatises. As religious renewal unfolded across Catholic countries, I claim that students of nature engaged with contested religious topics, often using their studies to propagate central doctrines of the Tridentine church. Catholic teachings thus found expression not only in theological treatises, sermons, and books of spiritual guidance but also in the content and iconography of secular texts on cosmography, astronomy, and navigation.

The significance of this phenomenon should be carefully placed in context. Rather than focus on the monolithic dogmatism that was often associated with Tridentine Catholicism, historians have instead, since the late twentieth century, reconceived the cultural dynamics of the era by employing "an alternative set of concepts" in which "education rather than repression" takes a central place.[10] The concern with strengthening the Catholic consciousness of believers during the Catholic Reformation manifested itself in diverse intellectual activities. The process of confessionalization involved an unprecedented deployment of "propaganda" in all print media and was undertaken by religious and secular authorities alike.[11] The arts also played a significant role in teaching and leading Catholics to live a life of faith and good works. Symbols of Catholicism were etched into the architecture of cathedrals and parochial churches, in the paintings that decorated palaces and city plazas, and in the engravings in pamphlets and other printed material.[12] As we shall see, cosmographers, too, discussed and reaffirmed Catholic tenets such as sacramental theology, the Eucharist and the conversion of substances, Marian devotion, and questions of predestination, divine election, and morality in politics. I claim that the interest in these topics was not coincidental. Instead, the sources reveal just as much about the culture of Counter-Reformation Spain as they do about the perceived configuration of the universe and the earth. Earth scholarship transmitted Tridentine views, playing a role in the renewal process that aimed to deepen piety.

While recognizing the blurry boundaries between religion and science in early modern Spain (as the involvement of Pedro de Medina in both worlds indicates), some readers might still ask why we should examine the works of lay writers in a study that otherwise deals with religious practitioners in science. The answer is simple: in order to show how the production of natural knowledge across imperial Spain was affected by and responded to larger Catholic debates and concerns, it is equally important to examine religious expressions in secular scholarship and place those expressions in conversation with works by religious authors. While tracing a line between certain theological ideas and their manifestation in nontheological treatises during a period of confessional disputes might seem superfluous, in that we should expect this from Catholic intellectuals, it remains vital to demonstrate this connection and not simply to assume it. As Henry Phillips has argued in the context of seventeenth-century France, "the safeguarding of the faith was not perceived only as the task of theologians. The new scientists were also conscious of the need to describe and explain their activity, not only in terms of its legitimacy in the study of the natural world, but of its importance in the space of religion itself."[13] Similarly, Ann Blair has argued that at the peak of the European wars of religion (ca. 1570–1630), religiously inspired writers developed natural philosophy according to the "divine light" of faith.[14] Applying this perspective to the field of cosmography in imperial Spain, this chapter presents the synergy between imperialism, Catholicism, and early modern science by considering the relevance of Catholic Reformation culture and thought for cosmography, arguably one of the most significant scholarly fields in the era of European expansion. The fact that Catholic teachings are apparent in cosmography alerts us to the propagandistic use of earth scholarship by religious actors in the subsequent chapters.

To be clear, the focus on representative Catholic expressions does not suggest that every cosmography printed in the period addressed matters of doctrine and piety, or that their religious content was always the same. This chapter plots common Catholic motifs found in a sample of works, often in passing, and explains the significance of the subject matter in historical context. To be sure, the brief theological commentary presented in cosmographies will not satisfy our curiosity as to their authors' positions regarding larger questions of politics and morality. Moreover, we will never know for certain whether cosmographers simply wrote as "Catholics" or whether they consciously used their writings to propagate church doctrine. But the question of intention is secondary to my objective here, which is to reconstruct the cultural imprint of an era. Studying those reflections in much the same way that recent historians have examined the Catholic Reformation's visual art, architecture, and material culture, we may gain a vantage point from which to detect the imprint of Catholicism on cosmographical culture in the Spanish world. Cosmographers safeguarded the Catholic faith by responding to, and incorporating, Catholic views into their writings, whether on the holy sacraments, Marian devotion, or morality. Emphasis on these specific topics reinforced Catholic conformity at a time when the church felt itself to be under attack.

Anthropocentrism, the Church, and Three Laws of Creation

In 1599, Ginés Rocamora y Torrano (1550–1612), *regidor* (town councilor) in his hometown of Murcia and an instructor of cosmography, published the cosmographical work *Esphera del universo*. The book included a Spanish edition of Johannes de Sacrobosco's (d. 1256) *De sphaera*, which was originally written in the first half of the thirteenth century and, through its many reprints and editions, became the standard cosmographical textbook of the era.[15] Grounded in Aristotelian natural philosophy and Ptolemaic cosmology, Rocamora y Torrano explored the division of celestial and elemental spheres, the climatic zones, geological processes, and navigation, and provided a short description of the four known continents. His *Esphera del universo* also stands out as a clear expression of Spanish religious culture. The book's first chapter begins with a tribute to the fields of mathematics and astrology, the study of which, the author believed, was a way to decipher the mysteries of the universe. Informed by sixteenth-century neo-Pythagorean currents, Rocamora y Torrano suggested that the secret to God's design could be found in numbers.[16] "Mathematics can provide us with an understanding of God through His causes," he wrote, advancing the idea that secular sciences offered insights into the mind of God and the act of creation.[17]

From the very beginning, it is clear that Rocamora y Torrano's *Esphera* is steeped in Catholic ideas and language. In the opening pages, Rocamora y Torrano unpacks the relationship between God's creation and the church by dwelling on the notion of Christian anthropocentrism. When God created "all the objects of the world," he wanted to sum up his work in a body that contained the essence of the other creations: vegetables, animals, and angels. Rocamora y Torrano then explains that the Holy Trinity "consulted" and "together created man" (*consultandolo las tres personas de la Santissima Trinidad, juntas todas hizieron al hombre*). This process of "consultation" reconciled Christian orthodox doctrine with the use of the plural in Genesis 1:26 ("And God said: Let us make man in *our* image, after *our* likeness"). The Christian concept of the Trinity—one God existing in three distinct persons (*hypostases*)—resolves the ambiguity and confusion caused by the biblical author when describing a monotheistic God in the plural. The anthropocentric idea that humans possess the essence of all creatures goes back to the early church, which appropriated Aristotle's division of the soul according to three functions: the vegetative soul (which allows life, including nourishment, growth, and reproduction), the sensitive soul (the power that allows sensation, perception, and movement), and the rational soul (specific to humans and responsible for reason, speech, and thinking).[18] Since human beings are composite beings who possess all three kinds of soul, they are at the top of the hierarchy (plants have only the lowest operations of the soul, i.e., the vegetative soul, and irrational animals possess both the vegetative and sensitive powers). "Only Man, not even angels," Rocamora y Torrano proclaims, could claim that he was created in the likeness of God, expressing the idea that the human tripartite soul has a trait of God by virtue of which it was created in his image (*solo el hombre, ni los Angeles, pudiessen dezir tener a Dios de su misma especie*).[19]

God thus created a composite perfect being (i.e., the human), but this creation was insufficient without God's church, which also played a key role in God's original design. Committed to the well-being of humanity, God subjected man not only to the laws of nature but also to the "laws of scripture and Grace."[20] In a sense, Rocamora y Torrano propagates here the edict of Trent's fourth session (1546), which confirmed unequivocally that both scripture and tradition were sources of faith. It stated that "[essential truths] are contained in the written books and unwritten traditions which have come down to us, having been received by the apostles from the mouth of Christ himself."[21] According to Rocamora y Torrano, there were three laws imposed on humanity: natural, scriptural, and that of grace. These three laws *together* guaranteed that man would "never degenerate nor deviate from his obligation."[22] Natural laws were incomplete without the Bible and the ecclesiastical behavior enshrined in church tradition. In the view of the Roman Catholic Church, these three laws were intrinsically linked. Interwoven in this manner, the study of nature came to the defense not only of sacred scripture but also of the church.

The taxonomy of three divine laws further echoes Alejo Venegas's trinity of books, discussed earlier. As we saw, Venegas proposed a typology of three "books," which were "translations" of the divine work: natural, revealed (sacred scripture), and rational (a guide to proper decorum and the way of Christian living). The tripartite division was an elegant way to sidestep the problematic

Fig. 4. The four elements and their qualities. From Ginés Rocamora y Torrano, *Sphera del universo* (Madrid: Iuan de Herrera, 1599), fol. 42r. Photo: Biblioteca Histórica de la Universidad Complutense de Madrid. BH FLL 27056.

dichotomy between the book of nature and scripture (two sources of divine revelation) by establishing the church as the vehicle for grace. In much the same way that Venegas's third book, the rational, provided a Catholic path to God, Rocamora y Torrano's "law of Grace" was placed at the doorstep of the church. In the post-Reformation world, where Protestants contended both that individual faith was sufficient for salvation and that *scripture alone* provided the foundation for faith, Rocamora y Torrano emphasized the necessity of the church and employed explanations garnered from the laws of nature to prove his point.

Visually, this relationship between natural studies and religion found expression in the following version of four elements and the four qualities (fig. 4).

According to Aristotelian physics, the sublunar region was composed of four elements: air, fire, earth, and water. The elements had natural qualities: air was hot and wet; fire, hot and dry; earth, cold and dry; water, cold and wet. On the surface, this was a typical diagram of Aristotle's elemental theory, depicting a square inscribed within another square, the corners of one being the classical elements and the corners of the other being the properties. Such geometric representations had decorated manuscripts since the early Middle Ages.[23] The diagram reproduced here features, at the very heart of the elemental system, the medieval Christogram IHS (with the three nails that symbolize the three monastic vows: obedience, chastity, poverty), itself a common, often Jesuit, signifier in the early modern era, plainly linking all changes in matter and qualities to the Christ monogram.

The symbolic meaning behind the diagram was not trivial. The nature of matter and its transformation were related to one of the more significant confessional disputes. As the scholar of visual culture David Morgan explains, religious images are fundamental to the "visual ordering and articulation of experience." They construct and maintain a sense of order by functioning as "a visual mediation of a particular group of humans and the forces that help to organize their world."[24] The particular imagery of the elemental system embodies a powerful belief that constructed Catholic time and space: the presence of Christ in his church. The transformation of form and matter stood at the heart of the question of what happened during the sacrament of the Eucharist, when the consecrated wine and bread are said to be transformed into the blood and body of Christ. This medieval mystery became a major point of contention between Catholics and Protestants. According to Catholic tradition, the central ritual of the Mass constituted a real, miraculous change in matter. This was quite different from the Protestant view of the sacrament, which saw in the ritual a symbolic union with Christ. In October 1551, the Council of Trent finalized decrees and canons on the doctrines of the real presence and transubstantiation, affirming the "real" corporal presence of Christ in the Eucharist. The Council explained that the Eucharist was "the holiest and most divine work that the Christian faithful" could carry out; the faithful received Christ "whole and entire."[25] Accordingly, there could be a miraculous change of substance without a change in the external appearance (of the bread or wine), an idea that became intrinsic to Catholic natural philosophy.[26]

In the context of a fundamentally different view of the essence of Catholic worship, then, the diagram in figure 4 stresses the mutable nature of matter and underlines the idea that *all* transformation in substance is dependent on God's will. The profane and the sacred joined together, providing a visual representation that gave coherence to Christian experience. The diagram visualizes the mysteries of faith and nature, their interconnectedness, and the fact that only when faith and nature are understood together can humanity understand the entire cosmos. The mutability in the elemental sphere was valid from a natural-philosophical perspective through the Aristotelian theory of matter, and it was also possible thanks to God's grace, in accord with the medieval scholastic theology that was later ratified by the church's councils. Conforming to Catholic doctrine, this diagram attributed a sense of order to reality and served as visual propaganda: Christ and his church were the basic building blocks of the earth.

Marian Devotion

As much as Christ was present in Spanish cosmographies, so too was Mary. A fully fledged partner in God's plan for salvation, Mary was portrayed as a merciful and forgiving mother who interceded between humans and God. Although Marian devotion was not new, the sixteenth century witnessed a resurgence in Marian piety that was manifest in prayer, Marian shrines and pilgrimages, feasts, and also in the visual arts, literature, and music. Moreover, the Council of Trent endorsed popular Marian devotion "against a background in which Reformation Christocentricity tended to downgrade Mary" and ratified the medieval veneration of the highest of the saints.[27] The veneration of Mary further intensified in the Spanish world after the victory over the Turks at the Battle of Lepanto in 1571, which Pope Pius V credited to the apparition of the Virgin Mary.[28] Popular devotion to the "Mother of God" was widespread overseas, as attested by the narrative surrounding the appearance of Mary before the peasant Juan Diego at Tepeyac near Mexico City in 1531, an apparition that came to signal for many believers God's protection of his expanding church.[29]

A representative example of Marian imagery can be found in the *Compendio del arte de navegar* (Compendium on the art of navigation), by Rodrigo Zamorano (1542–1620), a cosmographer of the Casa de la Contratación. This popular navigational manual was first published in Seville in 1581; it was reprinted five times over the next decade and translated into English by the mathematician Edward Wright in 1610.[30] Zamorano's *Compendio* includes diagrams and tables that aided practical mapmaking and navigation, and was considered one of the best handbooks of navigational techniques. Published sixteen years after the Battle of Lepanto, the 1588 edition contains a compass rose featuring the thirty-two winds and sixteen cardinal directions, with the Virgin Mary and Christ Child at its center (fig. 5).

Fig. 5. Compass rose. From Rodrigo Zamorano, *Compendio del arte de navegar* (Seville: Casa de Ioan de Leon, 1588), fol. 9v. Courtesy of the John Carter Brown Library, Brown University, Providence, RI.

Mary's place at the center of the compass rose reflected the widespread association of the Virgin with light and the sea. In the *Etymologies* by Isidore of Seville (ca. 560–636), Mary signified "inluminatrix, sive stella maris" (the one who illuminates or is the star of the sea).[31] By following Mary's guiding star, a striking symbol of voyage, the traveler reaches Christ and thereby salvation. Hymns for *stella maris* were an essential part of Hispanic medieval liturgy and religious poetry, which depicted the Virgin as a gateway to heaven: "The door of paradise, closed to all by Eve, is again opened by Mary."[32] Mary was understood as the patron of Spanish navigators and explorers, and countless ships crossing the oceans bore her name; she was believed to give ultimate protection to those aboard. As Amy G. Remensnyder has noted, this common appeal to Mary was incorporated into official imperial ideology, as shown in a portrait of the Virgin Mary housed at the chapel of the Casa de la Contratación in Seville. The painting, known as the *Virgin of the Seafarers*, was painted circa

Fig. 6. Alejo Fernández, *Virgin of the Seafarers*, ca. 1531–36. Oil on panel, 225 × 135 cm. Photo: Wikimedia Commons.

1531–36 by Alejo Fernández (fig. 6). It depicts a larger-than-life Mary, her arms outstretched above the Spanish royal family, various conquistadores and explorers, and natives, with ships on the ocean in the foreground. The altarpiece proudly announces Mary as the benevolent overseer of Spain's colonial project in the Indies. Its location at the headquarters of that enterprise further illustrates the Spanish claim to a Catholic empire across the sea.[33]

Returning to the compass rose in figure 5, while we cannot know for certain whether Zamorano himself was involved in the artistic choice of the imagery or whether its inclusion was the decision of the printer and publisher, the important fact is that the widely printed textbook expresses the church's fervent conviction of Mary's special place in the salvation of humanity. Like the diagram of the Aristotelian theory of matter (fig. 4), this image functioned as a visual mediation that provided a community with a sense of order by communicating the transcendent. Mary was not merely an emotional and metaphorical sanctuary but was pictured as a divine guide for those searching for their way in the world. In an instance of visual religious propaganda, Mary and Jesus are depicted as having symbolic control over the winds and, both theologically and nautically, point humanity in the right direction.

The Sacraments and Good Works

The presentation of the four elements in cosmographies was often used as a point of entry for religious instruction. Facing doubts regarding the necessity of the sacraments for salvation, Trent's reformers affirmed during the seventh session (1547) that all seven sacraments (i.e., baptism, confirmation, Eucharist or Holy Communion, penance or confession, extreme unction, holy orders, and matrimony) were vital for the Christian believer. In the Council's decrees and canons, "sacraments were not simply acts of worship, of honoring God, as evangelicals had defined them to be, but sites of access to God's grace."[34] Although all the sacraments were necessary for salvation, special weight was placed on baptism, which the Council defined as "the sacrament of faith, without which no man has ever been justified."[35] Appearing in 1566, Trent's catechism stated that unless they are "born again of water and the Holy Ghost," humans cannot enter the kingdom of God. It asserted that baptism "may be accurately and appropriately defined: 'The Sacrament of regeneration by water in the word.' By nature we are born from Adam, children of wrath; but by Baptism we are regenerated in Christ, children of mercy."[36]

References to baptism's special place could be found in cosmographic literature. Pedro de Syria's *Arte de la verdadera nauegacion* (Art of true navigation, 1602) was a practical nautical text that addressed such subjects as maritime charts, altitude measurements, and solar declinations. Syria's focus on the element of water served as a conduit to commentary on the sacrament of baptism. Water, Syria explained, was a "powerful element humid and cold" that also had spiritual importance. Like Rocamora y Torrano, Pedro de Syria had recourse to the biblical narrative of creation, in his case to explain water's special place in the formation of the world. He explained that according to scripture, water accumulated in the recesses of the earth and therefore could not "damage" the earth, and its collection in particular places allowed humankind to prosper: "Water does not cover the entire earth, as

God arranged at the beginning of the world, as the first chapter of Genesis concludes; commanding the waters to gather in order that men could inhabit the earth, and the earth could grow trees and plants. And as God arranges all things gently, He ordered that the earth would have cavities where the waters could naturally pool and could be there without force or any violence."[37]

Syria drew a spiritual connection between the law that God imposed on water and the ecclesiastical law imposed on humans. He concluded that "water is the medium of our spiritual life; God wanted our regeneration and baptism [to] be through the medium of water." He exploited this idea by referring to the power of the oceans, where God created salty water in order to protect and "preserve such an infinity of fish."[38] This passage demonstrates the "naturalization" of church law (sacrament) by the laws of nature (the forces of water). Syria employed explanations from the first law of nature according to scripture (the gathering of water in one place) in order to explain the spiritual force of regeneration behind the church's sacramental theology.

Some cosmographies also included sections on imaginary or symbolic space along with their geographical surveys of the terrestrial globe. A work called *Imagen del mundo* (1626), by the Spanish explorer Lorenzo Ferrer Maldonado (d. 1625), aimed to study all the components of the universe, "from the Empyrean Heaven to the center of the Earth."[39] Ferrer Maldonado, famously known for claiming to have traversed the mythical Strait of Anián, covered wide-ranging themes in his cosmography, including geography, astronomy, navigation, and hydrology.[40] However, he aimed to understand more than the visible realm and explored the place of both heaven and hell in his discussion of the element earth. Heaven, he claimed, was "the terrestrial paradise . . . a place, orchard, or a garden that God planted on earth at the beginning of the world." He evoked the biblical story of Eden and described the diversity of its trees, among them the Tree of Life and the Tree of Knowledge, which gave humankind the capacity to distinguish between good and evil. Ferrer Maldonado claimed that hell, by contrast, was "the place of the condemned; those who transgressed the precepts of the law of God" (*el infierno es el lugar de los condenados; los quales por aver traspassado los preceptos de la ley de Dios*). It was "the farthest place possible (among all that God created) from the Empyrean heavens."[41]

The notion that hell was a real, physical place situated at the center of the earth was important to the church's vision of the cosmos. The exact location of hell was never regarded as a tenet of Christian faith, however; most believers agreed that inside the earth there was a hot region where the souls of sinners were punished.[42] Such views shaped cosmographers' depiction of the world. For instance, Pedro de Medina stated that "Hell is at the deepest part and center of the Earth, which is the most remote and far place from heaven where, naturally, there is the most fierce and intolerable cold, and the deepest obscurity in all of the world, because rays of the Sun, moon, or the stars cannot penetrate there."[43] It was not uncommon to identify hellfire with the subterranean fire that was observed during volcanic eruptions (volcanoes were depicted as the mouth of hell). Such views were quite different from Aristotelian physics, which saw the element earth as cold and dry.[44]

Regardless of the coexistence of two very distinct views about the earth's interior, seventeenth-century church authorities were inclined to accept the idea that hell was located at the center of the earth. Cardinal Roberto Bellarmino (1542–1621), one of most important theologians of the Counter-Reformation church, for instance, explained that "the place of devils and wicked damned men should be as far as possible from the place where angels and blessed men will be forever. . . . The abode of the blessed (as our adversaries agree) is heaven, and no place is further removed from heaven than the center of the earth."[45] Francesco Ingoli, the influential secretary of Propaganda Fide (see chap. 4), objected to Galileo's heliocentric ideas for precisely this reason.[46] The question of the physical location of hell (and heaven) would continue to intrigue later Catholic writers. In the mid-seventeenth century, for example, the Franciscan Francisco Resta defended the view that volcanic fire during eruptions was the fire of hell.[47] Accepting the notion that hell was a distinct subterranean place, Ferrer Maldonado held that any legitimate model of the universe had to uphold the Catholic belief that heaven and hell existed on diametrically opposed sides of the universe.

Ferrer Maldonado's inclusion of heaven and hell in his cosmography allowed him to engage in a central theological dispute. For him, hell was where God sent those who transgressed his law (punishing deeds, and not executing an act of divine election). The Tree of Knowledge made possible humanity's ability to understand God's directions and choose to follow them or not. Thus Ferrer Maldonado's references to the biblical Eden, the Tree of Knowledge, and man's choice to follow (or disobey) the word of God in effect reinforced the church's persistent position on human free will. By stressing humanity's ability to distinguish between good and evil, Ferrer Maldonado sought to confirm the Catholic position on divine election. The emphasis on free will reflected uneasiness with the Calvinist notion of predestination and the relationship between grace and free will. Ferrer Maldonado's Catholic definition of the "condemned"—those who transgressed God's precepts—left little room for doubt. According to the Spanish cosmographer, God did not predetermine who would be saved and who would be damned (in opposition to Calvin's doctrine of double election). Additionally, God's grace was dependent on the good works of individuals who did not transgress the laws of God, an opinion that conflicted with the Protestant ideal of election by faith alone.

To be sure, both Protestants and Catholics believed that salvation came by faith. The Council of Trent clarified the Catholic position, asserting that faith should be seen as "the beginning of human salvation, the foundation and root of all justification without which it is impossible to please God."[48] In contrast, following Luther, Protestants championed the doctrine of *sola fide* (faith alone) as their soteriological principle. For Luther, as Robert Kolb explains, "reliance on works, including the ceremonial works of ritualistic religion, has no place in the Christian's life; those ceremonies serve to teach and guide, not as ways to earn God's favor."[49] During the sessions at the Council of Trent on the doctrine of justification, there was general agreement that the Protestants' notion of justification *per solam fidem* radically deviated from orthodoxy. It was also agreed that the Protestant doctrine presented a challenge to Christian life by excluding the "good works" that were required from believers (including confession, contrition, and penance). The Council issued a strong condemnation: "If anyone says that faith alone, without works, justifies the ungodly—that is, brings about their justification—in the sense in which the heretics of this age profess, as if nothing is required on the part of humanity except that they should believe, let him be condemned." To counter such ideas, and Luther's denial of the institution of the seven holy sacraments, a special focus was given to the relation between faith and good works, and the active role of human beings in justification.[50] Informed by these concerns, Ferrer Maldonado followed the Catholic theology of justification. His description of hell denied that faith alone was sufficient to procure salvation, implying that the law demanded certain actions from humans in order for them to be considered righteous and innocent before God. Exploring the topics of heaven and hell, Ferrer Maldonado's cosmography presented the sacraments as pivotal for salvation.

Enrico Martínez on Free Will

A key point for church reformers was establishing the proper relationship between free will and grace, a theological topic in which cosmographers also engaged in their astrological discussions. For early moderns, astrology was a mathematical discipline that explored the influence of the celestial bodies on the subaltern region. The field was essential for every student of the earth but at the same time involved certain theological complications.

The church's policy on astrology was hesitant and suspicious. On the one hand, the church accepted the practice of observing the stars and making potentially beneficial predictions on the basis of them (especially as they related to agriculture, navigation, medicine, etc.). On the other hand, the church was extremely concerned about the magical or "demonic" practices involved in astrology, especially when astrology was used to foretell the fortunes and destiny of human beings.[51] The Dominican Thomas Aquinas (1225–1274), who rigorously expounded upon each facet of Christian theology in his influential *Summa Theologiae*, claimed that the astrological prediction of future events was superstitious and wrong, and that it exposed the practitioner to contact with the devil: "foretelling the future was the very opposite of an act of religion: instead of looking to God for instruction, knowledge was sought by a tacit or explicit compact with the devil."[52] The thirteenth-century compilation of Castilian law, *Siete Partidas*, reiterated Aquinas's suspicion about the motives and methods of fortune-tellers, making the matter into an issue of criminal law. While the jurists who compiled the law recognized that divination by astronomy was not necessarily illicit, they attempted to regulate the practice and restrict access to the occult.[53] In the sixteenth century, the Council of Trent repeated the condemnation of judicial astrology, and, a number of years later, astrological books that predicted future events were placed on the Index of Prohibited Books issued in 1583 by the inquisitor-general of the Spanish Inquisition, Gaspar de Quiroga. However, the Index permitted astrological works on certain matters such as agriculture, medicine, and knowledge of an individual's inclinations and qualities.[54] Three years later, Pope Sixtus V condemned judicial astrology as contrary to the dogma of free will in a papal bull (1586) that also prohibited magical practices associated with astrology.[55]

These ambivalent attitudes toward astrology informed the Mexican engineer Enrico Martínez's (d. 1632) cosmography, *Reportorio de los tiempos y historia natural desta Nueua España* (Almanac of the climate and natural history of this New Spain) (1606). Born in Hamburg in the middle of the sixteenth century, Martínez was eight years old when his family moved to Spain and converted to Catholicism. In 1589, he left for the West Indies, where he designed an ambitious hydraulic project in the Valley of Mexico that aimed to prevent recurring floods. In addition to his occupations as official cosmographer, engineer, and one of the first printers and publishers in America, the well-connected Martínez worked as an interpreter for the Inquisition, which may explain his sensitivity to matters of heresy and orthodoxy.[56]

Martínez began his *Reportorio* by stating that "the divine architect created the world and all its parts with much admirable order and harmony" so that creation would reflect "the knowledge and power of divine providence." Viewing nature as a source of revelation, Martínez especially praised the capacity of astronomy to access the divine. "Of the human sciences, the one which most delights the soul is astronomy," he claimed, since it "most clearly shows us the greatness and majesty of God." So as not to risk defying the conventional view of astrology, he put aside the contentious elements of the field that were opposed by church orthodoxy. Instead, he concentrated on natural astrology, which he defined as "the science of the sky and stars." He divided this field further into two main areas: astronomy, which dealt with the general movements of the stars, and *astrología judiciaria*, which focused on the effects of the celestial bodies' constellation and movements on inferior bodies.[57]

Addressing the prevailing political conflicts, especially the relationship between rulers and state religions, which had ripped apart his own country of birth, Martínez expressed the church's vision on the inseparability of ethics and political authority. He was informed by the church's doctrine on human free will, and he objected to any attempt to limit or hinder such liberty: "Human acts depend on free will [and] are not subject to celestial influence." Yet Martínez not only commented on the stars and heavens but emphasized that free will could not be subjected to any earthly tyranny. He claimed that "kings and potentates can subject kingdoms, provinces, and cities with thousands of people to their dominion, but the free will of man cannot be coerced by any created thing."[58]

By emphasizing that not even a monarch could coerce an individual and violate his or her free will, Martínez rejected the divorce of politics from Christian ethics. The clearest example of separation between the two realms was articulated by the Italian political theorist Niccolò Machiavelli (1469–1527), who widened the gap between the raison d'état and the ideal Christian commonwealth. The church declared Machiavelli's work to be dangerous, and soon thereafter, in 1559, *Il Principe* was placed on the papal Index of Prohibited Books. In the social atmosphere of the Counter-Reformation and European wars of religion, Machiavelli's anticlerical views contributed to his widespread image as a wicked man advocating immoral behavior. The Dominican theologian Ambrogio Catarino (1484–1553), who was active at the Council of Trent and influenced the decision to ban Machiavelli's works, saw Machiavelli and Luther as "mirror images of each other," emphasizing that both were enemies of the church and the ethical (read, Catholic) state.[59]

There was also a close relationship between natural history and moral history in Machiavelli's thought, which provoked further debate. As Anthony Parel explains in his *Machiavellian Cosmos*, Machiavelli's political ideas were deeply indebted to an astrological worldview and to humoral theory, which accepted the idea that changes in the individual body and in the body politic were both linked to the movement of the heavens. The practicality of any political initiative depended on "naturalistic" constraints enforced on man. Enrico Martínez responded to the Machiavellian challenge by emphasizing free will and claiming that the divine origins of humans prevented them from being dependent upon or surrendering to any determinist forces.

As historian Robert Bireley argues in *Counter-Reformation Prince*, anti-Machiavellian attitudes shaped the ideas of Catholic political theorists as they investigated and defined the state's right of "dominion" over people. Contrary to the skeptical morality of Machiavelli, Catholic writers like the Italian Giovanni Botero (ca. 1544–1617) emphasized the Christian foundation beneath the prince's legitimacy to rule. Following the neo-Thomist interpretation of Francisco de Vitoria and the theologians of Salamanca, Botero asserted that the ruler must cling to virtues of piety and justice, and his legitimacy must receive the consent of the commonwealth.[60] Spanish writers of the first decades of the seventeenth century were attentive to the subordination of the monarchy to Christian ethics. Francisco de Quevedo underscored the Christian foundation of the state when he wrote, "Christ alone knew how to be king, and because of that only he who imitates Him will know how to be a king."[61] Juan de Solórzano Pereira (1575–1655), one of the prominent writers on the West Indies' legal system, concurred with Quevedo on the essence of the state: "the sure, certain buttress and foundation of empires consists in establishing, propagating, conserving and increasing the faith, religion and cult of our True God and Lord."[62] Such views equated the monarch who ignored the dictates of religion to a tyrant who threatened the moral and physical integrity of his realm.

Martínez supported the conclusion of Catholic theologians and political theorists, underlining the consensual nature of the monarch's subjects, whose hearts and minds could not be conquered even by a vast army, and whose futures could not be predicted or manipulated by the movements of the stars. In his cosmography, he articulated political visions and religious ideals that were passionately debated at the time. At the heart of Martínez's argument was a belief that emerged from the biblical narrative: "The infinite goodness of God our Lord created man in his image and after his likeness." According to scripture, Martínez explained, while Adam was created of ashes and earth, his soul was created in the likeness of God: "while it is true that man, insofar as the body comes from the earth and returns to the earth, desires earthly things; the soul, whose being is divine, is not satisfied by the things of the ground, because its core is God."[63] The belief that not even the most powerful ruler on earth could oppress the human soul was explained as a result of humanity's likeness to God. Like countless Iberian religious texts that expressed the divinity of the human soul, Martínez's writings echoed similar ideas, exposing the imbricated nature of Catholicism, politics, and the science of cosmography.

✦ ✦ ✦

The field of cosmography, which was essential for state and empire building, was also useful in supporting Catholic views. By identifying religious motifs in our sources, this chapter has shown how Spanish cosmographers used their writings to propagate Catholic norms and doctrines during a time of religious renewal. Students of the earth integrated confessional themes into their writings, including sacramental theology, Marian devotion, and partisan discussions on predestination, divine election, ethics, and the morality of the state. Early modern print culture was an important channel through which both Catholics and Protestants attempted to assert the validity of their respective worldviews. Printing created the potential for a broad audience and thereby could help sustain doctrinal conformity in a religiously fragmented world. The popularity of Spanish cosmographies aided this objective. The idea that cosmographies served as an important conduit for religious proliferation is not limited to Catholic Spain. For instance, the seventeenth-century English writer Peter Heylyn used his *Cosmographie* to support a "vision of the Anglican Church as Catholic and apostolic but independent of Rome," as Robert J. Mayhew puts it.[64] The propagandistic potential of cosmographic literature was recognized across confessions.

Natural philosophy also had social and moral implications, which gained greater significance as the Catholic Church sought to consolidate its control over matters of faith. The attempts to reveal the laws of nature that God imposed on earth served to clarify and justify the ecclesiastical law imposed on humankind. This understanding—that the two divine manifestations of God's power (grace and nature) were inseparable—drew a spiritual connection between the regularities observed in the operation of nature and the social and doctrinal conformity demanded by the Catholic Church. In this sense, the regulation of natural forces mirrored the regulation and conformity of faith, and thus "naturalized" church law. In the next chapter we shall see that the development was reciprocal; as much as religious concerns were manifest in secular cosmographical literature, cosmographical knowledge was central to Catholic authors, who incorporated that knowledge into pious church literature.

3
SOR MARÍA'S COSMOS

My King, may you be praised for your providence and marvels as are [found] in the world machine, with its multitude of adornment and diversity of plants, flowers, and fruits, animals and birds, which are sustained by waters and food . . . and [for] the large variety of fish, the great diversity of herbs possessing healing virtues for man, and if his ignorance were not so great and his knowledge so limited, what marvels and secrets of nature, which Your Highness has hidden, You would reveal to him.
—María de Jesús, *Redondez de la tierra* (ca. 1616)

Mysticism is typically understood as a cluster of religious ideas and attitudes that allow the individual to realize his or her quest for direct communion with God.[1] The mystical experience is often perceived in terms of a gradual, metaphorical journey of the contemplative soul that requires experiential practices in order to alter the self's state of being (even if, ultimately, the desired union is dependent upon God's grace). To the modern reader, it is hard to grasp any scientific foundation for such an endeavor. The merging of all created things with the sublime appears to stand in stark contrast to modern science's aim to reveal nature's systems and processes through critical observation and experimentation. In this sense, science and mysticism are widely perceived as separate and fundamentally opposed ways of approaching and understanding the world. The mystic's ultimate goal is not to discern the design and structure of nature but to be one with its creator. This was not the case for scholastic theologians whose training, following the medieval school curricula, reveals what might be called an embodied, holistic approach to knowledge. Furthermore, during the early modern era, the study of nature influenced a wide range of cultural domains, including the pursuit of a mystical connection with God, by applying and redirecting esoteric and hidden knowledge.[2] Occult writers—including Juan Eusebio Nieremberg in Spain and John Dee (1527–ca. 1608) in England—demonstrate the confluence of natural knowledge with physico-theological arguments that inspired the emerging science.[3] The study of nature by means of direct observation was incorporated into the mystical experience, the act of observation providing a basis upon which the pious could conceptualize and articulate their longing for God by conveying a new sense of wonder. The devotional tract *Redondez de la tierra*, attributed to the young Sor María de Jesús and most likely written in early seventeenth century, was penned in this spiritual environment. As Bernard McGinn points out, the ways in which "the presence of God" has been understood have varied across the centuries. Sor María's journey is one such variation that shows us how the mystical experience and the pursuit of knowledge supported each other in a specific time and place.

Sor María de Jesús de Ágreda (1602–1665) is no stranger to scholars today. The Franciscan-Conceptionist nun gained fame and acclaim during her lifetime, especially for her close ties with King Philip IV of Spain (r. 1621–65) and her extensive writings on a variety of doctrinal topics, including the then controversial doctrine of Immaculate Conception, which was officially sanctioned by the Catholic Church only in the nineteenth century. Significantly, Sor María also gained renown for her alleged supernatural ability to bilocate—to appear in two places simultaneously.[4] This special gift allowed her, according to the legend, to actively participate in the Catholic mission in New Mexico while never leaving her convent in Ágreda. Before her rise to fame, however, Sor María is said to have written *Tratado sobre la redondez de la tierra*, a treatise that records her mystical journey, in which she supposedly experienced the entire universe from a bird's-eye view.[5] As far as we know, the tract was probably written around 1616 and, while it was circulated widely in manuscript form, was only published in the twentieth century.[6] Critically, this text is an assemblage of cosmographical data that, though not original or advanced, offers a series of hypotheses and facts about the shape of the earth and the universe. As Clark Colahan has observed, Sor María's tract reproduced parts of cosmographies, geographies, and travel accounts to which the young girl had been exposed.[7] Rather than refer the reader to the specific texts, Sor María claimed that she came to this cosmographical knowledge by means of revelation, a mystical method she called "infused science" (*ciencia infusa*). In later years, her contention seems to have helped the Franciscans, and in particular an ambitious Portuguese friar by the name of Alonso de Benavides, employ the nun's story to promote the order's interests in New Mexico by placing Sor María at the heart of the American mission. In the Franciscan version of events, Sor María's communication with divine agents and her translocations on the wings of angels explained the "miraculous conversion" of the Jumano tribe by a mysterious *Dama Azul* (Lady in Blue), who would later be identified with Sor María.

By exploring the connection between the young Sor María's preternatural cosmography and later developments in New Mexico, this chapter examines the intersection between cosmographical knowledge, mysticism, and Franciscan corporate identity. By and large, historical literature has kept the two dramatic episodes in Sor María's biography separate, seeing her *Redondez* as a footnote in her biography, a "juvenile tract"[8] of a young mind, and concentrating instead on her later years, especially on her magnum opus, *La mística ciudad de Dios* (Madrid, 1670), which is considered a milestone in Marian veneration. Moreover, until recently, Sor María's earlier cosmographical visions have not been integrated into historical accounts of the Franciscan expansion into the American southwestern territories, which instead have focused on the identification of Sor María with the Lady in Blue.[9] For our purposes, the bilocation, levitations, and spiritual journeys of the Franciscan nun are secondary. The specific means by which Sor María traveled, a question that became paramount to her biography beginning with the first inquisitional investigation into Sor María in 1635, and the question of whether Sor María was the nun who preached to the Jumano tribe, as some Franciscans friars have suggested, must be left to the believer to decide. At stake here is how cosmographic information helped Sor María establish her authoritative voice and how, later, as a result of the nun's growing reputation, members of the Franciscan Order recruited Sor María for their own purposes. Put succinctly, I contend that Sor María made claims to cosmographical knowledge that were particularly appealing in her time and were later used by the Franciscan Order for this reason. Centered on the crossroads between knowledge and religion, this chapter connects the two facets of Sor María's biography, from her time as a young girl in Spain to her later years as an emerging transatlantic legend.

Even at the time of its composition, the content of the *Redondez* was of questionable scholarly value. It is quite easy to understand why, in the eighteenth century, "when Mary's *Mystical City of God* was under scrutiny in Rome and being compared with her other writings, the *Mapa* [i.e., *Redondez*] was rejected as not being her work."[10] The astronomic fantasies of the Franciscan nun did not follow the scientific conventions of the "Age of Enlightenment" and, even more important, did not support efforts to canonize her. In later centuries, the church hid the "embarrassing" evidence of the nun's past because the content of her work seemed "absurd." Though it might be tempting to dismiss Sor María's *Redondez* because it does not stand up to the cosmographic standards of her time, it is nonetheless important to note and analyze her self-representation as a mystical "cosmographer."

The flaws in Sor María's cosmographic knowledge notwithstanding, I see the *Redondez* as a fascinating example of popular knowledge about the arrangement and composition of the world. The interdependence of cosmography and spiritualty expressed in this text reflects a broader, thriving religious culture and offers an intriguing perspective on early modern society's engagement with nature. Claims for authority take preeminence in this historical interpretation. Historian Pamela Smith argues that in the Holy Roman Empire, alchemy functioned as a way to legitimate power: "Because alchemical knowledge was known to be revealed only to the most pious and success in transmutation was granted only to individuals of exceptional moral probity, it was proof of the humility and piety of the Catholic emperor that God granted transmutations at his court." Smith's framework can equally be applied to cosmography, which, not unlike alchemy, also possessed "a material and a metaphysical dimension" and functioned as a "language of mediation."[11] I propose in this chapter that cosmography served comparable purposes in imperial Spain. Similar perceptions of cosmology guided the Franciscans and can be observed in the way they employed Sor María's cosmographic revelations: her knowledge showed that she was one of the elect. As such, Sor María's *Redondez* attests to the importance of cosmographical knowledge in Spain even among religious participants who, like the Franciscans, aspired to a contemplative, "quietist," secluded spirituality, even as they aimed to fulfill their apostolic duties.[12] Sor María's engagement with cosmographical literature supported her spiritual quest, and it reveals a broader history of the Franciscan Order that carried a medieval spiritual tradition into an expanding world.

Furthermore, I claim that Sor María's resort to the notion of infused knowledge was a gendered strategy designed to enlarge the limited autonomy given to women in her time. In her pioneering work *Teresa of Avila and the Rhetoric of Femininity (1996)*, Alison Weber has studied the rhetorical choices of Teresa de Ávila and how she employed certain stereotypes about women's character. Through self-deprecation and belittlement, Teresa was able to sway the male-dominated church. Applying Weber's framework, I analyze the rhetorical choices—specifically Sor María's method of acquiring *experiential* cosmographical learning—that enabled her to overcome her lack of scholastic training. This perspective should enhance the scholarship of gendered religious experiences in Spain by bridging the history of science and knowledge with studies on women's agency in the religious world.[13]

Through an analysis and contextualization of the mystical journeys of a devout female visionary, this chapter explores the place of Renaissance cosmology in Hispanic religious culture. By focusing on a cloistered nun who never set foot on American soil, I seek to uncover the cultural capital of specialized knowledge of the earth across social ranks and genders.[14] The case of María de Jesús allows us to situate cosmology as a language of mediation between the center of empire and its colonial periphery, between the cloistered convent and the Franciscan Order, and between men and women. Cosmography, geography, and travel literature were central to a renewed church that incorporated profane knowledge into its pious literature.

Sor María de Jesús de Ágreda

In 1602, Sor María de Jesús was born to Francisco Coronel and Catalina Arana in Ágreda, a small town in the province of Soria, Castile, as María Coronel y Arana.[15] According to hagiographic accounts, she learned to read at a very young age and read spiritual and devotional works with great interest.[16] Her parents, who were probably of Jewish descent, scions of the prominent Jewish financier Abraham Senior, lived an extremely devout Catholic life and regularly performed rigorous ascetic practices and meditative prayer. Notably intense levels of personal and familial piety were on the rise in the first third of the seventeenth century, at the same time that the religious orders were expanding their numbers in the Iberian Peninsula. In this context, María's mother took the dramatic step of converting her husband's house into a convent. At the time, it was increasingly common for Spanish families to adopt a monastic lifestyle.[17] The process itself took several years, beginning with Catalina's claim to have been commanded by God to create the convent (after María's first vision in 1615) and ending with the convent's formal establishment in 1619.[18] Encouragement to carry out this task came by way of "miraculous voices and a vision of Saint Clara." With this heavenly help, Catalina and her two daughters persuaded the aging and ill Francisco to sign away his home, but the next hurdle came in licensing the convent.

The expansion of monastic orders in Spain had occurred at a remarkable rate. The Council of Castile was increasingly displeased with this trend and tried to limit, and even reduce, the number of existing religious houses. This obstacle did not deter Catalina, who persistently pushed her entire family to join the Franciscans. In 1617, Catalina's two sons left the family home to join the Franciscan Order in Burgos, and in 1618 Francisco joined the same order as a lay friar after helping with the renovations of his former family home.[19] On August 16, 1618, the new monastery was commenced and the first Mass was held on the day of the Immaculate Conception.

Catalina appears to have had clear opinions about just what type of convent her home was to become. She had the convent placed under the order of the Poor Clares ("the Second Order of St. Francis"), as a discalced Conceptionist sisterhood (at the time still linked to the Franciscan Order), following the more stringent practices of its followers, "like the nuns of the Caballero de Gracia convent in Madrid."[20] This choice had important implications for María's path in life.

The Portuguese aristocrat Beatriz de Silva had founded the Franciscan Conceptionist Order, so named for its particular devotion to the Immaculate Conception, in Toledo, Spain, around 1484. Gaining popularity in the sixteenth century, the order produced a number of famous visionary nuns. Conceptionist avidity in Spain even sparked the creation of a confraternity, devoted to the cause of the Immaculate Conception, which by the 1620s already had more than eighty thousand members. The reformed Franciscan and Conceptionist movements generally, and their convents in particular, played a key role in serving as a platform for women's spiritual writings in the sixteenth and seventeenth centuries, and they provided an important and productive backdrop to Sor María's own writings.[21]

Sor María was said to have had visionary and ecstatic outbursts (*exterioridades*) from an early age, usually attributed to her recovery from a critical illness at age thirteen that nearly ended her life.[22] She took her vows at age seventeen and was appointed abbess of the Convento de la Purisíma Concepción in 1627. She became an eminent spiritual leader, holding the position of abbess for the rest of her life.

Our understanding of Sor María's personality and legacy is largely shaped by later developments in her life, above all her supposed bilocation to America and her long correspondence with King Philip IV, which spanned twenty-two years.[23] The association of the Lady in Blue with the Conceptionist nun from Ágreda has thrilled not only zealous Christians but also modern historians who have studied the myth of the "miraculous conversion" of the Jumano tribe.²⁴ The narrative took root in the decade between 1625 and 1635.²⁵ In addition to Sor María's personal testimony, two Franciscans associated with the mission in New Mexico helped promote María as a "bilocating protomissionary": first, Gerónimo Zárate Salmerón, who briefly mentioned the nun in his *Relaciones de todas las cosas que en el Nuevo-Mexico se han visto y sabido* (dated 1629), and second, Alonso de Benavides, who penned three related texts that discuss Sor María and/or the Lady in Blue. In addition to these early sources, a third seventeenth-century Franciscan who contributed immensely to the growth of the myth was José Ximénez Samaniego, Sor María's biographer and, later, minister-general of the Franciscan Order. Samaniego wrote a holy biography of Sor María that was included as a preface in almost all editions of the *Mística ciudad de Dios* and thus, as Anna Nogar notes, "seems to have brought the narrative to the greatest number of general readers." However, Samaniego published his extremely popular *Vida* much later—around 1670, five years after Sor María's death.²⁶

Of the three promoters, the Portuguese Alonso de Benavides (ca. 1578–1635) was without a doubt the most significant in planting the seeds of the legend, and his contributions were made while Sor María was still alive (and before the Holy Office intervened in her case).²⁷ Benavides was born in São Miguel Island in the Azores, and his lifetime coincides almost exactly with the Iberian union between Spain and Portugal (1580–1640), following the Portuguese crisis of succession. In his *memorial*, Benavides, then the chief religious administrator of the *custodia* of New Mexico, described the route between San Bartolome in Nueva Vizcaya and Santa Fe, providing a geographical description of the region, including its people, climate, wildlife, crops, and other natural resources. Being an advocate of the Franciscan mission, Benavides included in his first report, written in 1630 and printed a year later in Madrid, the story of the Lady in Blue, who was said to have assisted with the evangelization of the local people, under the heading "Convesión Milagrosa de la Nación Xuamana." It was only later, in a 1631 letter to New Mexico's missionaries and the revised, second *memorial* (1634) that Benavides affirmed, as Gerónimo Zárate Salmerón implicitly had done, that the woman who helped the Franciscan mission was Sor María, a figure previously known to her confessors and fellow nuns for her mystical trips.²⁸ These reports by the Franciscan friars involved in the New Mexican mission confirmed the veracity of Sor María's mystical trips, which her earlier *Redondez* had documented.

Both Sor María's special relationship with the king, who consulted her in spiritual and political matters, and the posthumous publication of her celebrated opus, *The Mystical City of God*—a detailed biography of the Virgin Mary that narrates the secrets of creation and salvation based on supposed revelations by Mary herself—also influenced the perception of María de Jesús. But these episodes took place at a much later phase in her life. To understand how Sor María's reputation emerged, it is necessary to look back to the time before the many legends of Sor María shrouded the actual person. When María wrote her first known work, *Redondez de la tierra*, she had yet to capture the attention of those outside her hometown. Yet it was in these formative years that Sor María fashioned her image as a knowledgeable visionary and developed the distinctive authoritative voice that she and her order would deploy later in life.

Experiencing the World in a Gaze

The *Redondez* describes a mystical trip into the earth's interior, around the globe, and up into the firmament; Sor María served as the enthusiastic narrator of her own journey. The text represents a particular kind of travel literature (or *iter*, Latin for journey or path), that of an imagined or imaginary spiritual journey, penned as either poetry or prose. Such visionary travelogues, as Silvia Evangelisti has argued in her study of Spanish female mystics, reflect a diversity of religious experiences that aimed to promote a "female image of strength and dedication to the Catholic cause."[29] In narrating her peculiar journey, young Sor María additionally offered a summary of cosmographical knowledge, supposedly acquired by personal divine revelation. Her representation of the universe, however, had more mundane sources, as it was based on formulations of Christian-Aristotelian Scholasticism. The text is divided into chapters that examine the configuration of the Ptolemaic universe, the four Empedoclean elements, the celestial spheres, and the heavens.[30] She also dedicated a chapter to each continent: Europe, Africa, Asia, and America. In each, Sor María described the physical characteristics of the land, the terrain and climate, countries and provinces, and human and natural phenomena. It is clear that readers were not expected to be terribly knowledgeable in the field of cosmography; the work may have been intended for her fellow nuns.

The exact sources of Sor María's mystical cosmology are unclear. Her cosmos resembled the representation of the sphere by the thirteenth-century English monk John of Sacrobosco, which, thanks to its many translations and renditions, was one of the most popular cosmographies before the acceptance of Copernicus's heliocentric system. Clark Colahan has also noted that the list of countries, cities, and rivers in the description of the continents was taken nearly word for word from the popular cosmography of the German mathematician and astronomer Peter Apian (Apianus) (1495–1552).[31] Apian's work, *Cosmographicus Liber* (1524), explored the spheres and the division of the heavens, the theory of the climatic zones, winds, the basics of geography, the use of parallels, and meridians. Its main strength was the teaching of practical devices for measurements, including methods of calculating the latitude and longitude of a place and the use of triangulation to measure distances.[32] Sor María probably used the 1575 Castilian translation, which contained an appendix on America based on Francisco López de Gómara's work.[33]

Sor María provided an account of the large-scale structure of the universe in which she discussed the number of celestial spheres (or heavens) (fig. 7). Designating a distinct heavenly sphere to the moon, the Sun, and each of the five planets, she assigned the eighth heaven to the fixed stars. The ninth and tenth heavens were devoid of celestial bodies and frozen into the purest crystal, and were created by God as protective layers between the radiant heaven above and the lower heavens and the earth below. The tenth heaven also served as the "prime mover because with its movement it pulls with it all that is beneath it."[34] Lastly, the eleventh heaven, the "empyrean heaven," was "the home of angels and the blessed." For Sor María, it was the "celestial Jerusalem," a quiet place "where the great and magnificent king" dwelt.[35] The notion of an empyrean heaven had its origins in the early twelfth century, or possibly even earlier;[36] theologians and astronomers alike believed that it was an actual physical place. This model of the universe drew inspiration from the *Etymologies* of Isidoro de Seville (ca. 560–636), a work that Sor María must have known.[37]

Following cosmographical conventions, Sor María made general comments concerning the qualities of the celestial spheres: the sun, located in the fourth heaven, was "hot and dry"; Jupiter, in the sixth heaven, was "naturally hot and moist"; Saturn, in the seventh heaven, was "cold and dry."[38] As for representations of the earth, which stood "in the middle of the universe," Sor María detailed the measurements and structure of the planet, which she described as a "spherical body" that was "dense and very heavy." She erroneously suggested that its circumference was 9,280 leagues, eight hundred of which had yet to be discovered by humankind, and that its diameter was 2,502 leagues.[39] The earth was, she claimed, divided into three regions: the surface; the second layer, which absorbed the heat of the sun and other celestial bodies, thus generating earth's vapor and warmth (where minerals

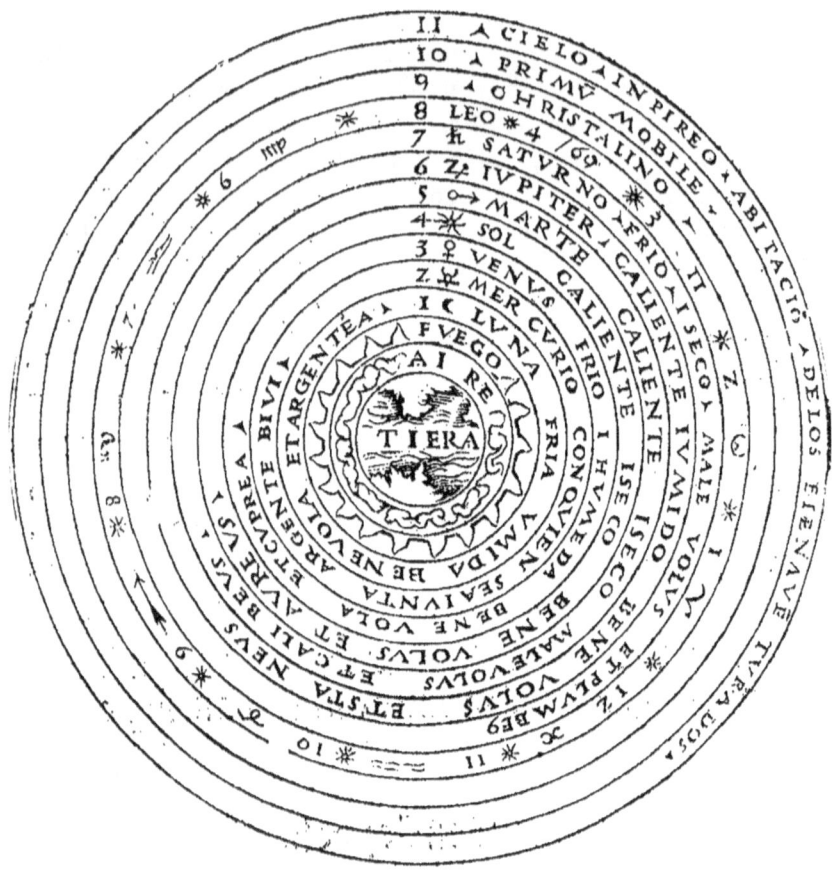

Fig. 7. Representation of the Christian cosmos in Martín Cortés's cosmography, one of the most comprehensive and widely read navigational texts of the sixteenth century. Sor María's mystical voyage similarly explored the cosmos by traversing the elemental and celestial spheres (eight spheres that comprised luminous bodies and two "aqueous" layers). From Martín Cortés, *Breue compendio de la sphera y de la arte de nauegar [. . .]* (Seville: Casa de Anton Aluarez, [1551]), fol. 13v. Courtesy of the Biblioteca Virtual de Andalucía.

and metals were formed); and the "pure and simple" core, where nothing was produced because light could not penetrate to such a distance. She situated hell, purgatory, and limbo in relation to places on earth, asserting that "purgatory is beneath Mount Calvary, with hell on one side and limbo on the other," the distance from Mount Calvary to purgatory being a remarkably exact 1,251 leagues.[40] Building on the creation of man from dirt, as described in Genesis 1, she claimed that "divine providence" was responsible for the fact that everyone's feet were oriented downward, toward the earth "from which we were formed," while our heads "pointed to the heavens," on which "we should meditate day and night." Humanity's final home, however, would be the "celestial Jerusalem for which we were created."[41]

Sor María provided her readers with a quantitative world picture: the first heaven was separated from the earth "by 6,247 leagues" and was the location of the moon, which had a circumference of "1,663 leagues"; it moved westward at "31,532 leagues per hour." In total, the first sphere contained 756,758 leagues and the crystal was 118,878 leagues thick.[42] For each of the other spheres, she specified the name of its planet, its distance from the earth, and its thickness and circumference, all measured in leagues. It is not clear whence Sor María derived these numbers, and they are clearly inaccurate. Nonetheless, Sor María's quantitative cosmos reflects the importance of Christian neo-Pythagoreanism to the Franciscans, as seen, for instance, in Francesco Giorgio's (or Giorgi's) (1466–1540) *De harmonia mundi totius* (1525). The Franciscan friar from Venice adopted the neo-Pythagorean idea that numbers convey the perfect harmony and order of creation.[43] Combining the Franciscan mystical tradition with Renaissance Neoplatonic ideas (in particular the Christian Kabbalistic teachings of Pico della Mirandola), Giorgio suggested a series of mathematical ratios that served as the foundational model of the cosmos. Giorgio claimed that God created the universe as a perfectly proportioned temple, based on numbers and in accordance with geometrical laws of proportion. Inspired by such trends, Sor María articulated a Christian vision of a mathematized cosmos.

Sor María aimed to praise God's creation and inspire devotion by expressing her sense of wonder at the vastness of the cosmos.[44] Many Spanish mystics of the time, especially women, typically chose to write either poetry that focused on the aesthetics of creation or tracts about their inner spiritual life (as Teresa de Ávila famously did in her *Interior Castle*). Sor María instead meditated on the arrangement and shape of the universe. As we have seen, observing nature was a path to spiritual truth; for Sor María, it was through the contemplation of the universe's harmonious order that God's care for humanity was revealed: "Wonderful is the Lord as seen in the entire world [*la redondez de la tierra*], in having created it, in its nature, and the order that governs it."[45]

Sor María's views echo widespread attitudes in the seventeenth-century Catholic world, including those expressed by the Italian Jesuit cardinal Roberto Bellarmino, on the encounter with God through the observation of creation. Written at roughly the same time as Sor María's *Redondez*, Bellarmino's *De ascensione mentis in Deum per scalas rerum creatorum* (The mind's ascent to

God by the ladder of created things) (1615), which enjoyed great popularity in Iberia, taught that each element in the universe had been designed by God as a sign of his attributes, and as such provided humanity with a "ladder" to the divine.[46] For example, Bellarmino believed that water was a sign of God's goodness, that God designed the sun's light as a sign of his wisdom and charity, and that the earth provided a safe haven for all creatures in the same way that the soul could find respite in the divine. Bellarmino proposed that the ladder had fifteen rungs "corresponding to fifteen steps by which people ascended to Solomon's temple."[47] The first step began with man observing himself; on the second, he contemplated the cosmos; the next four represented the elements (earth, water, air, and fire); the seventh consisted of the sun, moon, and stars, and so forth. Like Luis de Granada, discussed above, Bellarmino explained that since the entire universe mirrored God's perfection, and since no one creature could reflect that perfection completely, each one instead disclosed but a single aspect of it, and creation thus must be infinite. The diversity of nature's patterns and objects, Bellarmino argued, provided humans with the opportunity to "climb and ascend in order to see God."[48] While Bellarmino did not claim to be guided by a divine agent, he too subscribed to the idea that observing the universe in all its richness and fullness was the most appropriate way for humans to comprehend the benevolence and omnipotence of God.

In addition to mystical aspects of her divine encounter, Sor María's *Redondez* also points to important sociopolitical contexts. At a time when Europeans were extending their territories, Sor María's emphasis on the vastness of the earth and its multiple peoples underscored the pressing need for a vigorous mission. She often expressed sadness that people in many parts of the world still lived without the knowledge of God, in "darkness and blindness." By contrast, she portrayed Europe as the continent that most widely recognized God and suggested that Spain was "the most faithful" nation. If, of the many peoples of the earth, Spaniards were the most eager to serve God, then the Franciscans stood at the apogee of this constellation. Sor María repeatedly expressed her desire to inspire and motivate her "brothers and sisters": "I consider that the Lord has given me this light to know this truth so that with this science I could leave behind my ignorance and, having become skilled through experience, wanted it [i.e., her spiritual experience] to serve for health and as a medicine to not only rid me of my error but my brothers and sisters, too, of theirs." Sor María's visionary cosmography was thus intended to support the goal of the mission to save "those who blindly worship false gods."[49] As she wrote, the size of the earth was still unknown

Fig. 8. The twelve Franciscan "apostles" in Mexico erect the sacred cross and dispel the demons. From Diego Muñoz Camargo, "Historia de Tlaxcala [Descripción de la ciudad y provincia de Tlaxcala]," ca. 1585, fol. 239v. By permission of University of Glasgow Archives and Special Collections, MS Hunter 242 (U.3.15).

and there was need for a vast number of missionaries to spread the faith; the Franciscans, ready to traverse land and oceans in a global war against heresy, assumed that they were best suited to carry out the task.

Unlike that of medieval authors, Sor María's awareness of the world and its peoples went beyond the medieval *mappamundi* and included the West Indies, new to Christendom. While the *Redondez* describes the four known continents, it gives particular attention to America, where the Franciscans zealously built the foundation for the Catholic Church. Having arrived there in 1524, the Franciscans were the first mendicant order to come to the West Indies. Their mission began in the Valley of Mexico, with twelve friars who evangelized to the defeated Mexica people in what was perceived to be prefigured in the New Testament by the twelve apostles (fig. 8).[50] As Jaime Lara has demonstrated, the Franciscans, embracing the eschatological ideas of the thirteenth-century Joachim of Fiore and Nicholas of Lyra, built the New World's conversion complex, while in their minds they saw new Golgothas and Solomon's temples.[51] Franciscan chroniclers like Juan de Torquemada (ca. 1562–ca. 1624) celebrated their order's role in the revival of the ideals of the primitive church and in ushering in a new age of the Holy Spirit. In his monumental *Monarquía indiana* (1615), written at roughly the same time as Sor María's *Redondez*, Torquemada identified the Mexica deity as Satan and the city of Tenochtitlan as another Babylon, which Franciscans helped to uproot as they reconstructed the kingdom of God in the New World. This complex typological vision of history, so embedded in the American mission, became an essential part of Franciscan identity, shaping Sor María's description of America and the role of Spaniards in the redemption of humankind.

Sor María identified certain provinces of northern and central America, including New Spain, Guatemala and Yucatan, Honduras and Nicaragua, and Florida.[52] She described a land "very rich in gold and precious stones," surrounded almost entirely by an ocean (probably leaving the option for a land bridge such as the Northwest Passage to be discovered). Her fascination with the otherness of Amerindians dominates her narrative and attests to her familiarity with the depiction of exotic human groupings in medieval topographical and travel literature. As Lorraine Daston and Katharine Park have pointed out, medieval religious writers taught that marvels and wonders were most likely to appear on the margins of the world, where, in the words of the fourteenth-century monk Ranulph Higden, "Nature plays with greater freedom."[53] Writing about far-flung countries, Sor María suggested that the natives in America communicated by grunting and that their appearance was fundamentally different from that of Europeans, incorporating medieval descriptions of "four-footed" people with "long ears" into her descriptions.[54] Following observations made by notable Spanish writers, including José de Acosta, Sor María contended that the Indians were idolaters whom the "devil deceived" (*el Demonio los engaño*).[55]

Such ideas regarding the involvement of the devil in Amerindians' practices, as Fernando Cervantes has shown, emerged from the Franciscan nominalist school; for instance, the Basque friar Martín de Castañega discussed the various schemes imposed by the devil in order to resist and invert God's sacraments. In his 1529 treatise, Castañega asserted that there were only "two Churches in this world: one is the Catholic church, the other is diabolic church."[56] Following Castañega's demonological thinking, Fransican missionaries in America, including Andrés de Olmos, who translated Castañega's manual into Nahuatl in 1553, held, as Cervantes puts it, that "Satan had set up his own church [in America] as a mimetic inversion of the Catholic Church."[57] The importance of the Spanish mission in America lay not merely in saving human souls but also in undermining Satan's kingdom.

Nevertheless, Sor María asserted that her angel had told her that the natives were humans who "have a soul like you." Despite the somatic and mental differences between American natives and Europeans, "all [were] souls in your image and likeness."[58] We shall return to the significance of the angel in the next section; for now, it suffices that the fact that the natives had souls was considered proof that the American mission was necessary. Sor María's assertion conformed to the papal bull of 1537, "Sublimis Deus," which acknowledged that the native Americans were rational beings with souls who qualified as a collective group for Christian conversion.[59] She expressed her longing to join the mission, and even to be a "martyr" for "the defense of the faith that I so value and love."[60] Her rhetoric echoed that of male missionaries such as the Jesuit Francis Xavier (1506–1552), whose popular letters from the South Indian mission expressed his rejoicing in the dangers and difficulties "granted" by his service, which offered him fulfillment and spiritual growth.[61] Sor María longed, "even at the cost of my life and blood," to go to the New World and "spread the holy gospel from west to east and from north to south."[62]

This advocacy for the church's global mission is a crucial component in our understanding of her early work. With the rise of Protestantism and its persistent denunciation of clerical mediation, the sociopolitical atmosphere in Spain became hostile toward religious expressions that emphasized inward-turning practices and the unmediated contemplation of God.[63] As early as the 1520s, the Spanish Inquisition was concerned with self-proclaimed holy persons who could stir "enthusiastic" religious expressions.[64] This suspicion of individualistic spiritual practices often resulted in accusations that such persons were *alumbrados*—from the Spanish verb *alumbrar*, to illuminate, a rather loose category used to describe an unorthodox spiritual sect that had been prosecuted in sixteenth-century Spain for emphasizing interior manifestations of piety at the expense of church ritual. Sometimes self-proclaimed mystics were even called *ilusos*—"a term denoting people tricked by the devil into believing they had experienced 'true' mysticism."[65] The inquisitors sought Protestant sects everywhere, and such individuals, especially after 1558, under the policy set by Inquisitor-General Valdés, were associated with Protestants and targeted as Lutheran sympathizers who endangered the state and the religious establishment.[66] While Sor María could have been labeled a "false mystic" for claiming to have received wisdom directly from God, her cosmography did not contradict orthodox representations of the world or church teachings. Moreover, unlike those who renounced the world or practiced a passive union with God, her strong commitment to worldly affairs and to the global expansion of Christendom remained a powerful declaration of support for the Catholic Church.

Sor María's choice to use profane knowledge, particularly cosmography, in order to promote religious ideologies followed the Franciscan intellectual tradition. The Franciscans, in keeping with Saint Bonaventure's (ca. 1217–1274) attempt to integrate faith and reason, were influential in advancing the idea that the study of nature offered insights into the mind of God and the act of creation. From Roger Bacon, to William of Marseille, to Duns Scotus, Franciscans shared a keen interest in the field of cosmology.[67] The Franciscan reform movement gave new orientation to the study of the natural world, elevating God's "book of nature" to equal importance with scripture, as we saw in chapter 1.

Franciscans also participated widely in the study of nature throughout the Spanish realms and beyond, even though the historiography on Catholicism and early modern science tends to focus, perhaps too narrowly, on the Jesuits. The Franciscans were trained at seminaries and universities and had many libraries at their disposal.[68] Their monasteries were spread across the Spanish world and helped to gather local knowledge and materia medica, serving as chambers of knowledge long before Bacon envisioned the reform in natural philosophy through the establishment of Solomon's House.[69] For instance, based in the Franciscan Colegio de Santa Cruz in Tlatelolco, Bernardino de Sahagún (ca. 1499–1590) employed innovative empirical methodologies in order to gather social and geographical information regarding New Spain and its pre-Columbian past. Aided by a group of Nahua writers and artists from the college, Sahagún developed a research methodology that included extensive questionnaires and oral interviews with Nahua elders, which provided the sources for his study of Mexico.[70]

For the Franciscans, the prominence of cosmography within the natural sciences was unrivaled, for it permitted the observer to witness the "spectacle of nature." The Franciscan priest André Thevet (1516–1590), who served as royal cosmographer to four French kings, claimed that "there is no science, aside from theology, that has greater power to give us awareness of divine grandeur and power."[71] Thevet's popular geographical writings exposed European readers to the new discoveries (he wrote one of the first French works about America).[72] As we saw in chapter 2, it was commonly believed that cosmography exposed God's greatness and majesty, yet Thevet also described cosmography in a manner that was compatible with Franciscan identity, explaining that it revealed "the vanity upon which we dwell," thus "diminishing our arrogance."[73] This depiction of the spiritual advantages of cosmography echoes Saint Francis of Assisi's mendicant ideal of humility and humble

Fig. 9. The classical natural philosopher measuring the earth. From Diego Valadés, *Rhetorica christiana* (Perugia: Petrumiacobum Petrutium, 1579), 5. Getty Research Institute, Los Angeles (1388-209).

living.[74] Learning about the vastness of the cosmos would bring humans to humility, as the poor man of Assisi had preached.

In the Spanish realms, too, Franciscans noted cosmography's compelling features for Christian values and meanings. The engraving by the polyglot Diego Valadés of a natural philosopher measuring the earth (fig. 9) reveals the significance of cosmography among Franciscan missionaries. Born in 1533 in the city of Tlaxcala to a conquistador father and a Tlaxcalan mother, Valadés wrote his *Rhetorica christiana* (1579) for the purpose of guiding missionaries in America. His book, probably the first to be published in Europe by a Mexican-born mestizo (it came out in Perugia, Italy), reflects Valadés's broad humanist education under the Franciscan friar Pedro de Gante, as well as his strong commitment to the education of the natives. Valadés drew elaborate engravings that accompanied the written text, using them as a visual mnemonic device to help his readers retain the content.[75] In keeping with the book's objective, namely, supporting preaching to the nonbelievers, this engraving conveys the idea that studying the earth was crucial to the civilizing and Christian mission precisely because it allowed for deeper understanding of religious truths. This vibrant hybrid Franciscan cosmographical culture informed the manner in which Sor María chose to explore the divine and promote the triumph of the church.

Angelic Encounters and New Ways of Knowing

María de Jesús claimed that her knowledge of the universe came via a special type of divine revelation: *ciencia infusa*. In her words, she experienced the world by means of "an intellectual vision of the Lord" (*por visión intelectual del Señor*).[76] According to Sor María, after she had taken Communion but was still deep in contemplation, an angel appeared to her and told her that the lord wanted to reveal to her the mysteries of creation. God spoke to her, she later wrote: "My wife and my dove ... I created the heavens and the earth and the elements and the sea, and I want you to know what all of those were created for and of my providence and protection of man, and his service." God thus granted Sor María a special ability to see all of creation, from the smallest things in nature to the vast stretches of the earth, an ability she described as "infused knowledge of all things" (*ciencia infusa de todas las cosas*).[77] This curious testimony raises many questions about Sor María's conception of knowledge and mysticism. What did she mean by *ciencia infusa* and "intellectual vision"? Who was the angel that appeared before her? Why was she chosen? In order to answer these questions, let us continue by unpacking her mystical experience.

The notion of *experiencing* the earth—as Ann Blair has shown in her comprehensive study of Jean Bodin's *Universae naturae theatrum* (1596)—was more than a figurative expression used by mystics. It recalls the metaphor of *theatrum mundi*, the theater of the world, common to geographical works like that of the Flemish cartographer Abraham Ortelius (1527–1598), who compiled and edited the first modern-style atlas of the world, which first appeared in print in 1570 and was dedicated to King Philip II. Ortelius continually expanded and revised his compendium, *Theatrum orbis terrarum* (the Theater of the world), with new maps and geographical descriptions; by the end of the seventeenth century there were more than seventy editions (fig. 10). As the word "theater" indicates (from the root *theaomai*, to behold), Ortelius's *Theatrum* was a place to see a spectacle, the entire universe as it was represented in a standardized format. Through the metaphor of a theater, the world was displayed in visual fashion to humankind, presenting a spectacle of the beauty and order of divine creation for human edification.[78]

Furthermore, cosmography's authority was closely associated with a sense of experience. In 1564 the Bolognese Leonardo Fioravanti wrote, "Cosmography is a science that no man has ever been able to learn or know other than by experience: a fact that is most manifest, and has no need of proof."[79]

Fig. 10. Abraham Ortelius, *Theatrum orbis terrarum* (1570), frontispiece depicting the personification of the four known continents. Europe, following the Columbian voyages, is surrounded by globes above all the other figures/continents, symbolically representing the new world order. Photo: Wikimedia Commons.

While Sor María responded to such common perceptions, as a nun she could not *experience* the world outside her monastery other than by revelation.

María de Ágreda's conviction that God specifically wished *her* to be the spectator of his creation is rooted in Spanish mystical theology, in particular the teachings of the Dominican Luis de Granada, discussed in chapter 1. The Spanish theologian developed the idea that "God grants extraordinary knowledge to the selected righteous" (*una especial lumbre y sabiduría que nuestro Señor comunica a los justos*). Granada attributed knowledge to grace, describing it as "infused wisdom" (*prudencia infusa*). For him, "understanding" was a divine "gift": "These gifts are so many rays of light which proceed from the divine center of grace."[80] Granada's terminology had a striking impact on Sor María, who saw the sign and recognition of God's eternal love in the acquisition of complete knowledge. This perception of knowledge continued in her later works, especially, as Colahan has noted, in the *Mística ciudad de Dios*, where she described Mary's acquisition of universal knowledge in the days prior to her union with God. During this time, a total of nine days (*novena*), Sor María suggested that each day God imparted to Mary a ninth of the knowledge of all things.[81] Through this "gift," Mary could become a representative of God and an intermediary between God and humanity.

Sor María's cosmographic visions in the *Redondez* similarly follow this logic. Revelations elevated the status of both the Virgin Mary and Sor María, who could now act as intercessors for humankind. The Virgin Mary, who received total knowledge directly from God, was able to intercede and mediate on behalf of all humanity; Sor María, who received knowledge limited to things of the earth and time from God's messenger, was able to mediate on behalf of the Franciscans and Spain, as we shall see below.

In Counter-Reformation Spain, women were encouraged to live a devout life, and popular texts celebrated women's "natural" capacity to love and achieve spiritual perfection. For instance, the Spanish mathematician Juan Pérez de Moya (ca. 1513–ca. 1597) insisted that Adam was more responsible than Eve for original sin, and argued that while women are not as strong as men, they are "more devout and pious" and "in their spirit and virtue [*ánimo y virtud*] they greatly exceed men."[82] In his curious catalogue of notable women, *Varia historia de sanctas e ilustres mujeres* (A selected history of holy and illustrious women, 1583), Pérez de Moya provided several arguments for women's superior spirituality, including one based on the different material sources of men and women (i.e., man was made of dirt, woman from Adam's rib) and the idea that women were less inclined to offend God with grave crimes. In the spirit of the Marian veneration widespread in Iberia, Pérez de Moya also claimed that only a woman, quite naturally, could "be praised for anything more important than being the mother of God." From their role as nurturing mothers (albeit holy) to their spiritual qualities, Pérez de Moya saw women as predisposed to divine love. Sor María employed gendered perceptions of women's devotion and exceptional spirituality as a rhetorical device in order to project authority. She repeatedly insisted that the knowledge she had received was due neither to her unique intelligence nor to her personality; in an act of ostensible modesty, she depicted infused science as a passively received gift. But there was little modesty in her final work, and certainly not in her claim to have experienced all of creation. By employing stereotypes regarding women's propensity to devotion and love, and by invoking the concept of the divine gift of knowledge, Sor María could sidestep her lack of official theological training and claim autonomy in religious matters.

Although the notion of *ciencia infusa* emerged in a specific Spanish mystical context, and was used by Sor María as a gendered rhetorical strategy,

Sor María's interactions with higher authorities were part of a larger pan-European trend. Her claim to have received knowledge by communicating with an angel recalls John Dee, who also maintained, around the same time, that he conversed with angels for the sake of science. According to Deborah Harkness's *John Dee's Conversations with Angels*, the highly regarded natural philosopher and mathematician of Elizabethan England turned to angels in an attempt to unify religion, history, and natural philosophy. Dee believed that the restoration of human knowledge (after the Fall) needed help from above. Frustrated with the scholarly inability to reach wisdom solely through existing science and earthly arts, John Dee admitted to having a series of mysterious conversations with angels between 1581 and 1586, and again in 1607, which purportedly gave him the exegetical tools to understand the book of nature.

Written in two very distinct cultural geographies, both John Dee's and Sor María's contentions nonetheless reflected the growing skepticism of the late sixteenth century and the search for alternative ways of gaining knowledge by privileging supernatural explanations over the seemingly limited options presented by science and reason. These sentiments were not only shared by skeptical natural philosophers. Luis de Granada also praised "the university" of the visible world as superior to the prestigious "universities of Athens and Paris."[83] Nature provided a better understanding of theological matters than the established streams of knowledge that schools and universities promoted. Likewise, throughout her *Redondez*, Sor María expressed her frustration with the inadequate state of knowledge that resulted from humanity's condition after the Fall (which, for her, was expressed through humans' ingratitude to God). Bookish culture could not fill the gap. For the Franciscan nun (and for the English natural philosopher), "infused" knowledge of nature was privileged over other forms of knowledge because it reflected a transcendent reality and divine certainty.

Sor María's expectation that angels could reveal the secrets of nature to humankind is hardly surprising in the early modern context, where angelic intercessions in diverse human activities were not unheard of. Both theology and natural philosophy considered angels to be dwellers of the created world.[84] Their participation in the human realm helped explain nature's mysteries, which included global biodiversity, as we shall see in chapter 5. Angels' presence (though recognized as a spiritual matter) and continued involvement in earthly affairs was believed to help humans "acquire or imagine new forms of knowledge and new understandings of the relationship between God and man and of the arrangement of the natural world," as Joad Raymond points out.[85]

The church supported the engagement of angels in earthly matters and the pursuit of knowledge only as long as the angelic visions confirmed orthodox theology. In the tradition taught by Pseudo-Dionysius the Areopagite, whose *Celestial Hierarchy* depicted the nine orders of angels and was considered the most comprehensive on this topic of all patristic texts, angels were seen as mediating agents that provided a way of encountering God. The universe was understood through a chain of influences that emanated from God to the angels and thence to the entire world. According to this structure—often metaphorically described as "Jacob's Ladder"—the seventeenth-century Jesuit Juan Eusebio Nieremberg claimed, "The angels which go up and down are the ministers and executors of His Divine Majesty in the government of the world."[86] This chain that connected heaven and earth was also conceived as a metaphor for ascent.[87] For instance, the Franciscan Francesco Giorgio asserted that "just as God descended to the world by emanation through the angels, so humans might use the angels as a ladder to ascend to God."[88]

The post-Tridentine period witnessed a significant increase in the popularity of angels. In part, this blossoming interest was a direct response to the Reformation challenge, which continually undermined the scholastic tradition, including medieval angelology.[89] Catholic devotion to angels, as historian Alexandra Walsham argues in the context of England's religious strife, "acquired a distinctly confessional edge."[90] Angels were deployed in the protection of Catholics and in proving that Rome was the one and only true church. In 1586, Pope Sixtus V (1521–1590) proclaimed that every soul had a special heavenly companion. In 1608, Pope Paul V (1552–1621) announced a universal feast and office of the "Holy Guardian Angels," a feast that was first initiated by the Franciscan order according to an ordinance of the general chapter in 1500.[91] New confraternities dedicated to angels sprang up, and "their iconography was given a boost by a Church eager to harness the arts to enrich and enhance the experience of worship," as Walsham puts it.[92] Franciscan mystical literature was replete with references to guardian angels during the period.[93] Spaniards such as the neo-Thomist Jesuit Francisco de Suárez (1548–1617) played a key role in the renewed interest in angelology. With his comments on Aquinas's *Summa*, he provided "the most sustained and influential synthesis of scholastic angelology produced in the post-Tridentine period," in the words of historian Trevor Johnson.[94] Local feasts in honor of angels were held across Spain, including in Cordova, Toledo, and Valencia, even before Pope Paul V's announcement of the general feast.[95] Angelic devotions, regardless of monastic belonging, were encouraged and, especially after 1608, became mainstream in the Catholic world. In such an atmosphere, reports of communication with angels made their mark on knowledge culture in Catholic countries. In 1656, years after Sor María's *Redondez* was written, the Jesuit Athanasius Kircher wrote of a dream-state encounter with a guardian angel, Cosmiel, which resulted in his writing the cosmographical work *Itinerarium exstaticum* (The ecstatic journey).[96]

In the final analysis, Sor María's revelation, granted to her by "infused science," demonstrates points of convergence between mysticism, cosmographic knowledge, and the Iberian Atlantic expansion. While the content of the *Redondez* clearly did not contribute to the "advancement of learning," it nonetheless reveals a vernacular perception of cosmographical knowledge used by a devout young girl and her religious community. It was through the framework of cosmography that the visionary nun could articulate her ideas about spiritual perfection, ideas that also supported the global ambitions of the church. Sor María's narrative took a remarkable turn when the nun's fame reached destinations much farther than the province of Soria, where she lived all her life. The background on the intersection of cosmology and Franciscan religiosity provides a lens through which to understand how the legend of Sor María's bilocation evolved. The Franciscans, in particular Alonso de Benavides, learned of Sor María's reputation for divine translocation and appropriated it, further imbuing the nun's mystical journeys with a Franciscan hue. Fray Alonso had probably arrived in Mexico by 1598, and by 1603 he had joined the Franciscan Order and had served in Mexico City, Veracruz, and Puebla before being elected to the position of the third custodian of New Mexico in 1623.[97] We do not know whether Benavides was acquainted with the *Redondez*, but, as we shall soon see, we do know that he was familiar with Sor María's claims and reputation.

News of Sor María's mystical travels "circulated within the Franciscan order in the early 1620s."[98] In Franciscan circles and beyond, her "knowledge" of America and other parts of the world was presented as evidence of her claims. Gerónimo Zárate Salmerón mentioned Sor María in his *Relaciones* as he pleaded for the king's support in exploring further and searching for "new worlds" in the territory of New Mexico. Zárate Salmerón averred that "cosmography will aid in finding other kingdoms," a statement that concurred with Sor María's contention in the *Redondez* that the world contained parts still unknown.[99] Benavides similarly acknowledged Sor María's geographical knowledge, asserting that the nun described and reminded him of many details of New Mexico that he "himself could not recall."[100] Before Sor María was turned into a preacher, she was considered to be a person who knew the world. She was a divine cosmographer. It was through her cosmographical visions, recorded first in the *Redondez* and later in the testimony of her confessors, that the young nun from Ágreda became a suitable candidate for the Franciscan effort to advertise their mission in a competitive missionary environment. Though by the time of the Enlightenment her heavenly inspired cosmography might have been seen as an embarrassment by those who wished to elevate Sor María's status and sanction her theology, when imperial Spain was expanding during the Catholic Reformation, her familiarity with the shape of the earth underscored practical and spiritual dimensions that were too tempting to ignore. This was especially true for the Franciscans, who were in the process of reformulating their strategies and competing over resources with other Catholic orders. Sor María's visionary geographical journeys possessed cultural capital for those, like the Franciscans, who believed that such knowledge "was granted only to individuals of exceptional moral probity," and was a "proof of the humility and piety" of the saintly.[101] The elect, they believed, radiated their heavenly goodness and purity in the tradition of the poor man of Assisi upon the community.

Coming to America

In April 1631, three Franciscan friars—Francisco Andrés de Toro (Sor María's confessor), Sebastián Marcilla (her former confessor and the father provincial in Burgos), and Alonso de Benavides—arrived at the Purisíma Concepción convent in Ágreda to meet Sor María. The abbess had told her confessor a decade earlier about her frequent journeys to the New World, where she took part in the mission without leaving the confines of the convent. This account could probably have been ignored, dismissed, or, alternatively, attributed to demons, or evil deeds, had it not also allegedly been corroborated by the indigenous people of the northern missions. According to the famous narrative, the Jumanos who traded in the Rio Grande pueblos claimed that a mysterious young "woman in blue" guided the tribe in the knowledge of Christianity and urged them to beseech the missionaries in those territories to baptize them. Upon informing his superior of this dramatic testimony, Benavides, while still custodian in New Mexico, was instructed by the minister-general of his order, Fray Bernardino de Sena, to investigate the matter further.[102] In his first memorial (1630), written before the interview, Fray Alonso briefly mentioned the "miracle" without referring to Sor María: "we had asked the Indians [the Jumanos] to tell us why they pled with us so movingly for baptism and priests to teach them the ways of the Church. They answered that a woman like the one we had in a painting there (which was a portrait of Mother Luisa de Carrión) had preached to each one of them in their own language."[103] In Benavides's later inquiries, the virtuous woman was identified as Sor María, who had crossed the ocean in order to preach.

The precise nature of Sor María's mystical travels remained a matter of debate and interpretation. While Sor María was never officially charged and tried by the Inquisition, two investigations undertaken by the Holy Office during her lifetime focused on her supposed "journeys" (in 1635 and 1650), and interest in them continued long after her death. It is true that Sor María did not claim that she traveled *bodily* to America. Instead, she suggested that her supernatural experience could be explained either spiritually or physically. Yet she never objected to Benavides's version of the events during his lifetime. Only in 1650, when the Inquisition demanded a fuller explanation of her earlier mystical journeys, did she slightly modify her story, admitting to Father Manero from the Holy Office that some of the details Fray Alonso provided had been "exaggerated or misunderstood, and others added," and that she had been young and inexperienced at the time and therefore could not really explain the incident.[104] In 1631, however, she had written a letter to the Franciscan missionaries in which she confirmed her multiple visits to Amerindian communities, some of them yet to be discovered, omitting a detailed discussion of the exact nature of her journey (whether physical or spiritual). Sor María kept her description short and vague, yet she did refer to the physical assistance of angels (with their hands), writing, "I was taken by the will of God, and by the hand and aide of His angels I was carried wherever they took me, and I saw and did all that I have told the father." The letter was meant to encourage the Franciscan missionaries and strengthen their piety. Sor María exhorted the Franciscans in New Mexico, "Do not allow, my dear fathers and lords, that wishes of the Lord and His Holy Will be frustrated and permitted to fail because of the many insults and travails." For his part, following their meeting in Ágreda, Benavides added details about the "miraculous conversion" and Sor María. He called upon the missionaries in New Mexico to consider themselves fortunate that such "a blessed soul" supported their cause and was "looking after them" in their remote place.[105] Benavides sent his and Sor María's letters to America with one of his colleagues, remaining in Madrid so as to lobby for funding and to turn the *custodio* of New Mexico into a bishopric. "This moment was pivotal for the Lady in Blue narrative," writes Anna Nogar; "it was at this point formally associated with Sor María, and the letter circulated within the Franciscan Order and far beyond."[106] There was a larger, and specifically Franciscan, context for Benavides's actions.

By the seventeenth century, the initially optimistic missionary zeal had become harder to maintain in the face of mundane disputes and the quotidian routine of Catholic orders and squabbles over the continent's resources. In a crowded missionary market, the Franciscans, who wanted to continue the task of the twelve apostles of Mexico, had to reinvigorate their mission. Katie MacLean places the myth of the apparition of the Lady in Blue in the context of the Franciscan ambition to secure the future of the mission in New Spain, as "material and human resources were spread thin." The Franciscans, who had come to New Mexico in 1573, were keen to maintain their presence there. However, the Crown had never guaranteed that specific orders would be able to monopolize given areas. Moreover, after the 1570s, the church and the secular clergy "gradually curtailed the role of the religious orders" in urban areas.[107] In response, the religious orders increasingly moved to the periphery. This development quickly widened the gap between the orders. Those with better financing, like the Jesuits, soon enough used their material advantage and relationship with the elite to expand northward into New Mexico. The relations between the competing Franciscans, the secular clergy, and the Jesuit Order were not always cordial, despite their common goal of converting the natives.

Around 1616, the Franciscan superiors in Mexico City decided that the missions in New Mexico should be grouped together and elevated to the administrative unit of a custody (namely, the Custody of the Conversion of St. Paul). Their decision turned the missions of New Mexico into a semi-autonomous administrative unit under the Franciscan province in Mexico City.[108] However, the progress of the Franciscans was slowed by a constant state of underfunding and lack of supplies and manpower.[109] The Crown was slow to respond to the Franciscans' requests and demanded to see a material return on its investment. In response to these challenges, the Franciscans searched for innovative ways to inspire and recharge their earlier zeal. The idea that God might favor Sor María with a "special gift" that allowed her to instruct the indigenous peoples (along with other reports of divine intervention) supported the Franciscan efforts. The story about native evangelization by a gentle female figure was presented as proof of God's satisfaction with the Franciscans, and proved to be instrumental in assisting the order's goals in the region.

The appropriation of women's sanctity for political purposes was not unusual in Counter-Reformation Spain. The Franciscans' strategy in New Mexico is comparable to the efforts to elevate the newly canonized Teresa de Ávila to the position of a national co-patron saint of Spain, together with the older patron, Santiago (Saint James), a development that Erin Rowe has analyzed in *Saint and Nation*. These attempts spanned the years 1617 to 1630—coinciding almost exactly with Sor María's mystical trips and Benavides's investigations—and created much controversy between two factions that had very different visions of Spain's future. Teresa's supporters (Teresianos) believed that Spain's new challenges, particularly the danger of Protestantism and heresy, necessitated a modern patron saint better equipped to face contemporary problems, and Teresa was seen as an ideal candidate. In the bull issued in 1622 for her canonization, Pope Gregory XV called Teresa "the new Deborah" and lauded her ability to "overcome her feminine weakness and lead spiritual battles." Armed with the Counter-Reformation church's reassessment of sainthood, the Teresianos were "quick to fashion an image of their saint as the ideal choice to defend and sustain Spain." Franciscans were also part of the debate; in 1627, the discalced Franciscan and royal preacher Diego del Escurial conveyed his enthusiasm for Saint Teresa, stressing that, despite being a woman, she truly symbolized Spain's status as a defender of the faith.[110]

Teresa's role in defending the faith and safeguarding Spanish interests inspired many devoted women to take part in the church's triumph across the world. Teresa's posthumous miracles and the discourse surrounding the campaign to elevate her status lent credence to the case of other women, like Sor María, who claimed to have participated in a mission that was reserved for men. Through bilocation and her spiritual pursuits, Sor María could "overcome her feminine weakness" and successfully spread the Gospel like any other missionary. Just as the Teresianos appropriated Saint Teresa, the Franciscans longed for a unifying symbol, their own Joan of Arc or "new Deborah." The Franciscans needed an inspirational figure who could promote piety and reform, and they sought to capitalize on the growing popularity of the Immaculate Conception throughout the Hispanic world. Sor María's femininity and the fact that she was a Conceptionist added a provocative dimension to this effort to create spiritual momentum.

Beyond Teresa's model, there is a broader gendered context for the Franciscans' strategy in New Mexico. As Silvia Evangelisti has shown, between the mid-sixteenth and mid-eighteenth centuries there were a number of cases of cloistered nuns who claimed to have journeyed afar, and whose stories were recast in order to advance the goals of various Catholic orders. During their journeys, these women reportedly participated in the conversion of non-Christians, fought against heretical beliefs, and even joined Catholic soldiers on the battlefield. In several cases, they were also associated with the supposedly spontaneous conversion of pagan communities in regions where missionaries were active, again without ever leaving their convents. The pattern of capitalizing on female actors to promote Catholic and monastic goals was strong in the mid-seventeenth century and would continue after Sor María's lifetime. For example, Juana de Jesús María (1574–1650) was said to have traveled many times to the Ottoman Empire, the West Indies, and the Philippines. Writing more than twenty years after Juana's death, her biographer reported that in all these places Juana preached the Christian faith, carrying in her hand the "miraculous face of Christ."[111]

Among such stories, the myth of the Lady in Blue was clearly central to advancing the Franciscan goals in New Mexico. However, the study of the Dama Azul did not begin in the 1630s when the investigation of Sor María's bilocation began, or with the incorporation of her mystical experiences. The seeds of the legend are to be found in Sor María's own version of the mystical journey in the *Redondez*. Without acknowledging Sor María's description of herself, her claims to "infused science," and the mediating function of cosmographical knowledge, it is hard to comprehend how Sor María came to position herself as a candidate for the role of the Franciscan female "savior." Her earlier tract already contained the necessary ingredients for the later popular myth, a myth that the Franciscans helped foster on these bases.

The role of Fray Benavides in creating the myth of the Lady in Blue cannot be ignored. In his 1631 letter to the Custody of the Conversion of St. Paul, Benavides lamented the "scant information" on New Mexico back in Madrid, "as if God had not created it in this world."[112] Benavides wanted to rectify this lack, bringing the accomplishments of the Franciscans in the region to wider attention. Emphasizing the opportunities for financial and spiritual gain on the plains of New Mexico, he wrote the two *memoriales* after he had left the colony of New Mexico and reached Spain. The first edition (1630) was addressed to King Philip IV. It was published and read enthusiastically at court, including by the king himself, and was quickly translated into several European languages, including French, German, Latin, and Dutch.[113] Benavides formulated his first report according to the interests of both the Franciscan order and the Spanish state, hoping to garner human and financial resources through his propagandist efforts. He took great pride in the enthusiastic interest in his first memorial. In his letter, he informed his custody that his report was "well received in Spain" and that the king and members of the council "liked it so well that not only did they read it many times and learned it by heart, but they have repeatedly asked me for other copies."[114] The second, expanded version included revisions made after his interview with Sor María and was dedicated and offered in person to Pope Urban VIII in Rome.[115] The audience of the 1634 *memorial* may have been small, but it was important: "the text was meant to be read in Rome by the pope, and there is no evidence it was ever printed."[116] Notably, this was the same pope who ratified Teresa de Ávila's patronage status in 1627, only three years before the investigation of Sor María began, and, arguably, he was favorable to the idea of a pious woman in the service of the church. By implicating the Vatican in the progress of the mission, Fray Benavides and his superiors aspired to secure the establishment of a new diocese in New Mexico to be headed by the Franciscan order, preferably by Benavides himself.

Through his energetic campaign on both fronts, toward the Vatican and the Crown, Benavides stirred much excitement on the matter of the mysterious apparition. He went to interview Sor María in Spain and excitedly informed his order that the nun "recognized me as the one she had seen" at the baptism of the Pizos (i.e., Piros, a community in the Rio Grande region).[117] He tailored his narrative to please all Franciscans, both conventional and discalced, by paying close attention to unifying cultural codes and symbols: "the habit she wore most times was that of our father, Saint Francis; on other occasions it was that of the *Concepción* with its veil."[118] In his accounts, Benavides never doubted that Sor María's bilocation was a *physical* phenomenon, that she was simultaneously present in two separate locations.

We will never know for certain what Benavides actually believed. What concerns us here is the manner in which he transformed Sor María's visions into a Franciscan narrative. Benavides recorded Sor María's travels as fact, but he reshaped the story for the needs of the mission by accentuating a peculiar aspect of the Franciscan sensibility. For instance, while Sor María explained in the *Redondez* that she came to her geographical knowledge thanks to the revelation of a holy angel, in Benavides's version, the narrative of mystical trips was reworded so as to imply that Sor María was physically present in countries overseas. Benavides maintained that Sor María was elected through grace via angelic intervention (in Sor María's account, for the purpose of gaining infused cosmographical knowledge), but he altered the meaning of this intervention significantly by suggesting that she was chosen to serve as an agent of the mission. The mystical cosmographer was thereby turned into a preacher. Benavides explained the nun's miraculous journeys by appealing to the concept of angelic translocation: "His Majesty revealed to her all the savage nations in the world that do not know Him, and she was transported by the aid of angels that she has as guardians."[119]

Such stories about transportations by angels were woven into the early modern Catholic imagination, especially among Franciscans, who developed a rich and elaborate legacy of angelology.[120] The autobiography of Ana María de San José (1581–1632), a Poor Clare nun from Salamanca, describes how God invited her to travel to "the Indies," where she preached the Gospel to the local people. She was carried by "angels" and the "saints" to Japan as well, where God asked her to assist male missionaries who were worn out by the hardships of the mission. Coincidently or not, Ana María's stories about angelic travel were included in a biography written by yet another Franciscan friar, Juanetin Niño, who published his work in Spain in 1632, between the writings of Benavides's two accounts (1630 and 1634), on the miraculous conversion of the Jumanos.[121] We shall see in chapter 5 that angels were responsible not only for the transportation of nuns to overseas missions but, according to some, also for the migration of certain animals.

Benavides took care to identify the angels who transported Sor María from one place to another: "Her wings are Saint Michael and our father, Saint Francis."[122] By suggesting these particular angels, Benavides translated Sor María's experience into a Franciscan idiom. Francis of Assisi was, of course, the founder of the order. The Franciscans generated their understanding of spiritual perfection from the teachings of their radical founder, whose own encounter with the seraph on Mount Alverna left him with a "singular privilege," the stigmata: as David Keck points out, "no other founder of an order had been so holy and so favored by God that he had received the actual wounds of the Savior." From the thirteenth century onward, Saint Francis was associated with angels for three reasons: he was seraphic (by the power of the stigmata), he was the sixth angel of the Apocalypse (the angel who was to seal the elect and bear "the seal of the living God," Rev. 7:2–4), and he was the "angel of true peace." The last angelic association was particularly significant to the colonial expansion and Catholic mission to the pagans. Critically, Bonaventura promoted the image of Saint Francis as "a man who brings peace and triumphs over discord," a symbolic character who reflected the desire of the Franciscans in Benavides's time to convert the Amerindians with their harmonious cooperation (as reports on the Jumano tribe's conversion had suggested).[123]

Archangel Michael, for his part, symbolized the agent of Catholic triumph. Traditionally, Michael was considered the leader of the army of God, an ideal spiritual warrior fighting against pagans and evil forces both within and without. This narrative had its origin in the book of Revelation, which positioned Michael as the head of God's armies, triumphantly marching against Satan's forces. During the Counter-Reformation, the militant aide of angels was embraced in the fight against heresy and "demonic" forces. In short, Benavides enlisted the church's most powerful allies in his effort to establish the legitimacy of Sor María's narrative and the Franciscan enterprise (and thus to promote his campaign in New Mexico). The angelic leader of God's army and the angel of true peace were guarantors of the order's success in spreading the desired faith, whether peacefully or by the sword.

The Franciscan investigation of the appearance of the Lady in Blue in the southwestern desert of America emerged at a time of great unrest within the Castilian court and as religious orders were looking to renew themselves, which they did through, among other strategies, appropriating the deeds of saintly women. New realities demanded new leaders, voices, and visions. Holy women could intervene on behalf of their religious communities and enhance general piety at a critical time in the church's history. The appearance of the Conceptionist nun among nonbelievers in New Mexico followed conventions that attributed spiritual victory to a female figure. The incorporation of Sor María's mystical trips into the Franciscan repertoire, which legitimized her claims to preternatural cosmography, reinforced missionaries' identity as divinely inspired messengers of Christ, whose task was to eradicate heresy and idolatry through the light of the faith. God's grace was a constant theme in the narration of Sor María's life, first with her acquisition of knowledge through the assistance of an angel and then, later, as her visions were appropriated for the sake of the Franciscan mission. Her apparition was explained as a miraculous gift to the followers of Saint Francis and the native inhabitants of New Mexico.

The insertion of the Lady in Blue into the account of the mission was remarkably successful, and it led to the acquisition of important financial support from the royal treasury. The contract between the Franciscans and treasury officials increased the number of missionaries in New Spain; the Crown would now subsidize a total of sixty-six missionaries, along with thirty-two four-wheeled heavy freight wagons, almost one for every two missionaries.[124] While Alonso de Benavides did not return to America, but instead continued on to Goa, India, where he accepted the position of auxiliary bishop, his campaign put New Mexico on the map and reinvigorated the Franciscans' self-image.

✦ ✦ ✦

This chapter has examined Sor María de Jesús's visionary cosmography and legendary bilocation, highlighting the distinct place of geographical and cosmographical knowledge among the Franciscans, who were the first to begin the Catholic mission in the Americas. I have emphasized that cosmography provided young Sor María with a vehicle through which she could express her devotion and support of the global mission, suggesting also that her infused cosmographical learning was a gendered strategy to enlarge the limited autonomy given to women in her time. In subsequent years, the Franciscans deliberately appropriated María de Jesús's geographical visions and reputation in order to reinvigorate their missionary campaigns in New Mexico in the 1630s. The Franciscans needed a new symbol that would promote piety and unity, and they sought to capitalize on the growing popularity of the Immaculate Conception by adopting and remodeling Sor María's visions. Their use of Sor María as a female figure who protected Catholicism recalls similar discourses that had led to the proposal of Teresa de Ávila as the co-patron of Spain only several years earlier. Women of various monastic backgrounds could help promote Catholic ends by becoming agents of Christianization on a global stage. The later fashioning of the Franciscan Conceptionist nun, with the aid of Alonso de Benavides, who further imbued Sor María's mystical journeys with Franciscan symbolism, added new impetus to their mission in a faraway land.

Seen in this context, New World encounters not only shaped religious life in the colonies but also fostered forms of religious consciousness that developed in Iberian convents and monasteries. The expansion and popularity of travel writings and geographical works in the early modern Hispanic world informed Sor María's spirituality and her fascination with new territories and peoples. In the next chapter, we shall see how friars in the New World used geographical narratives to incorporate America into their monastic traditions. For them, as for Sor María, new cosmographic knowledge offered the opportunity to refine and extend their spiritual lexicon. After all, Sor María did more than merely reproduce cosmographic materials. Drawing upon various sources, she gave cosmographical information a new Catholic orientation by integrating new evidence into her mystical writings. Infused or not, natural knowledge validated Catholic piety and doctrine and contributed to the diversity of the Iberian religious experience.

4

DESCRIPCIÓN AND THE ART OF PIETY

How shall we sing the song of the Lord in a foreign land?
—Psalm 137:4

Adam's God-Given Knowledge Revealed

Writing in the mid-seventeenth century, José Antonio González de Salas (1588 or 1592–1651) presented a series of religious motivations for practicing geography in the preface to his *Compendio geográphico i histórico*, a translation of the first-century Iberian writer Pomponio Mela's work.[1] González de Salas, a renowned Spanish humanist, claimed that geographical information was imperative for theology, for without it "many occurrences would be not understood in both Testaments." Geography and chronology, he suggested, were "the pair of eyes of the artificial body of history" (*los dos ojos de el artificial cuerpo de la Historia*), without which it was impossible to "see" and thus understand religious truth.[2] Discussing the origins of the discipline, Salas linked geography to ancient wisdom by placing Mela in a long chain of geographers beginning with none other than Adam, the namer of all of creation.

Genesis 2:19 says that all the animals were brought before Adam, who named them according to their essence: "whatever the man called every living creature, that was its name." The enigmatic verse inspired many traditions that assigned to Adam God-given knowledge of nature's secrets.³ Accordingly, Salas asserted that since it was agreed that the "First Father" was "the master of the science of the stars," "by necessity [Adam was] also the master of the first geography," a subject that originated on the third day of creation, when the waters receded and earth became visible.⁴ In his account, Adam did not merely know the shape of the earth but was a geographer; "knowing" the created animals, land, and stars made Adam the first scientist.

The idea of linking geography to Adam is perplexing. The encounter in Eden with all the animals and plants on earth might have made Adam a "scientist," but it is unclear how he could have been the first geographer without leaving Eden and exploring the entire world prior to the Fall. Nonetheless, Salas's ambitious claim for a biblical starting point for geography deserves our attention. As geography evolved in his time, Salas evoked sacred scripture to provide the discipline with greater legitimacy and authority, which were further enhanced by citing Mela as a (Spanish) patriotic model for his geography.⁵ By according Adam the role of the first geographer, geographers could claim both access to and continuity with a tradition of divinely inspired learning. Adam enjoyed a privileged relationship with God and thus had access to true and authentic knowledge, of which the description of earth outside Eden was now a part. The suggestion that geography enjoyed continuity from biblical times to the seventeenth century was an insurance policy against claims of heresy. Uncovering new geographical findings, as Spaniards did in Salas's time, posed no threat to religion but was seen as a means of regaining prelapsarian knowledge.

The clear connection González de Salas made between religion and geography opens the door to considering the significance of the field to Hispanic religious life during a time of Catholic renewal and imperial expansion. Bearing in mind Salas's conclusions, this chapter turns to the definitive role that religion came to play in geographical knowledge and, conversely, how the field of geography supported the propagation of the Catholic faith.

Describing God's Kingdom

In his letter of March 10, 1625, to Friar Gregory Canali, the prior-general of the Carmelite Order, the Carmelite friar Antonio Vázquez de Espinosa expressed his desire to be appointed the commissary-general in the Indies. To impress his superior, Espinosa, who had spent much time in Spanish America, enclosed material that reflected both his religious calling and his experience as a land surveyor in the Indies. Espinosa sent Canali his four printed works, including the theological treatise *Confessionario general, luz y guía del cielo*. He also offered Friar Canali four maps of the Peruvian bishoprics and their descriptions, "in order that your excellency can see them and show them to his holiness [Pope Urban VIII]." Espinosa asserted that this geographical information was intended "to be of service to God and his Church." Unfortunately, these maps did not survive the intervening centuries; as early as the seventeenth century, a commentator reported on their poor condition.[6] Yet the correspondence between Espinosa and Canali is noteworthy because it reflects the keen interest of the church in geographical data about the American continent, an interest that was distinct from and independent of the official cartography of the Spanish Crown.

It was by no means unusual for a Spanish friar to transmit geographical information to his European peers. Thanks to monasteries, libraries, colleges, and transnational intellectual networks, members of religious orders were in an excellent position to take part in the global circulation of geographical knowledge.[7] Historian María Portuondo has stressed that sixteenth-century Spain endeavored to keep knowledge gained from "maps, geographic descriptions, and historical account about the Indies" a "state secret," hoping to prevent European rivals from making incursions into its overseas territories.[8] While this policy of censorship was enacted, alternative channels for producing and sharing geographical information emerged among Spanish subjects, in particular in the Western Hemisphere, where the land was surveyed by a large number of Catholic clergy who produced descriptions of unknown parts. Along with missionaries' role as ethnographers and "cultural translators" across the world, a role that has received considerable attention in scholarship because of the primacy of human encounters in missionary work, Spanish friars repeatedly acted as brokers of geographical knowledge.[9] In fact, Catholic friars proved to be indispensable to the transfer of geographical and cartographic materials from around the world to Europe, thus contributing to the development of scholarship back home.

The Portuguese Jesuit cartographer Luis Teixeira (1564–1604), for example, created a map of Japan on the basis of local Japanese cartography. In 1592, Teixeira apparently sent his map to Abraham Ortelius, who printed it in his *Theatrum orbis terrarum* in 1595, helping the map become the model for most Western maps of the archipelago and "the first which correctly located the Japanese islands between 30 degrees and 40 degrees north latitude."[10] The mission in Asia substantially augmented Europeans' knowledge of the Far East. For example, though he had never been to China, Juan González de

Mendoza (1545–1618), an Augustinian friar from Mexico, wrote a very important work on China based on missionaries' reports.[11] In the Portuguese context, as Ângela Barreto Xavier and Ines Županov have claimed, from the late sixteenth century, and especially after the Iberian union under the Spanish Habsburgs, the main producers of knowledge on Asia were ecclesiastics.[12] The Jesuit Order, including friars such as Luis Teixeira—frequently heralded in historical accounts as bringers of Catholic modernity—was not the only Catholic order to take a leading role in the global geographical enterprise. As we shall see, Jesuits were joined by mendicant friars, including Carmelites, Franciscans, Dominicans, and Hieronymites, whose geographical writings over distant and vast territories introduced rigorous standards to the field.

Geography, together with its related skills of navigation and cartography, was not a marginal discipline; on the contrary, it stood at the forefront of the scientific transformation of the early modern world.[13] As David Livingstone explains, "the fact that geography has always been a *practical* science is thus of central significance in its history, and all the more so because the triumph of experience over authority is seen by many as the fundamental ingredient in the emergence of experimental science in the West."[14] European consciousness of the world, together with the belief in scientific growth and progress, was dependent on the improvement of the accuracy of maps and geographical descriptions, including of parts of the earth, like India, eastern Asia, and Africa, that were to some extent previously known to Europeans.[15]

The growth of the complex field of geography, which was divided historically into three branches (mathematical, descriptive, and chorographical or local), is usually understood as intrinsic to European state-building and exploration.[16] Historians of various regions and periods have repeatedly drawn connections between geography, on the one hand, and political and commercial pragmatism, on the other, and especially have noted how colonial expansion played a decisive role in the field's development.[17] For instance, Jordan Branch claims that cartographic tools and innovative spatial practices first used in the colonial project in the Americas were then applied to European metropoles, paving the way for the modern system of sovereign territorial states.[18]

The relationship between religion and geography, by contrast, is often overlooked in modern scholarship, which instead has emphasized the prominent place of geography in forming abstract concepts, such as sovereignty and the nation, that permeate most interpretations of modern history. This secular perspective is especially true for historians of the Spanish world, who, until recent years, have directed their studies to challenging the "Black Legend," which depicted Spain as a backward state. As mentioned in chapter 1, these historians have successfully shown the achievements of Spain in various scientific fields, including geography, which has been studied from an imperial perspective (in terms of geography's importance to trade and commerce, patronage, military pursuits, and so forth).[19] The existing scholarship on the Jesuits notwithstanding, we should also examine the broader imprint of Tridentine Catholicism, since religion, as Stephen Gaukroger has observed, was crucial to the legitimation and formation of the scientific enterprise in the West. The field of geography was no different.

This chapter aims to address this lacuna by revealing the utilitarian approach of Spanish clergy to geography. I examine works by geographers affiliated with various Catholic orders, recognizing in these texts not merely the accomplishments of skillful scholars but the output connected with many religious and social sensibilities, all of which shaped the works' content. Rather than present an account of a Ptolemaic revolution in the period—a narrative that often assumes a turning point in which mathematical representations of earth's surface replaced symbolic and theological conceptions of space—I aim to demonstrate how geography was a powerful tool used to endow space with sacred meanings and to advance particular Catholic agendas that coexisted alongside imperial projects. The bulk of the chapter looks at representative case studies, through which I reconstruct the story of how Spanish missionaries in America, including Diego de Ocaña and Antonio Vázquez de Espinosa, appropriated local geographical descriptions in order to support Catholicism's evangelical dynamism. As Spanish imperial ventures opened new channels for amassing information, I claim that these Catholic friars and others, whom I call "confessional geographers" to highlight their distinctiveness, adapted and modified geographical writings to their own ends.

The *descripciónes*, as descriptive geographies were called in the Spanish realms, are multifaceted textual studies that depict a certain location primarily by noting its natural and human features. They can be read as individual reports, but it is essential to recognize that through their accumulation they formed a collective body of knowledge, reflecting what Lorraine Daston and Peter Galison have called "collective empiricism," which in subsequent years led to the standardization of geographical investigatory methods. Nonetheless, these colonial texts offered more than a dispassionate report on a specific area. The discipline of geography was from its early beginnings (as it is now) not merely an objective tool for the study of lands and countries but an efficient means of co-opting space, or, in Lefebvrian terms, producing it. One of the modern techniques that made the "invention of America" possible was the use of (European-style) geographical texts, a practice that remains effective today in the construction of religious, national, and ethnic identities.[20]

Descriptive geographies that originated in colonial settings shed light on the cross-fertilization of geography and religion and reveal hermeneutical methods of sacralizing "new" lands previously unfamiliar to Christianity. Since Durkheim, the concept of the sacred has permeated theoretical writings on the practice of religion.[21] The particular use of the term "sacred" for the spatial experience of religious communities has drawn our attention to, inter alia, the demarcation of special places set apart by ritual and symbolic performance (i.e., ceremonies, pilgrimages, prayers, etc.). One of the pioneers of twentieth-century religious studies, Mircea Eliade, has already noted that believers' need to find holiness in their surroundings generated multiple methods of consecrating space.[22] More recently, Thomas Tweed has also focused on the spatial image of religion in his thought-provoking *Crossing and Dwelling*, in which he argues that religions "involve homemaking." Building on Charles Long's *Signification*, Tweed develops the idea that people employ religious narratives and rituals in order to make homes and cross boundaries, making explicit the link between religion and the organization of space.[23] This process of finding one's place by symbolic religious practice was certainly something that affected Catholicism in premodern Iberia, where popular traditions emphasized community-centered devotions to local saints and holy sites.[24] Unlike in the Old World, where Catholic clergy inhabited a space made sacred by centuries-old Christian tradition, the Western Hemisphere's "virgin" landscape required the invention of new myths and legends, which often involved co-opting native sacred spatiality. With no multigenerational *geographia sacra* available, I argue, geographical writing was one technique used to integrate into Christendom a continent that had no previous record in church history. Infusing sacred meanings into foreign lands, the potential of geography was thus recognized not just by European courts but also by confessional geographers whose writings propagated the moral code of Counter-Reformation culture.

Early Modern Geography in Spain and Beyond

In only a few short decades, the modest-size kingdom of Spain, which was only unified by the marriage of Isabella I of Castile and Ferdinand II of Aragon in 1469, expanded into other parts of Europe, the Atlantic, and the Pacific, becoming the largest empire in the world. Running a global empire on which the "sun never set" was a serious business that required the aid of geographers and mapmakers in controlling and supervising immense territories. The first extensive geographical description of Spain is the unfinished *Descripción y cosmografía de España* (1517) by Hernando Colón. Two years later, Martín Fernández de Enciso included America in his world geography.

Historians have pointed to both personal and institutional motives for the success of geography in the Spanish realms, including the personal involvement of curious monarchs such as Philip II (r. 1556–98), who insisted on personally reading reports about the empire's perimeters, and the establishment of a bureaucratic administration that promoted the study of the environment and population across Spanish possessions.[25] The nature of some of Spain's more ambitious projects—such as the Padrón Real, the Crown's master map, housed in Seville, which was routinely updated as returning flotillas brought back new details of maritime routes and discovered lands, and the *Relaciones geográficas de Indias*, a rich trove of geographical information amassed from standardized questionnaires dispatched to the various regions of Spanish America—required networks of informants and craftsmen who specialized in geography and nautical cartography.[26] Such complex projects exemplified Spain's state-of-the-art empirical practices, making it arguably one of the most advanced nations, in geographical knowledge, in sixteenth-century Europe.

Coinciding with Iberian maritime expeditions, geography developed into an independent discipline beginning in the late Renaissance, and gradually separated itself from its parent field of cosmography.[27] While the study of geography gained new momentum as a result of the "rediscovery" of Ptolemaic geography in the early fifteenth century, the representation of the surface of the earth as a modern cartographic abstraction was a slow process that did not fully mature until the ability to measure longitude was finally achieved in the eighteenth century.[28] The description of space "continued to depend in one way or another upon the measure of distance and direction," as Ricardo Padrón observes.[29] Nonetheless, between the time that Johannes Werner published his commentary on Ptolemy's *Geography* (1514) until the appearance of Bernhard Varenius's *Geographia generalis* in 1650, European writers provided geography with an epistemological foundation by making explicit programmatic assertions about the field's objectives and scope. Spanish geographers were part of this intellectual dialogue. They saw geography as a distinct, recognizable discipline and sought to define a standardized method of presenting spatial data that would eventually shed the romantic and fabulous embellishments that characterized medieval travel

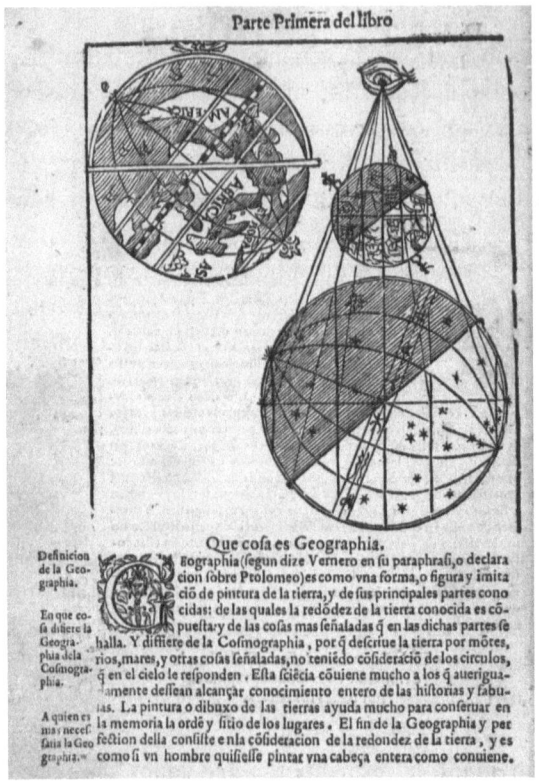

Fig. 11. "What is geography?" An example of the programmatic assertions about the objectives of geography, the "pintura de la tierra," common in contemporary literature. From the translation of *Cosmography* by Petrus Apianus and Gemma Frisius, *La Cosmographia de Pedro Apiano, corregida y añadida por Gemma Frisio* (Antwerp: Iuan Withagio, 1575), fol. 1v. Photo: Biblioteca Histórica de la Universidad Complutense de Madrid. BH FLL 20759.

narratives.[30] Part of this trend involved a growing number of methodological reflections on what constituted geography and what sort of facts were to be collected and reported in geographical inquiries (fig. 11).[31]

These analytical attempts at developing criteria or guidelines for the geographical tradition, inherited from classical authors such as Ptolemy, Strabo, and Mela, responded to a wider transformation of the European system of knowledge. Just as in the sixteenth-century natural history was separated from medicine and natural philosophy by naturalists who developed specialized techniques for "the science of describing" flora and fauna, contemporary geographers delineated a field of knowledge based on information collected incrementally over time.[32] Rather than describing plants and animals, they aimed to describe places and spaces with precision, to provide an account of the relationship between people and their environments. According to the conventions they developed, spatial description incorporated elements of human activity that today would be part of ethnography and cultural anthropology rather than human geography.[33] As with so many other intellectual activities and disciplines, the consolidation of geography supported new claims to scientific authority. Instead of copying Greco-Roman materials, the new geographers required that spatial investigation be based on empirical research and transparent criteria—in fact, whenever possible, on firsthand experience. For instance, Alejo Venegas, introduced earlier, distinguished between geography and other descriptive scholarly fields by dividing the study of the earth into five separate but interconnected branches. The first, cosmography, described the entire world, both land and water, and its intricate relationship with the celestial sphere. The second, hydrography, studied the maritime and coastal regions; the third, geography, focused on the earth's surface. The fourth, chorographia, explored the "locations of populations, mountains, valleys, rivers, fields, or marine coasts." The fifth, topographia, consisted of descriptions of a particular region.[34] Geography, according to Venegas, provided the physical and political description of the earth's surface (*la tierra y las provincias*). He considered this discipline "the most difficult" to pursue, owing to the ontological difficulty of recording physical space in words as a result "of the many mutations in the landscape."[35] Gerónimo Girava, a Spanish resident of Milan and the author of various cosmographical works, sought to resolve this difficulty by calling for a "nueva descripcion" and providing a template with which to carry it out. The scope of descriptive geography was, he explained in 1556, the research of places through their human and natural elements.[36] The description should delineate the subsections of the earth (*partes de la tierra*), their respective political subdivisions (states, republics, provinces), and should then provide the principal cities, islands, rivers, mountains, and, ultimately, the practices and way of life of their inhabitants.

The results of these methodological reflections can be seen in *Relationi universali* (Rome, 1591—translated into Spanish as *Relaciones vniuersales del mundo in 1603*) by the Italian political thinker and ex-Jesuit Giovanni Botero, a work that helped shape a new, modern vision of the world. Botero's work became a standard reference for world geography, comprising four books with descriptive material on the cities and countries found on the four known continents.[37] By the end of the seventeenth century, this influential geography had appeared in more than sixty editions and translations (either in full or in part) in various European languages. Reflecting his Jesuit education and the universalist vision of the church, Botero devoted a large portion of his work to the East and West Indies. He benefited greatly from on-the-ground Iberian informants, most notably the Jesuit José de Acosta (on whom more in the following chapter), who provided him with necessary information about places Botero himself had never had the opportunity to explore.[38]

Fig. 12. The union between compass and sword. From Bernardo de Vargas Machuca, *Milicia y descripción de las Indias* (Madrid: Pedro Madrigal, 1599), frontispiece. Courtesy of the John Carter Brown Library, Brown University, Providence, RI.

As Spaniards continued their explorations of vast oceans and lands, the reputation of Spanish geography was elevated, signaling progress and innovation.[39] For this reason, the veteran conquistador Bernardo de Vargas Machuca (ca. 1557–1622) depicted himself in the frontispiece of his book, *Milicia y descripción de las Indias* (1599), as an erudite geographer surrounded by navigational instruments and cartographic elements (fig. 12). Portraying Vargas Machuca holding a sword in one hand and dividers pointing to the Western Hemisphere on a globe in the other, the portrait, along with the famous inscription ("By the sword and the compass, more and more and more and more"), conveys the pretensions of Spanish geography. The image shows how the compass and the sword were viewed as equal partners in Habsburg overseas ventures. Much like the map historian John Harley's oft-quoted statement, "As much as guns and warships, maps have been the weapon of imperialism," Vargas Machuca's illustration points to the place of geographical knowledge in enabling European hegemonic power.[40]

Catholic Clergy and the Imperial Geographical Project

Spanish clergy shared in the contemporary appreciation of geography. From the late sixteenth century onward, they wrote dozens of *descripciónes* and *memoriales* (histories), introducing different parts of the world to a European audience in great detail. In Spanish America, both secular (diocesan) priests like Baltasar Ramírez and ordained priests like the Dominican Reginaldo de Lizárraga typically followed the method of itinerary, which, as Ricardo Padrón has shown, served Spanish officials' need to supervise and administer colonial space. As descriptive itineraries, these texts instructed the reader how to travel to and traverse Spanish territories and were often meant to work in tandem with visual representations of the land.[41] The utilitarian aspect of the friars' geographical production is clear. Geography offered a vantage point that allowed the state and the church to oversee each diocese and to catalogue territories for the expansion of Christian communities. Obviously, rich spatial description was not uncommon in the Christian literary tradition or in purely religious literary genres.[42] Even so, pilgrimage and evangelical accounts never strove to follow objective criteria, nor did they gain their authority from adherence to a particular methodology. Descriptive geography was quite different in this respect. But as much as these textual "cartographic" sources demonstrate the technical skills of the individual friars and their engagement with existing literature, the networks and global distribution of members of religious orders facilitated the production of this kind of work.

To govern its new colonies effectively, Spain needed people on the ground, especially individuals skilled in making maps and other geographical materials. Spanish clergy such as the Franciscan Alonso de Benavides, the Hieronymite Diego de Ocaña, the Carmelite Antonio Vázquez de Espinosa, and the Dominican Francisco de Burgoa were obvious candidates for such a task because they were often stationed at, or passed through, the farthest reaches of the earth. From the mid-sixteenth century on, state laws and provisions instructed ecclesiastical officials to compile and submit, based on their experience, *relaciones* to the Council of the Indies, "for the best service of our Lord."[43] The persistence of this method demonstrates the continued dependence of the Spanish state on data provided by church personnel. Recognizing their usefulness, the Spanish Crown frequently consulted friars skilled in these pursuits. Confessional geographers provided Spain with advice on matters of politics and security, based on their firsthand knowledge and often their years of experience in the mission. Monks like the Mercederian Francisco Ponce de León not only sent *descripciónes* of a particular region to the Crown (in his case, the kingdom of Chile) but also advised the king about necessary defensive measures, recommending the fortification of the kingdom in order to combat Spain's imperial enemies.

For their part, friars offered their services to the Crown, using their cosmographical knowledge and navigation skills to obtain work in a bourgeoning enterprise. From the very beginning, they were welcomed into the principal institutions responsible for the colonial process, including the Council of the Indies and Casa de la Contratación.[44] Catholic priests were also vital to geographical expeditions around the world. Basque Augustinians were key players in early voyages to the Philippines, with Fray Andrés Urdaneta (1498–1568) serving as a leading personality, navigator, and expert on the Pacific in the 1560s.[45] Fray Martín de Rada (1533–1578), a famous contributor to the early development of Catholic sinology, accompanied Urdaneta in the Legazpi expedition (1565) and took astronomical observations and measurements to determine longitude.[46] Half a century later, the Discalced Carmelite friar Antonio de la Ascensión played an important role in an expedition along the coast of California that sailed from Acapulco in 1602. Fray Antonio studied cosmography at Salamanca, where he was born, and had also been trained in the School of Navigation opened by the Casa de la Contratación. He conducted a remarkably detailed study of the region, collecting information about various deltas and bays (including data relevant for anchoring and going ashore), taking daily solar and stellar readings as well as noting landmarks, ports, reefs, and various resources along the coast.⁴⁷ Like other confessional geographers, Antonio de la Ascensión left us with a descriptive account of the area, noting the wealth of minerals, species of fish, abundance of animals, fertile land, and advice for "pacification and settlement" in California. The expedition's precise geographical descriptions and coastal charts remained the standard for years.⁴⁸

The church similarly saw in the work of overseas friars the opportunity to collect information about the world outside Rome.⁴⁹ In chapter 2, we saw the enthusiasm surrounding Alonso de Benavides's 1634 *Memorial*, which was composed especially for Pope Urban VIII and the church in Rome. More than mere spectators, cardinals and papal secretaries also actively supported the creation and spread of geographical knowledge. Already in the fifteenth and sixteenth centuries, as Zur Shalev reminds us, the church was "the primary patron of geographical learning. In Italy, for example, almost all the significant figures in the recovery of Claudius Ptolemy's geography and other classical geographers were either clerics or scholars who worked under the Church's patronage."⁵⁰ New Roman universalism demanded greater involvement in world affairs and culminated in the establishment of Propaganda Fide under the direction of the formidable secretary Francesco Ingoli (1578–1649), who supported the efforts of gathering geographical information on "the four parts of the world." Created under Pope Gregory XV (r. 1621–23) in January 1622, the *Sacra Congregatio de Propaganda Fide* (Sacred Congregation for the Propagation of the Faith) was intended to serve as the missionary headquarters of the church, responsible for raising funds and keeping records and reports of missionaries, among other duties. From its inauguration, Propaganda Fide directed its energies both to countries that had fallen under the sway of Protestantism and to "heathen" lands, where the church hoped to evangelize to the indigenous people. Geographical information was needed and reports and personal correspondence were continually gathered and sent to Rome.

The benefits of geography to the church were not only utilitarian but also propagandistic. While Christian factions claimed to be the exclusive caretakers of the truth enshrined in sacred texts, the description of the world lent the appearance of universality to the various parties' claims. Unlike controversial fields such as alchemy, astrology, and astronomy, the field of geography did not threaten the church or sacred scripture. In John Larner's words, "It did not involve gods and goddesses or pagan morality. It did not depend upon philosophies or attitudes which could be thought of as striking at foundations of Christianity."⁵¹ To the contrary, geography was easily incorporated into Catholic ideals. The end result of geographical inquiry, which depicted a particular location or the entire terrestrial globe in a text, was the public display of Catholic grandeur and triumph. Geography communicated a message of universalism in an expanding world, a point that will become clearer through concrete examples.

Let us continue by closely analyzing the itineraries of two friars, the Hieronymite Diego de Ocaña and the Carmelite Antonio Vázquez de Espinosa, whose "prose cartography" offers insights into the sophisticated way in which geography was practiced by confessional geographers.[52] Studying these figures illustrates how disparate monastic stories were woven into such geographical narratives. The focus on textual analysis here is imperative, as it reveals how descriptive geography encouraged both the harnessing of imperial science to monastic objectives and the hermeneutics of sacralizing the unfamiliar New World for Christianity.

The Madonna and the Compass

Born in Ocaña, a small town near Toledo, the Castilian Hieronymite monk Diego de Ocaña (ca. 1570–1608) was a gifted writer and painter who used his skills to propagate his order's interests in South America. Ocaña came to the famous Extremaduran shrine of Guadalupe in his youth and formally professed his vows to the Hieronymites on June 8, 1588.[53] From the monastery in Extremadura, Ocaña was sent to the West Indies in early 1599 along with the senior friar, Martín de Posada. On the basis of his travels between 1599 and 1605, Ocaña wrote a multilayered text, known today under the title *Relación del viaje de Fray Diego de Ocaña por el Nuevo Mundo*.[54] Ocaña's *Relación* (account) blended multiple literary genres, including travelogue and comedy, as well as sketched maps and paintings of indigenous people aimed at satisfying the enormous anthropological curiosity about the New World. Beyond the complexity and richness of the text, one element is especially prominent. Ocaña surveyed natural and economic resources and noted specific milestones such as towns, seaports, irrigation networks, and religious sites along his journey. He included two informative sections of *descripción*, one on Chile and the other on Tucumán and Paraguay; he also compiled a list of latitudes of the ports on the Peruvian coastline between Panama and the Strait of Magellan.[55] Taken as a whole, Ocaña's treatise is an instructive description of Spanish America that exemplifies the importance to the Spanish Crown and the Hieronymites of compiling overseas geographical data.

The Order of Saint Jerome was well connected and decisively Iberian, founded near Toledo in the late fourteenth century by Pedro Fernández

Pecha and Fernando Yañez de Figueroa. The founders envisioned a community of monks who would emulate the life of one of the eminent fathers of the church, the fifth-century hermit and biblical scholar Saint Jerome, who translated the Bible into Latin (the Vulgate) and, of relevance to Ocaña's goals, a significant promoter of Marian theology.[56] The Hieronymites were officially recognized by Pope Gregory XI in 1373 as a religious order under the Rule of Saint Augustine. Yet, unlike certain other orders, the Hieronymite Order allowed its members to practice their professions, most notably law and medicine, which contributed to the order's overall wealth and prosperity. Significantly, the Hieronymites enjoyed the powerful patronage of the Spanish Crown, allowing them to take a leading role in sixteenth-century Iberian society, which made them a particularly prosperous order not only in Spain but in Europe. Their intimate connections to the monarchy also helped them gain control over several of the most prestigious monasteries in the kingdom, including the monastery of Guadalupe as of 1389 and later (in 1584) the monastery in San Lorenzo de El Escorial, Spain's royal palace and burial site, which was built under King Philip II.[57]

The monastery of Guadalupe, the starting point in Ocaña's journey, was a sanctuary for the sacred image of Nuestra Señora de Guadalupe (Our Lady of Guadalupe), a supposed relic of the Virgin Mary that was "discovered" on the bank of the Guadalupe River. As the guardians of this revered Madonna, the Hieronymites enjoyed financial privileges, including the right to collect alms throughout the kingdom to support the monastery and the pilgrimage site.[58] Ocaña and Posada's task in America was to increase the collection of alms for their monastery and propagate the Guadalupan cult in Peru and Mexico. To these ends, among his various activities, Ocaña wrote plays and painted images of the Madonna for the local population.[59]

Posada and Ocaña began their American journey in the Caribbean and the Isthmus of Panama; from there, they continued to the Viceroyalty of Peru. In September 1599, Fray Posada, whose health had deteriorated during the voyage, passed away, and Ocaña continued his assignment alone. He continued to travel extensively until 1605 through the western and southern parts of the Viceroyalty of Peru, including the present-day territories of Peru, Bolivia, Paraguay, Argentina, and Chile. He embarked for Mexico in 1604, and between his departure and his death in Mexico City in 1608, we have no information about his whereabouts.

In a study of Ocaña's *Relación*, Kenneth Mills has emphasized that this rich account functioned as an "epideictic" text by adapting and paraphrasing "Christian story telling across the centuries."[60] While this is true, Ocaña did not write merely a devotional tract or strictly religious literature. Much like Benavides's *memoriales* and Sor María's *Redondez*, discussed in the previous chapter, Ocaña's rendering of Catholic tales and *milagros* (miracles) was informed by early modern cosmographical culture and is therefore strikingly different from earlier examples found in the apostolic literary tradition. The authority of Ocaña's text was original insofar as he employed a geographical narrative that conformed to the techniques of colonial itineraries and the literature of European expansion.

Ocaña's reports owed much to earlier works and to the continuing influence of the expanding Spanish bureaucratic apparatus in surveying the Americas. By the early 1600s, when Ocaña wrote his treatise, there was already a tradition of descriptions of the West Indies that went back to Martín Fernández de Enciso's *Suma de geographía* (1519), the first printed text in Spain to include a description of the New World.[61] Enciso's work, a descriptive narrative of the entire known world, beginning with Spain, is best known today for a description of American geography that favored a reasoned approach over the fabulous.

Ocaña's writings followed on the heels of a much larger and extensive project of the Council of the Indies to gather and analyze cosmographical information about the West Indies.[62] While formal inquiries about American nature had begun after the inauguration of the council, they entered a critical new phase in the 1570s, when Juan de Ovando y Godoy (1515–1575), a *licenciado* and priest, was appointed president of the council and began improving the quality of information through a series of bureaucratic initiatives, including the use of systematic questionnaires.[63] In 1569, Ovando, then the *visitador* (inspector) of the Council of the Indies, had drafted a questionnaire with more than thirty chapters, which was distributed to provincial officials throughout Spanish America in order to gather information about the various regions and their peoples. Two years later, the council had produced an extensive questionnaire that included two hundred headings and reflected the desire to solicit information in a way that served the utilitarian purposes of the state.[64] This *ordenza*, dated September 24, 1571, provided the legal framework for investigation, requiring "exact and complete investigations and descriptions of all matters concerning the Indies, pertaining to the land and well as the sea, the natural and the moral, of enduring or of passing interest, religious and secular . . . and arranged in the order and form of the title of descriptions."[65] The detailed instructions provided the guidelines and method for the *Book of Descriptions*, as it was called, and were therefore critical to the development of a body of knowledge based on empirical evidence. Emphasis was placed on assembling geographical and hydrological data (e.g., articles 70, 75, and 76 in the council's guidelines). The guidelines also explicitly demanded that diocesan priests of all ranks and the various superiors of religious orders provide such information.⁶⁶ This expansive endeavor was pursued further by Ovando's successor, the *cronista-cósmografo* (cosmographer-chronicler major) Juan López de Velasco, who wrote his *Geografía y descripción universal de las Indias* between the years 1571 and 1574, using the material that had been collected. The reports of Spanish clergy were important resources for Velasco's synthesis of geographical knowledge, as the case of the topographic description of the bishopric of Antequera in New Spain shows.⁶⁷ The Spanish approach to the acquisition of knowledge, an approach that was soon adopted in other imperial contexts, was to take advantage of the movement of people around the world for the benefit of the state by instructing individuals to send relevant information.⁶⁸ The court's "epistemic setting," to employ Arndt Brendecke's terminology, influenced the types of information that local actors such as Diego de Ocaña provided.⁶⁹ Responding to the imperial intentions of the Crown, confessional geographers negotiated and actively transformed the meaning of bureaucracies' initiatives and new information channels for their benefit.

Partaking in this culture of observation and reporting, Diego de Ocaña paid significant attention to Chile, which during his lifetime remained largely uncharted territory at the far end of the Spanish realm. Ocaña's section on Chile took the form of a Habsburg "itinerary map," relying on measurements and distances from one spot to the next and offering occasional longitudinal coordinates. He included vital information on topography, hydrology, and natural resources, and commented on human activity and demographic features, making a clear distinction between the Indian pueblos and the Spanish settlements.

Ocaña conveyed a sense of tireless dedication to his mission, attesting, "I did not stop traversing the land and sailing the ocean until I reached the last tip of the land of Chile, namely, the city of Osorno, and the island of Chiloé, which is next to the Strait of Magellan."⁷⁰ Writing that he arrived from Lima by sea, Ocaña stated that he began his Chilean journey in Copiapó Valley, which was "populated with Indians" and marked the beginning of the territory. From there he traveled "to the city of Coquimbo, which was the first Spanish settlement. . . . The town is located above the sea and the port is located two leagues from it, at 29 degrees [latitude]."⁷¹ Ocaña claimed that he continued to the southern tip of Chile, which was believed to be the southernmost point of the earth.

Ocaña's special interest in Chile is understandable in the context of the Araucanian wars, the struggle between the Spaniards and the Mapuche people, which had taken a dramatic turn shortly before he arrived in America. Following their invasion of the Araucanía region, Spaniards had founded several strongholds and settlements on the southern frontier, including Concepción, Valdivia, Imperial, Villarrica, and Angol. Yet, by the mid-sixteenth century, sporadic but continual skirmishes had halted the colonial progression in Mapuche territory. The Spaniards' resounding defeat at the Battle of Curalaba in December 1598, in which Governor Martín García Óñez de Loyola and his soldiers were ambushed and killed by Mapuche warriors, triggered a general Indian uprising that lasted several years, during which the Spaniards had to withdraw south of the Biobío River. The Spanish cities and forts within the territory were abandoned and destroyed, in what came to be known as the Destruction of the Seven Cities. These events colored Ocaña's description, and he went to great lengths to report on the war and the massive destruction. He chronicled the events matter-of-factly: "Chillán is located at 34 degrees, ten leagues from the ocean and ten leagues from the cordillera . . . [and] is where the Indians began the war." He noted deserted cities that had been abandoned as a result of the uprising. He further explained the nomadic nature of the indigenous peoples in the southern border, "who live in the mountains without having fixed settlements," making "this land very difficult to conquer."[72]

Despite the devastation in parts of the land, Ocaña emphasized Chile's potential for Spanish settlement, stressing the region's richness and plenty, especially for agriculture and mining. Describing the area around Coquimbo, he noted the abundance of wheat, grapes, corn, and fruits from Castile, and local produce such as pacay (*pacaes*), lucuma, guayaba, sweet cucumber (*pepinos*), and sweet potatoes. He also emphasized the wealth of metals, including lead, copper, and, most important, the many deposits of gold. The gold, he explained, was not buried but was on the surface and easily panned. However, he acknowledged the demographic collapse, adding that the settlers were poor "because of the shortage of Indian laborers."[73]

Together with the description, Ocaña included four maps that he had sketched of the region, to which he refers in the text (fig. 13).[74] Maps, as John Harley explains, functioned as tools of "pacification, civilization and exploitation" that served "to legitimate the reality of conquest and empire."[75] Ocaña's written descriptions and maps functioned together as a means of demonstrating control of and familiarity with a troubled land, allowing for symbolic ownership and appropriation of the same contested space. The

Fig. 13. "Desde la ciudad de la Imperial a la Concepciòn." One of the four maps in Ocaña's description of Chile. From Diego de Ocaña, *Relación del viaje de Fray Diego de Ocaña por el Nuevo Mundo* (1599–1605). Photo: Universidad de Oviedo, Oviedo, Spain.

maps, supplemented by the descriptive text, do not "convey a wonder-filled vision of exoticism and otherness" but confirm a "sense of familiarity and ease of comprehension" that historian Heidi Scott has detected in the writings of Spanish explorers in colonial Peru, writings that helped create an impression of a "New World accessible to a distant European readership."[76] Such a tangible and recognizable representation of Chile allowed Ocaña to appropriate imperial territory for his own ends, imbuing the "end of the earth" in the Southern Hemisphere with a Hieronymite presence.

Beatriz Peña Núñez contends that Ocaña never traveled to Chile and that such a voyage, south of the Biobío River, was "unrealistic" in 1600 (when Ocaña claims to have reached those parts) because of the Araucanian rebellion.[77] Even if Peña Núñez is right, Ocaña's insistence on reproducing geographical information about the contested region demonstrates the cultural capital of geography. Describing travel through Chile made for a powerful statement. In writing his treatise, Ocaña could argue that the Hieronymites had reached the end of the earth despite the turbulent times in those parts, confirming the resilience of Catholicism and of his order.

Throughout his travels in South America, Ocaña consistently wove a religious message into his narrative, especially as he told of extreme conditions. In one instance, on the way from Portobello to Panama, he described a particularly difficult pass, the Paso del Credo, which was considered so treacherous that to ensure safe travels, one was advised to recite the credo and know "the entire Christian doctrine." Not far from there, he described how he and his companions had to make a difficult river crossing. All of his clothes and belongings were soaked. Miraculously, "300 volumes of *la historia de nuestra*

Señora" were saved "by the Virgin," along with the five donkeys who carried them: "none of the books fell because it seems that Our Lady saved them."[78] Written by Gabriel de Talavera, who served as prior of the Extremaduran monastery during the years 1595–98 and again from 1617 until his death in 1620, and printed in Toledo in 1597, these books were a history of the image of Guadalupe that chronicled the many wonders associated with it.[79] The volumes were part of the Hieronymite campaign to spread the word about the Virgin of Guadalupe and her miracles. "The Holy Mother" also came to Ocaña's aide in the passage through Pariacaca, a range of snowy peaks in the Peruvian province of Yauyos, in which Ocaña described a near-death experience while traversing "the most severe *puna* [high-altitude plateau] in all Peru." On an extremely snowy night in 1603, Ocaña became separated from his traveling party. Echoing the lamentation of his order's spiritual father, Saint Jerome (who, while living in solitude in the Syrian desert, yearned for the "pleasures of Rome"), Ocaña, fighting for his life alone in the "desert," longed for his home, the monastery of Guadalupe, where the monks were "well fed and comfortable in their cells" under the protection of the Virgin.[80] Ocaña survived the night and again credited the Virgin of Guadalupe's intercession. Crediting Mary's intervention was certainly a common practice in Ocaña's time, yet for the Hieronymites who guarded the sacred image of this Black Madonna, there was a particularly Spanish angle to their relationship with the Virgin Mary, deeply rooted in the epic of exploration and the *reconquista*.

The shrine of Guadalupe in Extremadura, whence Ocaña began his voyage, was the pride of the Hieronymites.[81] Unlike many representations of Mary as a young European woman, the image of Mary at the shrine depicts her as a black-skinned mother sitting on a chair with the Christ Child on her lap. The history of the small statue is said to be connected to Saint Leander of Seville, Pope Gregory the Great, and, some argue, to Saint Luke the Evangelist (who according to certain accounts was the sculptor).[82] When the Moors invaded Iberia in the early eighth century, legend has it that the mysterious statue of Mary was hidden. As the story goes, Mary later appeared to a Spanish shepherd and asked that a monastery be built in her honor on the spot where her statue would be found. Following the victory in 1340 over the Marinid and Nasrid forces at the Battle of Tarifa, which prevented Moorish forces from invading Iberia, Alfonso XI of Castile elevated the Black Madonna to its status as one of the most celebrated relics of the kingdom. From this period onward, the Guadalupe shrine evolved into a notable pilgrimage destination, and beginning in 1389 served as the residence of the

Hieronymites, in a sense cementing the relationship between the Spanish Crown, the Order of Saint Jerome, and the Virgin of Guadalupe. The veneration of the prominent icon of Iberian Catholicism had crossed the Atlantic Ocean before Ocaña's voyage to America. Columbus himself probably visited the Hieronymite monastery before his second voyage, and he named one of the first islands he found "Guadalupe" in honor of the Virgin.[83] The belief that the Black Madonna aided Spanish military victories undoubtedly contributed to her popularity among Extremaduran conquistadores such as Hernán Cortés and Francisco Pizarro, who paid tribute to the shrine.

Placed at the heart of his narrative, Ocaña's story of the intercession of the Virgin Mary brought to life the monastic imagination of the Order of Saint Jerome and promoted the cult of Guadalupe. The continued presence of "the Holy Mother" in his account reminds us of one of the Hieronymites' original tasks in sending Ocaña and Martín de Posada to Spanish America, namely, to promote the Guadalupan cult in South America and regulate localized patterns of piety toward her. Yet, to Ocaña's dismay, as Amy Remensnyder has noted, "he discovered that the material and spiritual fruits of devotions to these New World images of Guadalupe were not being ferried across the Atlantic to his home monastery. The local people considered these Madonnas their own, not representatives of one located thousands of miles away."[84] Nevertheless, Ocaña's geographical efforts prepared the ground for more Hieronymites to come and report on alms collecting and devotional sites, among them Pedro de Puerto, who noted Ocaña's work in his own 1624 report.[85]

Ocaña's narrative thus reveals the subordination of descriptive geography to monastic needs. While the legal and institutional infrastructure set up by the Council of the Indies stimulated the geographical inquiries made by the Catholic monk, Ocaña mindfully incorporated this literature and new information into the rhetorical arsenal of his order. We cannot know for certain whether Ocaña's talents as a geographer and artist prompted his order to choose him for the American mission, but it is clear that these abilities served the Hieronymite cause well. Writing to advance the Hieronymites' alms collecting and the Marian cult, geographical narrative provided the monk a platform from which to connect to centuries-old monastic ideals, while molding those ideals for an age of colonization. From placing the Hieronymites at the border of the Southern Hemisphere in order to convey the power of his order, to the miraculous intervention and safekeeping of the Madonna along his path, the narrative is saturated with Hieronymite ideals and visions. Just as the circulation of pilgrimage guidebooks could have "revolutionary potential in that [they] offered the clergy an opportunity to promote their cults to wider audiences removed from aural and visual immediacy,"[86] geographical texts could serve propagandistic objectives. Geography as practiced by Diego de Ocaña was a practical discipline that required know-how and experience, yet it was codified in a symbolic knowledge that provided the ultimate meaning to the confessional geographer's endeavor. The practicality and symbolism of geography were intrinsically linked, as both supported the transformation of a foreign land into an imperial Catholic space.

Vázquez de Espinosa: Portrait of a Confessional Geographer

In his *Compendio y descripción de las Indias Occidentales,* the Carmelite friar Antonio Vázquez de Espinosa remarked that the village of Carabuco, in the Peruvian province of Omasuyo, was reputed for possessing a unique pre-Columbian item. The village was blessed with a "miraculous cross," which, according to Espinosa, the Indians believed had been carried to their village by "a man of divine origin, child of the Sun."[87] The cross, as inscribed in their *quipos* (a system of knotted strings used in the Andes to record information), had been placed there by "one of the Holy Apostles" (whom Espinosa identifies as Saint Thomas),[88] who "had passed through preaching the Holy Gospel" to the locals and had "left it there as a sign to attest to and commemorate" (*testimonio y memoria*) his presence. Espinosa admitted that over the years many details regarding what had truly transpired had been forgotten, largely because the tribes "had no written language, nor any histories, but their *quipos.*" Despite the lack of a local written history, Espinosa stressed that "the miracles which God has worked through it among these new Christians [were there] to anchor them in our holy faith."[89]

Divided into two parts that explored the viceroyalties of New Spain and Peru, respectively, Espinosa's *Compendio y descripción* is an expansive geographical study written as a descriptive itinerary.[90] This descriptive geography included useful data on the climate, topography, flora, and fauna of the West Indies, along with anthropological observations. Espinosa completed the manuscript in the last months of 1629 and received royal license for its publication, but his sudden death in January 1630 prevented its publication until the twentieth century. Like Diego de Ocaña, Espinosa employed geography to support the goals of his order, the Carmelites, whose renewal movement became a model for the redefinition of piety and faith during the Catholic Reformation. The reporting of a miraculous cross demonstrates the ways in which Espinosa fashioned his *descripción* to bolster the church, in this case by uncovering the sacred in the land through the recognition of various local "miracles." To use Daniel's parable, "the writing was on the wall" for Espinosa; God had left such signs as a statement to be read by the righteous later in history, and geography was the perfect tool for recording and connecting these sites. Espinosa's readers are thus not merely introduced to sites along the author's route but also learn, often in passing, that each location carried with it the potential to tell a religious story. The reference to a purportedly ancient Christian relic should not take away from a basic fact, critical to Espinosa's geography—namely, that America remained a relatively new world for the Carmelites, one that had to be assimilated into the order's worldview. This Christian order was committed to both solitary prayer and apostolic service and attempted from an early stage to find the right balance between these two callings. For this reason, I argue, Espinosa presented America as both a space where evangelical work was much needed and, at the same time, as a new world that offered much room in which to re-create a spiritual Carmelite haven and return to the order's early hermitic focus.

Espinosa was born in the late sixteenth century in Castilleja de la Cuesta, a village in the vicinity of Seville. We know very little about his life before his journey to the Americas, and no information survives about why he joined the Carmelites. It is notable that Espinosa decided to join that order at a time when it enjoyed significant influence in Spanish life. Though the Carmelite tradition traces its origins to the biblical prophet Elijah and claims a special relationship with Mary, the order probably emerged around 1200 among a community of hermits on the slopes of Mount Carmel in Palestine.[91] The founders of the Carmelites are unknown; the only hint at the order's origins is a formula of life that focused on eremitic, simple life, granted by Albert, the patriarch of Jerusalem, in the early thirteen century. As the Carmelites began to migrate to European countries around the mid-thirteenth century, they deemphasized the place of solitude and seclusion from society in their regimen, and evolved, following the success of the Franciscans and Dominicans, into a mendicant order (the Carmelite Order received full mendicant privileges in 1326). After these early years, there were a few attempts to restore the order's early hermitic focus, a sign of the continual pull between the two poles of the order's identity, the eremitical and the apostolic. Most important, in mid-sixteenth-century Spain, the Carmelites went through one of the most influential renewals of any existing order, a turning point in Catholic worship in Iberia and beyond.[92]

From the Convent of San José in Ávila, the nun Teresa de Jesús set herself the task of restoring the mendicant ideals among the Carmelites. She focused her spirituality on maintaining an ascetic lifestyle, upholding the virtue of solitude and leading a life of poverty. Her approach was to impart a method of personal and communal prayer that, among her followers, became a doctrinal means of living a pious life.[93] The reforms caused a divide within the Carmelite Order between those who embraced the changes (the discalced, or shoeless, who preached an abandonment of comfort symbolized by footwear) and their opponents (the original branch of the order). Nonetheless, by the seventeenth century, the tensions between the two branches of Carmelite tradition had mostly dissipated. Though the inner schism was irreversible, Teresian restoration of contemplative life became the model of Carmelite spirituality on both sides of the divide, certainly after the Touraine Reform of the original Carmelites (later, the Ancient Observance), which began around 1600.

Though Espinosa joined the original Order of Carmel rather than the discalced branch, it is evident that the image of Teresa and her stance against heresy informed his religiosity. Espinosa called Teresa "a nun of my Holy Order." Lauding her renewal movement, he wrote, "She was like a Spanish apostle and had a man's valor, illuminated by the light of the Holy Ghost."[94] Her death in 1582, Espinosa noted, was said to coincide with a major earthquake in the kingdom of Peru, leaving the reader to connect the dots.

Espinosa's statements came at a time of heated debate over state patronage (1617–30) in which, as noted in chapter 3, the reformist camp wished to proclaim Teresa de Ávila the co-patron saint of Spain. To justify their campaign, Teresa's supporters emphasized her capacity to protect Spain against heresy and lead the nation to spiritual reinvigoration.[95] Espinosa's views reflected the Carmelites' interest in elevating their own holy saint to the position of co-patron, thus cementing the order's prominent role in the future direction of Spain. For Espinosa, Saint Teresa's revered image symbolized his order's dedication to Catholic renewal. Furthermore, by associating Teresa's death in Spain with a geological phenomenon in America, Espinosa was able to integrate the Carmelites' sacred history into American nature, implicitly making an ideological claim about the Carmelites' place in the American mission.

The early seventeenth century, when Espinosa arrived in the Americas, also saw a dramatic change in the way the Carmelites reconceived of their role within the Catholic mission. While the mendicant orders had been granted permission to found convents in Spanish America according to the terms of the 1552 bull of Pope Adrian VI (known as the Omnímoda), the Carmelites' interest in missionary work in the Indies grew noticeably only after the election of Juan Bautista Rubeo de Ravena in 1562 as general of the Carmelites.[96] In 1568, Carmelite friars founded a monastery in Santa Fe de Bogotá, though they abandoned it only a few years later.[97] In 1585, the Discalced Carmelites received permission from the Crown to establish a province in New Spain, the province of Saint Albert, initiating a new era for the Carmelite mission and bringing members of both the discalced and unreformed Carmelites to the New World.[98]

Against this backdrop, Espinosa set sail for America in 1608, working under the auspices of both the Spanish Crown and the Catholic Church as a member of the Carmelite Order. These two axes would inform much of his work. While Espinosa did not give an exact account of his journey, his detailed descriptions and frequent allusions to events and places in his *Compendio* confirm various journeys through Mexico, Central America, and Peru. After returning to Spain in 1622, Espinosa set about speedily publishing several works, including the *Tratado verdadero del viaje y navegación* (Malaga, 1623), in which he told of the challenges and calamities experienced by the Spanish fleet on its journey from New Spain to Cadiz, Spain. The same year, he also published three shorter treatises, *Confessionario general, luz y guía del cielo*; *Sumario de indulgencias*; and *Los tratos y contratos de las Indias del Perú y Nueva España*.

Espinosa's life and works straddled the sometimes contentious relationship between the Spanish Crown and the Catholic Church. Both institutions were natural allies in the colonial expansion in America, but they also had their own separate agendas. In the early 1620s, the tensions between Rome and the Spanish state were palpable (having emerged already by the 1560s), and the disadvantages faced by the "Iberian *Patronato* and Padroado were becoming manifest," as Robert Bireley reminds us.[99] Philip II had rejected the efforts of Pius V, in 1568, and of Gregory XIII, in 1572, to intervene in the control of the church in Spanish America. In time, as the church set out to establish new bases, geography became even more prominent. Rome had to create its own channels for knowledge.

Part of this transition can be observed in the creation of Propaganda Fide, which aimed to separate missionary efforts from the mundane interests of the state. While Propaganda Fide never succeeded significantly in Spanish America owing to the strong opposition of the Spanish Crown, the institution was central in promoting new Roman universalism, and in this sense it influenced missionaries everywhere. In fact, under Secretary Francesco Ingoli, one of Propaganda Fide's central tasks was to include more religious orders in the mission, including the Carmelites.[100] Critically, though the idea of creating a missionary headquarters had been proposed since the Council of Trent, it was a Carmelite theologian, Tomás de Jesús (1564–1627), who appears to have provided a blueprint for its mission and form. Nine years before the establishment of Propaganda Fide, in his *De procuranda salute omnium gentium* (On procuring the salvation of all peoples), the prominent Carmelite theologian suggested the creation of a central body under papal control to oversee the church's missionary activities.[101] Tomás de Jesús promoted the first mission of the Discalced Order, and in particular emphasized the importance of the evangelical enterprise in America.[102] To these ends, he initiated new educational programs for prospective missionaries, which provided specialized training for Carmelites who had completed their regular studies and wanted to join the mission. In 1621, he inaugurated the missionary seminary at Louvain, and similar mission seminaries were established in Malta and Goa in 1630.[103] Friars spent two years at the mission seminary, studying linguistics, dialectics, applied theology, and natural sciences, after which they returned to their home provinces, ready to depart for their missionary assignments on short notice.

Seen together, these developments within the church, the state, and the Carmelites led by the 1620s to a convergence of forces that set the stage for Espinosa's *Compendio*: the Carmelite order was undergoing a formative period of growth with respect to its apostolic identity, and both the discalced and unreformed branches were eager to play a larger part in the American mission. Such tendencies within the Carmelite community coincided with a new impetus and vision within the papal curia, which demanded the global expansion of Christendom. All of these developments formed the context for the Carmelites' discovery of America.

Upon his return to Spain, Espinosa set about advancing his career through contacts with the Carmelite Order and the Crown. From approximately 1623 to his death in 1630, he wore a number of different hats that reflected his growing stature in both the religious and the secular spheres. In 1624, he served on at least several occasions as a consultant to the Council of the Indies on matters regarding the archbishopric of Santa Fe in New Granada.[104] During the same period, he served as consultant to the Holy Office of the Inquisition.[105] A man of apparently inexhaustible energy, he simultaneously worked himself into the political life of the court by becoming a client to the *conde-duque* de Olivares. Espinosa served the count-duke and his wife as a personal chaplain and confessor, while at the same time lending his extensive knowledge of the New World to the count-duke, thereby advancing the latter's political agenda in government.[106] In 1625, he participated in several sessions of the Council of War of the Indies and, according to his later writings, advised the Crown on matters relating to the imperial fleet.[107]

Throughout the 1620s, Espinosa also corresponded regularly with Rome. In 1623, he wrote to the prior-general of the Carmelite Order, Sebastián Fantoni, describing his time in the West Indies. Espinosa also used the occasion to voice his desire to travel to Rome to obtain apostolic confirmation of his mission. Fantoni relayed the contents of Espinosa's letter to the newly established Propaganda Fide and highlighted Espinosa's qualifications and years of experience as a missionary. Through these channels, Espinosa sought recognition for his work, and it would appear that he received it. This included seeking permission to become a doctor of theology, which he received from Fantoni in 1624.[108]

In the same year, Espinosa appealed to the cardinal protector of the Carmelites to support his request to be declared vicar-general of the Carmelite missions in Spanish America. In 1625, he began making more concrete plans to return to the West Indies. He was granted license to return to Peru by the newly appointed general of the order, Gregorio Caneli, and in 1627 was appointed to the office of apostolic commissary to the Indies (and was given the administration of the province of Casanga by General Caneli). In late 1629, a royal *cédula* addressed to the viceroy of Peru asked that Espinosa be assigned a vacant post.[109]

While Espinosa prepared for his return to the West Indies, he wrote various letters, *relaciones*, and *memoriales* both for the state (to the Council of the Indies) and for the church, and penned his *Compendio*. In early 1625, he sent the general of the order maps and descriptions of the Indies. Naturally, the order and the newly founded Propaganda Fide were keenly interested in such materials, and it appears to have been critical to Espinosa to linger on geographical descriptions of the dioceses themselves. By exploring the area according to ecclesiastical divisions, he was in a position to advise officials on administrative matters of the church. In one instance, Espinosa suggested creating a new diocese in the city of Arica so that the area would be "manageable and have sufficient income and be better administered." Espinosa positioned himself as an agent in the curia's task of overseeing its global mission. Like Diego de Ocaña, he emphasized his personal experience and attention to detail: "I verified, having traveled, observed, and considered with special care when I was in that country, and I noted everything and informed, with a desire for improvement."[110] At the same time, Espinosa sent geographical information to the Crown. Between 1626 and 1630 he wrote a number of *memoriales* and *relaciones* to the Council of the Indies, hoping to elicit the attention of Madrid.

Searching for Mount Carmel

While Espinosa's death prevented the publication of his work, several contemporaries, including Antonio de León Pinelo, read his manuscript and lauded its achievements, praising Espinosa for being "well versed and proficient in all matters pertaining to the Indies."[111] Indeed, the utility of geography is evident throughout the work. Espinosa provided descriptions of routes and places largely taken from his own experience, as well as distances and cartographic references. His writings demonstrated his talent for evocative depictions that allowed his readers to step into the landscape. Describing the coastal areas, for instance, he recalled how mariners, "upon recognizing Sierra Nevada, which is close to Santa Marta, they sail West-North-West until they see the light-colored water of the Río Grande, and then they steer South-West."[112] Showing off his cartographic skills and deep familiarity with nautical charts, he included references to the latitudes of possible maritime routes to the coastlines of the Indies and back to Spain (in both summer and winter). In describing the land, Espinosa was no less careful. Like Ocaña, he provided the relative position of various locations and settlements as well as distances and cardinal points to orient the reader (and possible traveler) along the itinerary's stations. Espinosa made mention of the different dioceses and told of their history and economy, providing a remarkably detailed description of them.

As opposed to certain religious writers who saw American nature as full of signs to be deciphered, Espinosa took a more practical interest in compiling lists of natural resources.[113] Mindful of new opportunities for settlement and commercial exploitation, he focused less on the unique or extraordinary and more on the abundance that America had to offer, frequently employing the notion of paradise to these ends. In his account of his travels through the diocese of Nicaragua in 1613, Espinosa wrote, "The province and village of Viejo is 3 leagues West-North-West of Realejo; this is all groves and forests, and among them are some streams and rivers of sweet and crystal-clear water, and a great diversity of birds and animals."[114] The land was "abundant with corn and all kinds of native fruits," like "a piece of paradise" (*un pedazo de paraíso*). Espinosa repeated the phrase *pedazo de paraíso* in his descriptions of Omereque Valley, Arequipa and Huanta Valleys, Rio Bermejo, Hilo Valley, and the Caribbean.

To be sure, the fertility of the new continent was a recurring theme in the work of other seventeenth-century writers, which even prompted some of them, including the Franciscan friar Buenaventura de Salinas y Córdoba and Antonio de León Pinelo, to propose that the Garden of Eden might be found in the Americas.[115] But Espinosa appears not to have been searching for the biblical paradise, as certain other authors did; instead, he used the phrase as a rhetorical device, both to stress the bounty of a land ripe for further settlement and to urge his order to play a greater role in carrying the cross to America. A few years before Espinosa wrote his opus, Antonio de la Ascensión, a Discalced Carmelite, also noted the "mild climate and the great abundance of good fish," along with the resources that made California ideal for the Catholic mission. Fray Antonio concluded, "it is the best place in the world for the maintenance and way of life of the Discalced Carmelites, who, by order of the king, our lord, have charge of the conversion of the realm, and for their abstemious and penitent life."[116] As Carmelites of both branches tried to expand and establish themselves alongside other Catholic orders in the Americas, they evoked the beauty of various regions to articulate how "natural" their presence in the area was and how the land could support their hermitic lifestyle.[117] For Espinosa, paradise was a transformative idea that merged his spatial and visionary thinking. It was a promise that could be achieved by sending more pious Carmelites to the American mission.

Espinosa made a strong declaration of orthodox Catholic cosmography and historical consciousness. After explaining the spherical nature of the earth and its five climatic zones, he continued with geographical facts that stressed the vast physical reaches of the Spanish Empire and the role of Habsburg Spain in expanding Christianity. As in the writings of Diego de Ocaña, Chile conveyed the magnitude of the Habsburgs' global monarchy: "If one considers the lands in the Indies from Cartagena, which is 10° above the tropic of Cancer, to the city of Castro in the Kingdom of Chile, in the Chiloé islands, which are 43° to the Antarctic pole, there is a distance of over 1,440 leagues, in which there is a retardation of the sun between its rising and setting; . . . so consequently when it is day in Spain, there it is night." By describing the location and relationship between Chile and Spain in the language of geography, Espinosa articulated the universalist aspirations of the church. Around the world, Espinosa enthusiastically argued, "gracious sacrifice is always being made and offered to God in over 70,000 churches." The sun, as he remarked, never set on Catholic lands, and "all the hours of the day, without pause, a sacred sacrifice is celebrated: that of the Mass."[118] Espinosa continued by presenting the church's anthropological standpoint. European writers, and Spanish friars in particular, turned to a variety of postdiluvian stories to suggest a possible Old World origin for the Amerindians, including Atlantis, Carthage, ancient Spain, Ophir, and even the lost tribes of Israel.[119] Espinosa evoked tales of the biblical flood and the Tower of Babel, tracing the origins of the natives to the lost tribes of Israel, "the best people who were in the world at that time."[120] In this way, Espinosa echoed and confirmed the Catholic doctrine that all human beings had descended from Adam. Moreover, he offered a plausible historical account that included the Amerindians in God's plan for human salvation. After all, the ten lost tribes, and by extension the Amerindians, disappeared without a trace before Christ lived and therefore never rejected his message, a fact that gave their conversion greater urgency.

This information about the earth and its peoples, found at the very beginning of Espinosa's work, confirmed and justified the efforts of Catholic missionaries. During Espinosa's lifetime, Catholics were struggling for the hearts and minds of people across the world. In Espinosa's estimation, the church and the Spanish monarchy waged a critical battle against all the nations "who have not known God or served Him," including the inhabitants of the Protestant nations, whom Espinosa dubbed "the perfidious heretics of the North."[121] Espinosa signaled the significance of the American front in that struggle, highlighting the natives' need "for light, which will banish the darkness and ignorance."[122] He repeatedly wrote about Indians in the Americas "who desired to become Christians." Some had even built churches but, he lamented, they could not be converted for want of prelates or priests: "for the few [missionaries] that are there cannot fill the need."[123]

Espinosa composed his descriptive geography to serve Carmelite propagandistic goals, turning to both the church and the Spanish monarchy to point out the essential role that his order ought to play in America. He opened his description of the Americas with a short vignette about the island of Hispaniola, "the home of the first Christians in the Indies" and a "city of refuge." The island served, in Espinosa's account, as "mother" and "womb" for the American mission. The description of Hispaniola as the maternal cradle of faith reflects the missionary spirit that pervaded Espinosa's work. Applying Marian metaphors to the mission, Espinosa connected his geographical account with God's plan for human salvation, highlighting the significance of the Americas in this divine drama.

In the following pages, Espinosa infused his descriptive geography with a clearly confessional agenda, pointing to the presence of the divine in the landscape. Like other friars, he conveyed a strong typological consciousness that employed the Bible as the ultimate reference system to elucidate mundane experiences.[124] Another well-traveled friar, the Jesuit Gerónymo Pallas, likened the experience of the West Indies missionary enterprise to that of Moses in Exodus. He proclaimed that Catholic missionaries were struggling to liberate the Indians from "the servitude of Egypt" by guiding them through the desert to reach "the promised land of the Catholic Church," where "the milk and honey" signified God's understanding and love (*la leche del conoscimiento de las cosas de Dios y con la miel de su Divino amor*).[125] Similarly, by connecting new sites to biblical landscapes and narratives, Espinosa opened up the possibility of reading the sacred into the New World. For instance, he used biblical scenes in his description of the natural landscape: one Mexican sierra recalled for him Jerusalem and looked "like Mount Zion" because "it has many groves on its slopes," complete with "cypresses, pines, and oaks." Another site reminded him of Mount Carmel, the mythological home of his order.[126] Insisting on inherent similarities between the West Indies and the land of Canaan, Espinosa reconceptualized space by relating concrete sites in America to the Catholic imagination.

Espinosa further infused geographic locations with Catholic meaning by linking them to familiar biblical narratives. He described a town near a "mighty river" in the province of Casquin, set upon a hill with four hundred houses surrounded by a bountiful country "all full of corn, fruit, and other luxuries." He told how a native chief in the region appealed to the Spanish governor to beg God for rain, since the Christians "had a better God than theirs" and the land was suffering from drought. In a display of religious power, the governor and his men erected "a large cross" before which the Christians prayed, "and it rained well that night." The scene, as Espinosa painted it, was especially dramatic, and was witnessed by more than "20,000 infidels," who yelled "at intervals while the Spaniards were praying." The natives "were greatly comforted and held the Holy Cross in deep veneration."[127]

Stories of deities demonstrating their power by answering prayers for rain in times of drought are not unique and appear in many variations in ancient mythology. But there is one story with a particular Carmelite importance. The book of 1 Kings recounts the story of the prophet Elijah the Tishbite's prayer on Mount Carmel, which ended a devastating famine in the northern kingdom of Israel. The story pits Elijah against the prophets of Baal and Asher, both sides attempting to prove their ability to persuade the divine entities to accept their offerings and grant their respective pleas. The pagan prophets fail (and are later slaughtered by Elijah), even though

Baal was considered the supreme god in Canaanite mythology, controlling rain and fertility. But God accepts Elijah's sacrifice by miraculously setting it alight (much to the amazement of witnesses, who collectively affirm the Hebrew God's divinity). Elijah proceeds to climb to the summit of Mount Carmel, where he crouches down in prayer. The biblical chapter ends with the sudden appearance of dark clouds that finally bring heavy rains to the parched land. The tale of Elijah on the slopes of Mount Carmel teaches about both the power of prayer and the significance of preaching and evangelical work. For Carmelites, Elijah's self-styled disciples, this particular biblical story showed the zeal of the enigmatic prophet—the sole survivor among God's prophets during Ahab's murderous reign—and highlighted his intimate relationship to God. Thanks to Elijah's deeds atop Mount Carmel, the Israelites were able to behold God's power and abandon their false deities.[128]

To be sure, Espinosa's story differed from the biblical account, in that there was no need for a spectacular competition between deities or their loyal servants; Espinosa says that the indigenous people from the beginning recognized that the Christian God was stronger than their gods and merely pleaded that he be asked properly (i.e., through a Christian prayer) in order that the rain come. These differences aside, Espinosa's anecdote recalls key parts of the Elijan narrative, for both Espinosa and 1 Kings 18 tell of how a pagan people were able to appeal to God for help through a devout intercessor at a time of serious drought. Moreover, Elijah was able to turn the northern Israelites back to God by defeating the pagan prophets and their powerless deities Baal and Asherah. Similarly, the Spaniards converted the Indians by convincing them of the supremacy of the Christian God. Just as Elijah erected an altar to God on the spot (with twelve stones, one for each of the tribes descended from Jacob), the Spaniards placed a great cross at the location where they had prayed. Both narratives display the power of prayer on the part of God's chosen people, bringing the blessing of heavy rain to a dry landscape. Both stories find their dramatic climax as the Israelites, in one version, and Indians, in the other, are reminded of the power of the one true God. The pathos of the American version is further intensified given Espinosa's belief that the first settlers of the West Indies were none other than the Israelite tribes. Espinosa's rendering thus implicitly tells how (the now Christianized) God brought rain to the descendants of the Israelites, who once again witnessed God's omnipotence.

Moreover, in recounting a tale that any educated Christian would recognize, but one that particularly resonated with Carmelite typological consciousness, Espinosa invoked a biblical narrative starring his order's mythical spiritual founder, the prophet Elijah. For seventeenth-century Carmelites, who continuously wrestled with the two aspects of their collective identity—eremitical life and apostolic work—the story of Elijah on Mount Carmel could reconcile the tension between two opposite callings. In the New World, Spanish missionaries collectively followed Elijah's lead and continued his legacy, serving as intercessors between God and the native peoples. Espinosa's retelling of the Elijan legend at Mount Carmel offered a rationale for his order's dual pursuits: prayer and apostolic service. This Catholic miracle in the New World gave new, sacred meaning to a foreign land and emphasized the need for the mission (and particularly, Carmelite participation in it).

Espinosa also attempted to ground his observations in firsthand experience, culled from his travels. He could evoke Catholic and specifically Carmelite symbols of piety in his personal reflections. Reflecting on his 1616 journey through the desert of Pacará, Espinosa wrote several years later, "I was astounded as I carefully contemplated the greatest wonder of the world (in my opinion), which God created in that spot so that He might be glorified there by His creatures, and I gave Him infinite thanks for it." Specifically, he pointed to the "many cliffs of alabaster and other precious stones in so many shapes," which "God in His divine providence created." All the more impressive for the Spanish friar was the fact that some of these cliffs and stones resembled "armored horsemen," while others looked like "saints."[129]

Espinosa's assertion that God left a trace for human contemplation had its roots in Christian natural theology and appears to have been influenced by Catholic ideas that were popularized in his time. These included the theological works of Roberto Bellarmino and Luis de Granada, discussed above, who had developed methods of ascending to God through observing creation. Following Augustinian teachings, Espinosa held that created objects, in this case the very stones and minerals of the Pacará desert, attested that God was their creator. Espinosa might also have been responding to the indigenous sacralization of natural topographic features. As Carolyn Dean shows, the pre-Hispanic Inca valued not only carved stones but also rocks in their natural environment. The Inca's special relationship to rocks extended to sacred places where Andeans could interact with powerful numina, in a sense creating kinds of "natural temples" in the outdoors.[130] Espinosa's encounter with the extraordinary beauty of the Chilean desert was thus not only an encounter between human and nature but also a meeting point between Catholic natural theology and Amerindians' "culture of stone," which, in his estimation, provided definite proof of God's magnificence and power. Perhaps with the intention of co-opting native sacred spatiality, Espinosa saw nature as a space that could facilitate connection and communication between God and humans.

Espinosa did not simply see ordinary human figures in the stones of Pacará but "saints" and "holy men." The trope of saints and knights fits neatly with popular Catholic iconography. As Simon Ditchfield reminds us, saints were "not just a kinetic expression of religious devotion nor—together with the Eucharist—the most visible mark of Roman Catholic identity in a confessionally divided world." They were also "essential describers of sacred geography, particularly on the contested frontiers of Roman Catholicism."[131] While Espinosa, unfortunately, did not specify what made these images recognizable as saints, the means by which he identified the stones is less important than the fact that he saw in them tropes of Catholic power.

Furthermore, Espinosa contended that other stones looked like armored cavalry, one of the important symbols of the militant church in its crusade against infidels at home and overseas. Such militant symbolism was reinforced when Espinosa reminded his readers that *pacará* meant stronghold or fortress. The soldierly noble horseman was an iconic symbol in all of Europe, but in Iberian Catholicism the image of the caballero held particular importance, as it was frequently employed to depict the patron saint, the apostle Santiago (Saint James), who united the Christian communities in the peninsula against Islamic forces during the *reconquista*. In the Spanish imagination, the common visual representation of Santiago saw him in full armor, carrying a raised sword and riding a warhorse. Santiago had a dual role in the Spanish mind: he was both a spiritual/evangelical patron and a militant symbol of continuous holy war. The supposed discovery of the apostle's corpse in Compostela, Spain, made the location one of the most important pilgrimage sites in Christendom, simultaneously offering indisputable "evidence" of the apostolic foundation of the Spanish church.[132] As Spain became a world power, Santiago's image conveyed the imperial idea that Spaniards were the new "chosen people" and were obeying a divine call to spread the Gospel around the globe. He was credited with intervening on at least thirteen occasions in South America and New Spain.[133] Unlike the mystical trips of bilocating nuns described in chapter 3, Santiago did not come to America as an "apostle" or messenger of peace but as a supernatural conquistador. Stories of his apparition in the midst of battles were used to explain how just a few Spaniards succeeded in overthrowing vast native empires.

Espinosa's allusion to the caballero, perhaps a veiled allusion to Santiago, struck a chord. Santiago supported those who carried God's word; his image was a powerful symbol of unity in the Hispanic world, invoked in times of need. Nevertheless, unlike the fierce warrior storming forth from the heavens, Espinosa's caballero does not appear at the decisive moment of a battle but in a moment of solitude in the desert. In keeping with the spiritual focus of the Order of Carmel, the image inspired the Carmelite friar's contemplation and solitary prayer. Recall that prayer, for his patron, Teresa de Ávila, "was as powerful a weapon against heresy as preaching, and more effective than the sword."[134]

The narrative of the "discovery" of saints and holy men (or women, in the case of Teresa de Ávila) in the desert and its effect on the Carmelite missionary was well orchestrated. The desert was an authoritative metaphor in the Carmelite spiritual lexicon. After challenging the prophets of Baal, Elijah fled deep into the southern desert, a solitary place where he encountered God. It was in the desert south of Beer Sheva, at the cave of Mount Horeb, that God revealed himself to Elijah in a dramatic scene that has left an imprint on generations of Carmelite (and other) mystics. In a particularly poetic biblical passage, God is said to have come to Elijah not in the wind, not in a great noise (sometimes translated as an earthquake) or in a fire, but in a "still small sound" (1 Kings 19:11–12), an encounter that clearly influenced the order's profound desire for quiet and solitary retreat in the desert. The prior-general of the order between 1266 and 1271, Nicholas Gallicus, stated that "the citadel of Carmel is not the walled town but the open desert." In the solitude of the desert, he claimed, the Carmelite was alone except for the various creatures living there, who brought "comfort as our companions." The desert animals, "though silent . . . preach in wondrous wise words and excite our inner soul to the promise of the Creator." For Espinosa, the Chilean desert evoked a desire for solitary prayer, in which God could be thanked and, echoing Nicholas of France, "glorified by His creatures." Perhaps alluding to Elijah's revelation at the cave of Mount Horeb, Espinosa also made a point of noting the "caves and caverns" that dominated the cliffs in and around Pacará, where "people can live" and take shelter from storms. While the Carmelites evolved to become a mendicant order and became committed to apostolic service in urban settings, the order had never "forgotten the 'smell of the desert'" and the longing for an intimate encounter with God.[135]

The notion of the desert as both a physical space and a spiritual concept played a critical role in Carmelite spirituality during the Catholic Reformation. In the 1590s, not long after the Carmelites had joined other mendicant orders in America, the Discalced Carmelites began undertaking a project of creating "deserts" or wildernesses in rural areas, which became essential to the order's renewal.[136] The first Carmelite deserts were established in Spain and supported by the most important Discalced Carmelite theologian of the seventeenth century, Tomás de Jesús, who, while pushing the Carmelites toward a global mission, was also influenced by the interior religiosity of Teresa de Ávila and Juan de la Cruz.[137] These fabricated spaces, cultivated by human hands, were attempts to re-create both the original eremitical geography of Mount Carmel and a "simulacrum" of Eden. After the Touraine Reform, the original branch of the Carmelites also established similar hermitage houses and deserts. The seventeenth-century Carmelite deserts aspired to offer Carmelite friars a unique kind of terrestrial paradise in which they could live apart from society and devote their energies to solitary contemplation and worship. In a sense, these deserts allowed the Carmelites to turn back to the "primitive spirit" of the order, balancing the increasing burden of apostolic service with the original Carmelite ideals of solitude and simplicity. Some of these sites were located in the colonies and thus offered the opportunity to sacralize non-Christian environments by the very presence and holy work of pious Carmelite friars.

For example, Espinosa told of a Carmelite *desierto* located three leagues from Mexico City, in the hills of San Pedro Quauhximalpan in the *corregimiento* of Coyoacán. Established in the early seventeenth century by the Discalced Carmelites, this *desierto* functioned as a remote spiritual retreat for Carmelites who had worked in the local mission or were preparing to travel to the Philippines. Because it was designed to provide respite and foster spiritual rejuvenation, the clergy living there were not deemed responsible for the religious life of locals and remained separate from them. This caused some consternation among the local Nahuas and Spanish residents, who complained about the grant of the land to the Carmelites.[138]

This unique space, "one of the first in the world in size . . . and sanctity," evoked a distinctive imaginary geography. As Espinosa noted, "Its hilly site, its springs" lent it the impression that it was in fact "another Mount Carmel and Holy Land in that Land of Promise in the New World." Espinosa described the isolated complex, complete with a church, convent, and dormitories, and wrote that it seemed "like paradise, because of the disposition of the Heavens." He was equally taken with the secluded hermitage "a quarter league" away, where "the friars live like the hermits of the primitive Church."[139]

In thus describing "this Wilderness and new Mount Carmel," Espinosa infused his geographical itinerary with a distinctive Carmelite message. Such phrasing also had a practical angle, highlighting the need for increased Carmelite participation in the American mission. This description followed on the heels of another section in which Espinosa protested the forced abandonment of a Carmelite college in Coyoacán. According to Espinosa, a *visitador* from Spain "unreasonably" ordered the closure, "taking away consolation from many in the city." Espinosa encouraged his readers to share his anger at the decision of the small-minded Spanish official, and to sympathize with the goals of the Carmelite mission. On a continent where "the harvest is truly great, but the laborers are few" (Luke 10:2 and Matt. 9:37), Espinosa wrote, more friars needed to come.[140] And for those unable to visit and take respite in this new Mount Carmel, Espinosa catalogued these faraway sites, presenting them via a geographic corpus.

Espinosa wrote at a critical juncture, when the Carmelites were beginning their mission in Spanish America and the church was seeking ways to coordinate its larger mission in the world. His *descripción* reflects the convergence of these developments. Attempting to assimilate new knowledge about the earth into the church's consciousness, Espinosa's geography amounted to a literary assemblage of religious visions and images. In addition to providing geographical facts desired by the Spanish state, his itinerary offered a path along which the reader could both enter a sacralized landscape and participate in a Carmelite morality tale. Espinosa cited Catholic and specifically Carmelite images of piety, biblical landscapes and typologies (Mount Carmel, Mount Zion), and Catholic saints and holy people. Crafting geography allowed Espinosa to re-create multiple *carmelos* in a new world. The descriptive geography, embellished with tales of miracles and transmitted to a wider audience, made local images global, propagating the many signs of Catholic power for those who could not make the long and dangerous transatlantic journey. In Espinosa's narrative, typological thinking joined the representation of space, and the Spanish missionaries were collectively viewed as those who continued Elijah's mission in the New World. The *descripción* encouraged Elijah's most faithful followers, the Carmelites, to persist in their search for a terrestrial paradise that would assure the expansion and regeneration of their order.

The author of Psalm 137, which opens this chapter, asks, "How shall we sing the song of the Lord in a foreign land?" In more than one sense, the propagandists discussed in this chapter confronted a similar challenge as they reached a foreign continent and chose, among other options, to use geographical writings to advance their causes. While geography indeed remained an essential tool in the arsenal of imperialism, and while its early use in the Spanish colonies can be attributed to administrative reforms carried out for the purpose of gathering cosmographical information, it was also quickly adopted and embraced by religious writers who used their "book of descriptions" to take possession of new lands and souls. Confessional geographers, as we have seen especially in the examples of Espinosa and Ocaña, were well versed in the geographical literature and navigation manuals of their time. They wrote solid geographies that described places, catalogued resources, and reported the right spatial relationships from one point to the next, including measures of distance, direction, and latitude. As such, their writings highlight the pragmatism of a scholarly discipline that mirrored the centralizing tendencies of churches and governments alike, which began in the early sixteenth century. This fact reminds us that the discipline of geography did not develop naturally or neutrally; from the beginning, spatial description was implicated in and bound to political projects that sought to learn about and take possession of ever greater sections of the globe.

This chapter has also shown how, on an ideological level, geography provided a platform for the transmission of religious visions, thus helping construct a Catholic realm on an unknown continent that lacked a long-standing Christian presence. While sacralizing space has ancient roots in the Christian tradition, the use of an emerging scientific discipline did not. Saint Jerome did not write a geography while traversing the Syrian desert, as the seventeenth-century Hieronymite Diego de Ocaña did in the New World. Geography offered techniques for "consecrating space," to use Mircea Eliade's terminology, for those who can only live in "an atmosphere impregnated with the sacred."[141] Similarly, in describing Catholic iconography in the natural landscape, Espinosa not only joined the ranks of other Counter-Reformation propagandists in Europe but also placed America in a privileged position within the parameters of Catholic ideology. To be sure, this circulation of miracles via geographic works served not only spiritual needs but also encouraged the allocation of material resources. In the case of Espinosa, the objective was clear: to recruit both Madrid and Rome (and their vast resources) for the support of the Carmelite mission. His goal was no different from that of Alonso de Benavides, discussed in chapter 3, who also used his geographic itinerary to garner aid, financing, and attention for the mission in New Mexico. The growing appreciation of the geographical empiricist program profoundly influenced the choice by religious actors to use geography for material gain and to propagate the Catholic worldview. Espinosa, Ocaña, Antonio de la Ascensión, and Alonso de Benavides are a few among many who fit the social profile of confessional geographers discussed in this chapter.[142] Their hybrid writings and maps demonstrate the ways in which confessional geographers promoted distinct ambitions that they transmitted along with the vision of a universal monarchy promoted by the Crown. Geographies thus became a tool of propaganda, making the local global and spreading Catholic devotion via the study of the terrestrial globe.

Considering the coexistence and multilayered perceptions of space, the history of Spanish friars' production of *descripciónes* is linked to a broader trend in the consolidation of geography as an emerging field of knowledge, which was not restricted to Spaniards or even to Catholics. Historiography by and large focuses on state formation as the reason for the development of geographical practices, and overwhelmingly portrays the field as an administrative secular science that inspired the Baconian program "to study Nature rather than Books."[143] Yet this fragmentary depiction overlooks how Catholic friars, from New France and the Andes to the Philippines, Goa, and Ceylon, were critical interlocutors in the "geographic turn" of early modernity. Their systematic descriptions, though heavily imbued with Catholic universalism, joined the efforts of leading geographers in other parts of world, who defined the field and prepared the ground for a major epistemic shift in the methods of gathering knowledge by incremental and inductive procedures. Assembling up-to-date geographical evidence did not hinder the evangelical duties of Catholic friars. On the contrary, in an age of scientific growth, it was through geography that they recorded new myths and legends and brought them into a sacred spatial repertoire.

5

THE ORIGIN OF (AMERICAN) SPECIES

In the previous chapter, we saw how religious writers sacralized landscapes in Spanish America by crafting geographic itineraries that brought foreign locations intimately closer to Catholic consciousness. This chapter continues the theme of the Catholic co-option of American nature by shedding light on the theories that emerged to explain the continent's diverse wildlife. Why did the existence of alpacas, iguanas, armadillos, and other exotic animal species at the far reaches of the earth profoundly trouble Spanish theologians and missionaries? In what follows, I examine this seemingly simple and perhaps even naive question, demonstrating the complexities that underlie it. The publication of *Historia natural y moral de las Indias* (1590) by the renowned Jesuit natural philosopher José de Acosta provoked a lively discussion about the reasons for the dissimilarities between life-forms found in the known world and those in the isolated Americas. Acosta's attempt to reconcile the "new" zoological world with knowledge about animals based in scripture caught the attention of Catholic writers, such as Gregorio García, Juan Eusebio Nieremberg, Barnabé Cobo, and Athanasius Kircher, who continued to speculate on the theme of biological diversity throughout the seventeenth century. Long before Linnaeus and, later, Darwin fundamentally changed the essence of biology, these discussions provided a conceptual framework that explained biodiversity and differences among animal populations.

Zoological theories were not at the forefront of theologians' minds, to be sure. However, reconciling scripture, in particular the story of Noah's flood, with zoological evidence was one piece in a mysterious puzzle that connected the continents and justified the Christian mission to all humankind. Central to these discussions was an assessment of divine providence and, with it, the complete denial of chance in creation. Strikingly, we can still hear echoes today of the claims that were made by Spanish observers centuries ago. Chance and design are two of the "big ideas" that frequently divide the public regarding species variation. The role of "chance" in evolutionary biology, in particular, preoccupies thinkers and religious leaders.[1] From Richard Dawkins's assertion that "the evidence of evolution reveals a universe without design" to Pope Francis's statement at the Vatican's Pontifical Academy of Science in 2014 that "evolution presupposes the creation of beings that evolve," design versus chance has arguably been at the heart of the intersection between religion and life sciences ever since Darwin penned his thoughts on evolution by means of natural selection in 1859.

The aim of this chapter, needless to say, is not to justify any theological or secular position but to revisit the rise of flood zoology and reconstruct its fundamental tenets in the context of the Spanish early encounter with American animal species. I examine how speculations on the animal kingdom led to a religious conundrum, as theologians struggled to place the fauna of far-flung places within the hexameral narrative. As we saw earlier, in the case of geography and cosmography, the field of natural history was profoundly embedded in Christian theology and was shaped by Catholic concerns. I claim that the perceived overlapping of the three sources of knowledge—scripture, church tradition, and the "book of nature"—led erudite Spanish friars to focus their attention on South American camelids, wildcats, and reptiles. For them, the observant gaze of an unfamiliar ecology reaffirmed the correspondence between God, the church, and humanity.

The idea of animal testimony held particular significance in Spain, where miracles performed by animals proclaimed the glory of the Roman Catholic Church, and animals signified, in the tradition of Saint Ambrose's *Hexameron*, Christian virtues and moral lessons. Drawing on the didactic compendiums of medieval bestiaries, animals communicated complex Christian messages. The Augustinian Hieronymo Román y Zamora (1536–1597), for example, praised the moral lesson we could learn from each and every animal: nobility from elephants, loyalty from horses, and love from dogs. To his mind, "God placed in animals many useful properties for humans, so that they could learn moral virtues and also the way of life."[2] Taking special interest in animals, early modern books of emblems offered political advice and guidance for living a virtuous life. The Dominican Andrés Ferrer de Valdecebro (1620–1680), for instance, expanded on the moral lessons humans ought to learn from terrestrial animals and birds in his two-part *Gobierno general, moral y político*.[3]

Recognized for their ability to sense natural and supernatural events, animals could also explain the present condition of humankind and were believed to hold secrets to the past.[4] In European biblical culture, especially after the discovery of the New World, the "testimony" of animals could transmit important information regarding human history. Catholic thinkers attempted to place America within the Christian narrative of salvation, and within this narrative tried to understand the anthropological and biological diversity of the continent.[5] This understanding was particularly important since, according to the classic theory of five climate zones, the area below the torrid zone, as a result of its proximity to the sun, should have been uninhabitable because of its extreme heat.[6] Quite to the contrary, however, the existence and variety of life in that area was stunning.

"I have found a continent," one early commentator exclaimed, "more densely peopled and abounding in animals than our Europe or Asia or Africa."[7] In the words of another observer, this new world was "the best land in the world . . . land on which the cattle was abundant and marvelously varied."[8] Early observers were especially keen to report the diversity of autochthonous creatures who were fortunate to live in a land of "perpetual spring and perpetual autumn."[9] Describing Andean "sheep" (llamas and alpacas), Pedro de Cieza de León stated that these brutes were among "the most excellent animals that God had created" (fig. 14).[10] Tales of the strange and wondrous attributes of American nature, like those detailed by Peter Martyr and Cieza de León, were outdone only by stories of the Americas' vast abundance.

In this context, the discovery of unknown animal species in America troubled biblical exegetes and naturalists with unsettling questions: were the animals native to America different from those in the known world? If so, how did they come to be there? How could animals have developed into the likenesses that were observed in America? Were such animals contrary to nature (*contra naturam*)? Catholic writers reckoned that in answering such questions they might help understand the events that followed the universal deluge, including the question of how all living beings were dispersed across the planet soon after Noah, his family, and the surviving creatures disembarked from the ark. Animals thus acted as witnesses who could reveal

Fig. 14. Llamas (or *vicuñas*). From Pedro de Cieza de León, *Parte primera dela chronica del Peru* (Seville: Martín de Montesdoca, 1553), fol. 122v. Courtesy of the John Carter Brown Library, Brown University, Providence, RI.

the untold story of Adam's descendants in the fourth part of the world. At stake was far more than mere intellectual curiosity. Placing all members of humanity under the same family tree was an ideological necessity in order to justify the church's global mission, in which the Spanish monarchy after the Valladolid debate (1550–51) was heavily invested. This debate, which took place in the Dominican College of San Gregorio at Valladolid and concerned the Spanish right to America and the justification for converting its inhabitants, was an important stage, in which the bishop of Chiapas, Bartolomé de las Casas (1484–1566), criticized the colonial exploitation of the Amerindians and advocated nonviolent policies for their peaceful conversion to Christianity. "Recognition of the humanity of the Indians," as the historian Jacques Lafaye noted, "made them fellow creatures, souls capable of salvation."[11] Such discussions about America's nature and peoples took place at a moment when the robust search for schemes of classification was beginning to dominate the life sciences in earnest.[12]

Against the backdrop of Spain's endeavors to obtain credible knowledge about American nature, this chapter analyzes the different theories proposed by Spanish theologians to account for the existence of unique animals in the West Indies. I demonstrate how a particular set of exegetical concerns, primarily raised by José de Acosta, resulted in a series of bioenvironmental arguments that explained variations among animal populations. The chapter essentially makes a twofold argument related to the scientific and religious repercussions of the "conquest of American nature."[13] First, the chapter emphasizes that the isolated fourth continent not only provided exhaustive examples of never-before-seen vegetation and animals for a European audience but also presented an opportunity to conceive a novel interpretive framework for the "origin of species." The unprecedented treasure trove of biological data allowed observers to fashion terminology based on religious concepts that would have a lasting impact on animal taxonomies, including on the category of species, biogeography, animal migration, and the development, degradation, and extinction of species. Second, I contend that the information that was solicited and generated, including new zoological findings, was assimilated into Catholic outlooks.

Just as the chapter juxtaposes zoological thinking with biblical commentaries, it also situates the various hypotheses on the question of the origin of American animals in the context of power struggles within the church. In particular, I place the Dominican Gregorio García's exposition on the animal kingdom within the context of the competition between the Jesuits and the Dominicans over their respective claims to authority, showing how zoological information from the New World could be recruited to support scholastic doctrines. It is no coincidence, therefore, that formulations of the Dominican Thomas Aquinas became no less important than zoological findings in the attempt to account for nature's variations. Aquinas, known as the Angelic Doctor, whose significance to the church's renewal was clearly reflected in the sessions at Trent, offered a dense and intellectually rigorous philosophical system to explain Christian theology, in which he included sections about the creation of animal species. Aquinas was profoundly significant for medieval and early modern culture, and he was especially influential on the Dominican order, to which García belonged.

Acosta and García were both missionaries in Spanish America who had direct experience with the new plants and animals that inhabited the land and, of no less importance, had an impressive command of scripture and its interpretations. Their treatises are, however, profoundly different from one another. While Acosta was interested in analytical inquiry into American natural and human particularities, García's *Origen de los Indios* (1607) was a scholastic composition that had one aim: to present a Catholic perspective on the origins of Amerindians and stress the single origin of humankind. Because of these differences, Acosta and García's works have been granted very different status and prestige among modern scholars. Acosta is considered an acclaimed naturalist and anthropologist who developed novel theories based on empirical evidence. In contrast, owing to García's old-fashioned scholastic style and subject matter—the mythical origins of the Indians—his work is seen as belonging to a curious and "medieval" literary genre, which has determined our perception of his ideas. For our purposes, however, García's and Acosta's treatments of animals represent the interrelatedness of exegetical impulses and the study of nature during an era of global exploration. Both writers accepted completely the validity of the Bible, which was employed as a cornerstone to rationalize the natural history of America.

Despite the scholarly fascination with the European encounter with the New World's fauna, historians of colonial Latin America have typically been more interested in the practical aspect of the animals' "discovery" than in the biblical imagination of Spanish friars.[14] The focus on American animals in historical literature, such as Miguel de Asúa and Roger French's *New World of Animals*, has emphasized the depictions of living organisms in America, exposing the utilitarian approaches that sought to exploit their medical and commercial potential. Such studies thus focus on practical applications rather than on theoretical considerations in the study of animals; consequently, they provide only limited discussion of the theological framework of zoology and reach some ambivalent conclusions.[15] As for the general literature on natural history, by contrast, scholars of early modern zoology usually omit or belittle the early contributions made by Spaniards, especially those of friars in the colonies.[16]

My choice to concentrate on scriptural exegesis requires a word of explanation. After all, early modern zoological learning gradually evolved into an experiential field that brought skilled naturalists and amateurs alike into scientific networks that exchanged natural information throughout the world.[17] The production of zoological knowledge over time came to depend on new techniques, including animal anatomy based on vivisection and the use of the newly invented microscope, along with the sophisticated use of animal illustrations, which circulated more widely than ever thanks to the printing revolution.[18] But over the past two decades, this metanarrative on zoology has been steadily waning, along with previous understandings of the so-called Scientific Revolution. Historians have turned away from the focus on major scientific breakthroughs, showing instead the multiple approaches in life sciences, an important aspect of which includes awareness of how textual traditions continued to dominate the field.[19] In a world in which texts remained the primary way for intellectuals to learn about different species, and in which, for the majority of writers, "the description of a griffin was as credible as that of a gorilla," scriptural commentaries were still an essential body of knowledge that shaped and framed natural sciences.[20] The idea that the world was a book, and that the same interpretative frameworks could therefore be applied to both nature and written texts, further allowed for the application of commentary to the study of nature.[21] Theoretical frameworks employed in the debate on the origin of the New World's animals advanced zoological learning by shaping a nomenclature that explained the existence of, and differences among, animal populations. By turning to old knowledge to explain new kinds of animals, Spanish clergy offered innovative theories about the animal kingdom.

Filling in Pliny's Missing Pages

From the time of the Columbian voyages, the unfamiliarity with the variety of animals in America drew much attention. In a well-known letter attributed to Amerigo Vespucci, the author commented that the animal species that thrived on the isolated continent were barely mentioned in Pliny's magnum opus. "If I were to seek to recount in detail what things are there and to write concerning the numerous species of animals [*numerosis animalium generibus*] and the great number of them, it would be a matter all too prolix and vast. And I truly believe that our Pliny did not touch upon a thousandth part of the species of parrots and other birds and the animals, too, which exist in those same regions."[22] The author of the letter essentially pointed to a cluster of ideas that would have lasting influence on the taxonomy of American species throughout the century and can be reduced to three principles: first, the West Indies had an abundance of living organisms; second, these creatures, in terms of their biological classification, represented a multitude of distinct animal species; and third, these species were "new" in the sense that classic Greek and Roman natural philosophers did not know (and could not have known) of their existence. After exploring more of the West Indies, Vespucci remarked that he saw new animal species in such abundance that they "could not fit in Noah's ark."²³ This was a striking comment that, even if were merely meant to convey a sense of wonder, went completely against the orthodox interpretation of scripture. According to the biblical narrative and Christian exegetical tradition, all animals were believed to have been saved by Noah's ark. As we shall see, Vespucci's observation had significant implications for both theology and zoology.

The Italian humanist and *cronista* of the Spanish court Peter Martyr d'Anghera (1457–1526) agreed with Vespucci's conclusions about the newness and diversity of animal species in the Americas. Peter Martyr never crossed the Atlantic, but he managed to assemble news through his acquaintance with the leading figures in the discovery of America, including Columbus himself.²⁴ In his collected letters, *De orbe novo decades* (*The Decades of the New World*), Peter Martyr briefly suggested that the fauna along the coasts of Paria were all new: "Even the animals, reptiles, insects, and quadrupeds are different from ours, and exhibit innumerable and strange species."²⁵ While the abundance of America had been a common trope since the letters of Columbus and Cortés (and continued to be so in the modern era), the crux of Vespucci's and Peter Martyr's argument, which was that the continent was inhabited by "numerous" new species, was not universally accepted until the end of the sixteenth century.²⁶

Early reports on the West Indies revealed ambivalence, if not confusion, when describing indigenous life-forms. A telling example may be found in the work of Peter Martyr himself, who, though he recognized the newness of American nature, stretched the boundaries of his readers' imagination when describing peculiar unidentified animals. For example, he said that one "prodigious" animal (perhaps a tapir?) was as "as large as a bull, and has a trunk like an elephant and yet it is not an elephant. Its hide is like a bull's; and yet it is not a bull. Its hoofs resemble those of a horse, but it is not a horse. It has ears like an elephant's, though smaller and drooping, yet they are larger than those of any other animal."²⁷ Recognizing the differences but comparing this animal to familiar ones, Peter Martyr drew no conclusion about the proper classification of the creature but merely noted its unusual appearance. Moreover, as in other parts of his work, he was silent on the question of the ancients' knowledge of this animal. In fact, in gathering descriptions of American animals, whether real or fantastic, Peter Martyr attempted by analogy to find similarities between the Old and the New World's zoological variety. In another telling example, Peter Martyr described an opossum: "An extraordinary animal inhabits these trees, of which the muzzle is that of the fox, while the tail resembles that of a marmoset, and the ears those of a bat.

Its hands are like man's, and its feet like those of an ape. This beast carries its young wherever it goes in a sort of exterior pouch, or large bag."[28] As Sabine MacCormack has observed in relation to the native peoples' customs, European writers "integrated what was new and strange about America into a context of what was familiar and known."[29] Their "limits of understanding" also created much confusion about categories used to describe unfamiliar animal species.

The chronicler Francisco López de Gómara saw similar ambiguity in American nature at midcentury. Celebrating Hernán Cortés's victorious conquest of Mexico, Gómara accepted Peter Martyr's premise that Spaniards had reached the New World, which, in Gómara's view, was "the greatest event since the creation of the world" (excluding the Incarnation and death of Christ). While he claimed that the New World was aptly named given "all the very different things from the ones in our world," including terrestrial animals and birds, he expressed reservations about estimating the total number of new animal groupings (fig. 15). Like Peter Martyr, Gómara did not travel to the Americas but relied on the testimony of those who had participated in Cortés's expedition. This did not prevent him from suggesting that in terms

Fig. 15. The American bison. From Francisco López de Gómara, *Primera y segunda parte dela historia general de las Indias [. . .]* (Zaragoza: A Costa de Miguel Capila, 1553), fol. 116v. Courtesy of the John Carter Brown Library, Brown University, Providence, RI.

of quantity there were only a "few species" in America that were different (*los animales en general, aunque son pocos en especie, son de otra manera*).³⁰ The question of how many animal species in fact populated America and how many were utterly new to European readers continued to puzzle Spaniards and remained unsolved.

The biological classification of the strange life-forms that did not easily conform to descriptions found in Pliny's and Aristotle's texts reached the highest authorities in Spain. Even a small lizard like the iguana attracted writers who were undecided as to whether the reptile was a land animal, a fish, or a kind of crocodile (fig. 16).³¹ This was a serious matter for a monarchy that depended on reliable information to oversee its colonial enterprise. At the request of King Charles V, Gonzalo Fernández de Oviedo y Valdés (1478–1557), who later in the 1530s would become the first person appointed by the Crown to organize information about American natural history, was the first to write an entire work exclusively on the topic.³² Oviedo dedicated no fewer than fifty of the eighty-six chapters (chaps. 11–61) of his *De la natural historia de las Indias* (1526), the bulk of the work also known as the *Sumario*, to zoological findings in the New World. Beginning with "tiger" (an American wildcat) and ending with crabs, spiders, and toads, Oviedo described from memory what he saw as the profound strangeness and novelty of "a land that until our own era was incognita," stressing that most of the animals found in his pages "could not have been learned about from the ancients."³³ Unlike previous authors who relied on correspondence and conversations to depict American nature, eyewitness testimony formed the core of Oviedo's source base. Taking his *Sumario* together with his more elaborate and detailed work, the *Historia general y natural de las Indias* (published in 1535 and 1547), Oviedo described 250 species of animals and plants.³⁴ He was also one of the first to suggest a biogeographical explanation based on the American constellation and climate, which he thought might account for the differences in animal populations. "It is true," he wrote, "as seen from the marvels of the world and the radical differences among animals [*los extremos que las criaturas*], that [these differences] are greater in some places than in others, according to the diverse localities and constellations under which the animals live."³⁵ This understanding that different habitats created peculiar variations within "species" would reappear in later accounts, including Francisco Hernández's writings and Conrad Gessner's *Historia animalium*.³⁶ Yet, working in Pliny's tradition of natural history and *not* as a philosopher of nature, Oviedo did not offer in his miscellaneous catalogue

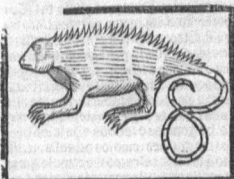

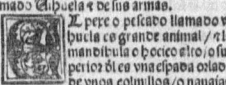

Fig. 16. Lizard (iguana). From Gonzalo Fernández de Oviedo, *La historia general delas Indias* (Seville: Iuam Cromberger, 1535), fol. 103v. Courtesy of the John Carter Brown Library, Brown University, Providence, RI.

a comprehensive, overarching theory of animal difference that could merge his astute observations with European religious and philosophical bodies of knowledge. But this was not Oviedo's objective. His desire to reveal the newness of American nature drove his selection of subject matter: "I ask Your Majesty to pardon any lack of order or arrangement that may be found in my content ... but I should like you to observe *the new things in it, for this has been my purpose.*"[37]

In 1532, the Crown appointed Oviedo to the position of "chronicler of the Indies" (*cronista de Indias*). Oviedo's appointment, along with other institutional reforms that took place in the same decade, signaled a turning point in Spain's approach to natural history in America.[38] The early rhetoric of wonder surrounding American nature became increasingly consolidated into a large-scale biological survey that aimed to improve Spain's exploitation of the West Indies' natural resources. Spanish expeditions and questionnaires, both relying heavily on the assistance and knowledge of the native peoples, generated an empirical base for early American zoology in the second half of the sixteenth century. As noted above, in 1570 Philip II appointed his court physician, Francisco Hernández, to conduct the first natural-historical expedition on the new continent, the results of which were circulated in manuscript form and later published in various editions.[39] Using words and drawings, Hernández described local fauna, provided their Indian names, and gave close attention to the use of animals by indigenous peoples. The Council of the Indies also gathered firsthand information about America, as we have seen, through the use of official questionnaires sent to Spanish dependencies overseas. The elaborate instructions prepared by Juan de Ovando y Godoy and the Council of the Indies in 1573 reflected the expectation that the responses should include information about local animals. It requested that "any person, lay or religious," who traveled the Indies collect information about the many animals, both domesticated and wild, that lived on land and in the sea—from "ferocious and wild" animals of the land to insects and snakes—as well as their various uses and benefits and how they could be hunted, caught, or raised.[40] Later provisions, such as the fifty-chapter questionnaires administered by Juan López de Velasco, compiled in 1577 and reprinted in 1584, continued to solicit zoological information, addressing both native species and the adaptation of European animals that had been sent overseas.[41] The responses to Velasco's 1577 questionnaire (*Instrucción y memoria*) form the material for the ambitious *Relaciones geográficas*, which provided, along with ethnographic and geographic data, considerable information about the biological diversity of Spanish America (fig. 17). Such administrative undertakings not only enlarged the amount of empirical data gathered but also recognized, more than ever before, the regional diversity within a land mass that had previously been thought of as a single "new world."[42] But the intricate zoological world that slowly became visible through words and paintings, reports, expeditions, and questionnaires still had to be reconciled with Eurocentric epistemology, which was deeply rooted in Christian concepts. The humanistically trained Oviedo did not have the tools, either philological or theological, to deal with the religious implications of these empirical findings, and neither did the royal physician Hernández or the cosmographers at Seville's Casa de la Contratación. Toward the end of the sixteenth century, this situation was changed by the brilliant theologian José de Acosta, who, more than any of his predecessors, reoriented zoological findings in light of Catholic tradition and scriptural commentaries.

Fig. 17. Armadillo. At bottom center of a map in *Relación de las minas de Temazcaltepeque en Nueva España*. Responding to question 27 in the royal *cédula* of 1577, the author described the native mammal in words and a drawing. Courtesy of Ministerio de Cultura y Deporte, Archivo General de Indias. AGI, MP-MEXICO, 21 Pueblo de Texcaltitlán.

José de Acosta and the Emergence of Flood Zoology

Then God said to Noah, "Come out of the ark. . . . Bring out every kind of living creature that is with you—the birds, the animals, and all the creatures that move along the ground—so they can multiply on the earth and be fruitful and increase in number on it."
—Genesis 8:15–16

To modern historians, Acosta is perhaps better known for his three-tier anthropological classification of the "barbarian," which began an influential tradition of describing the origin and progression of humankind. Yet Acosta's *Historia natural y moral de las Indias* also set the parameters for a heated debate about the origin of animal species in America.[43] Responding to Jesuit instructions to missionaries, including the urging of Ignacio de Loyola himself, to give attention to "extraordinary" news and details of animals and plants, Acosta confirmed the conclusions of earlier writers, that there were species in the West Indies not found on any other continent. Acosta noted that some thinkers had attempted to equate the local beasts and birds with known varieties in the Old World, but he likened this "to call[ing] an egg a chestnut."⁴⁴ Animals were not identical across the Atlantic, he emphatically determined, and given the diversity within the animal kingdom, the differences could not be considered accidental but were *essential*.

Jesuits' contribution to early modern science is by now a well-known story. Emphasizing the significance of secular knowledge to faith, the founder, Ignacio de Loyola (1491–1556), recognized that Jesuit missionaries around the world had access to valuable information and actively encouraged them to share it in their reports. In a letter to Gaspar Barzaeus, the Jesuit superior in Goa, in 1554, Ignacio specifically requested "details about animals and plants that either are not known at all, or not of such a size, etc."⁴⁵ Thanks to the circulation of such reports, Acosta was well informed about natural history in other parts of the world. He noted that rare kinds of animals were not unique to the Americas; Africa and Asia similarly contained unique animal species, like elephants, that could be found only in certain environments.⁴⁶ Unlike Oviedo, who aspired to inform the Spanish court about the richness of American biodiversity, the Jesuit theologian found that the existence of certain animals in America (and other geographical parts) provoked challenging questions about the proper reading of scripture, particularly the story of Noah's ark.

> It is more difficult to find out the beginnings of different animals that are found in the Indies and not in our world here [in Europe]. . . . If we say that all these species of animals were preserved in Noah's Ark, it follows that these animals, too, went to the Indies from this continent, and also that the animals that are not found in other parts of the world must have done the same. *And this being so, I must ask why their species did not remain here. Why are they found only in foreign and strange places?* Truly it is a question that has perplexed me for a long time.⁴⁷ (Emphasis added)

Acosta's speculations formed the core of flood zoology, which had a major impact on the science of life in subsequent years.

José de Acosta was born around 1540 in Medina del Campo. He began studying with the Jesuit order at a young age and was ordained a priest in 1566. Previously, Acosta had studied at the Universidad de Alcalá de Henares, where he learned theology, law, and natural history. From 1567 to 1571, he taught at several Jesuit institutions in Spain and Portugal. During that time, he made several requests to travel to America. Upon receiving permission, Acosta departed in 1571, residing first in Peru and then traveling extensively.

He served in important positions, including as president of the Jesuit college in Lima (appointed in 1572) and leading the order in South America as the provincial of the Jesuits in Peru (1576–82). He spent a year (1586–87) in Mexico before returning to Spain, where he continued his academic career until his death in 1600. His seventeen years in the Americas signaled a "watershed in the history of Jesuit missionary and scientific enterprises in South America," as Andrés Prieto observes.[48]

Sharing aspects of what María Portuondo has called the "Spanish disquiet" (i.e., the preoccupation of a generation of Spanish scholars with their inability to comprehend nature only through the knowledge they already possessed), Acosta was determined to confront the contradictions between empirical evidence and classical philosophical theory.[49] Critical and well read, Acosta famously confessed his amusement when he himself experienced the mistakes in Aristotelian natural philosophy while crossing the equator: "Since I had read what the philosophers and poets say about the Torrid Zone, I was persuaded that when I reached the equator I would be unable to withstand the terrible heat; but it was in fact the opposite, for as I was crossing it I was so cold, that several times I had to stand in the sun to warm. . . . And here I confess I laughed and mocked Aristotle's *Meteorology* and his philosophy."[50] In an attempt to correct such errors, he wrote a brief text in Latin, *De natura novi orbis* (Rome, 1583), which he followed with a significantly enlarged Spanish-language version, his magnum opus, the *Historia natural y moral de las Indias*. Beyond demarcating a field for Jesuit natural science, Acosta's *Historia* was the most significant study of America at that time, and was translated within a decade into Latin, German, Dutch, French, and Italian.[51] His objective was to place America within a coherent theory of the world. From the beginning, he declared that, rather than merely describe each natural phenomenon, as previous authors, including Oviedo, had done, he intended to identify the natural "causes and reasons" for the "new and strange things discovered in those lands" through philosophical inquiry.[52] Acosta's work is thus thematically very diverse, demonstrating his broad erudition in natural sciences, cosmography, and the cultures of the indigenous peoples.[53]

Acosta's *Historia* represents a fusion of empirical and rational observations of the physical world with the profound Catholic sensibilities that underpinned the Jesuit curriculum.[54] The notion that the "world machine," a rationally ordered system that harnessed diverse elements to the same end, testified to the greatness of God was especially significant in Acosta's writings.[55] This metaphor arose in the late fourteenth century, when the invention of the mechanical clock prompted the French theologian Nicole Oresme (ca. 1320–1382) and others to equate celestial movements with those of a material clock. Explaining the particular characteristics of the continent on the basis of universal principles, Acosta was determined to integrate the Western Hemisphere into the representation of a world machine. Following Ignacio de Loyola's view that science and spiritual life were interrelated, Acosta believed that revealing God's hidden laws through the proper study of nature served as a path to God. Acosta justified his desire to examine the many "metals, plants, and animals" of the region, insisting that "whoever looks at the created things with this philosophy . . . can extract the fruits of his understanding and consideration, making use of them in order to know and glorify the author of everything."[56]

Although direct observation and experience provided Acosta with facts about nature's workings, for him and his contemporaries, scripture contained many physical and biological truths. Scripture was, therefore, in Acosta's estimation, to guide the natural philosopher in his inquiries. It was the task of natural philosophers to reconcile the two bodies of knowledge (nature and revelation); the quality and value of philosophical systems depended on their success. Acosta's treatment of the origin of West Indies fauna was thus shaped by the Bible and exegetical tradition. He added another layer to an investigation that had already taken place, the classification of animals, by relating the new species to Noachian animals. Whereas Vespucci noted in passing that it was difficult to imagine that Noah's ark had room for all the living creatures he had encountered in the West Indies, Acosta refuted this skeptical idea by providing a blueprint that explained nature's diversity. Everything about animal life was believed to agree with the narrative of creation and animals' rescue by humankind during the universal deluge, as told in Genesis. The biblical story, however, said nothing about animals' geographical distribution at the time of creation or after the flood.

To be sure, Acosta endeavored to do more than merely outline the peregrinations of animals. As Abel Alver demonstrates in his *Animals of Spain*, the interactions between humans and animals in early modern Spain affirmed, and often generated, perceptions about *Homo sapiens* themselves. Acosta's treatment of animals mirrors this tendency. Writing two generations after the famous Valladolid debate, he aimed to incorporate the Amerindians into the biblical narrative by associating them with Adam's family, a precondition for the mission.[57] As with the modern theory of evolution, at stake was not merely the study of animals but that of humanity. In the Augustinian tradition, animals were preserved in Noah's ark "not so much for the sake of renewing the stock, as of prefiguring the various nations which were to be saved in the Church," in the words of Augustine.[58] As Christendom expanded into the territory of unknown nations, the link between the rescued animals and the ark (and, by extension, the church) gained new historical impetus. Animals thus became reluctant witnesses who could testify to past events in human history by revealing the possible migration path of human tribes to America. Knowledge of the route(s) that brought animals from Noah's time and place to America, and of their experience once there, held out the possibility of bringing together the populations across the Atlantic into the same family. While most writers did not believe that a definitive answer would be found, they believed, like most people of the period, in monogenism, which posited a single origin of humanity. It was thus crucial to Acosta to prove that the New World animals descended from Noah's ark and shared the same history that was told in scripture.[59] The story of animals had to be universally applicable.

Acosta proposed a natural explanation built on what can be abridged into four exegetical propositions: that everyone was on the boat, that everyone came off the boat, that there was no second boat, and that creation was a unique and perfect event (based on Genesis 2:1–2 and church interpretive tradition).[60] Following scripture, Acosta maintained that "all the beasts and animals on earth perished except those that were preserved in Noah's Ark for the continuation of their kind." Thus the newly found animal species must have experienced the same trajectory as the animals in Europe. This contention implied a second principle: that all the rescued animals, having left the ark, began their migration from the same place on earth. "We must reduce the propagation of all those animals to those that emerged from the Ark," Acosta wrote.[61] Acosta explicitly dismissed any alternative, imaginative rescue story: "Certainly, we are not to think that there was a second Noah's Ark in which men were brought to the Indies, nor much less that a certain angel brought the first inhabitants of this world holding them by the hair, as did an angel with the prophet Habakkuk."[62]

Acosta's rejection of a second ark followed Christian exegetical tradition, which typically considered a "second" ark to be a metaphor that pointed to the ark of the covenant.[63] However, the same cannot be said for his refusal to consider the possibility that an angel had carried the animals to the continent. Unlike a second-ark theory, bio-distribution by angels was considered an acceptable option. In *The City of God*, Augustine raised the possibility that angels had carried animals from the ark to various islands. In this way, Augustine attempted to reconcile the apparent difficulties posed by scriptural doctrine, which stressed that all animals on the planet were descended from those saved by Noah, and the realities of nature, according to which animals incapable of swimming populated distant and isolated lands. "It cannot be denied," Augustine wrote, "that by the intervention of angels they might be transferred by God's order or permission."[64] Acosta would have none of this; he denied and even ridiculed this solution to bio-distribution.

Instead, Acosta considered an alternative theory: the possibility that animals were re-created in the New World after the waters of the flood had receded, an idea that Augustine had also proposed as a solution to the bio-distribution found on islands. Yet, unlike Augustine's symbolic interpretations of biblical narratives, Acosta took a very literal approach to the text and ultimately rejected the possibility of a postdiluvian re-creation for two reasons. First, the idea of re-creation obviated the need for the rescue of animals on Noah's ark in the first place. And scripture maintained that all animals on earth had descended from those on the ark. Second, any narrative of re-creation contradicted Genesis 1, which insisted that creation was completed in six days.

Given that all existing species originated from those on the ark, Acosta argued that American animals were the descendants of those who had migrated from where the ark had come to rest on Mount Ararat.[65] He postulated that these animals migrated via a land bridge yet to be discovered, since the vastness of the oceans precluded swimming. Naturally, he could not have known about geological time or about the ice age that had opened the Bering Strait to the migration of animal and human populations. The possibility that humans could have brought the animals across the oceans was equally unlikely, since Acosta could see little reason why humans would transport vicious beasts by ship. Having resolved this issue to his satisfaction, Acosta considered the conundrum that certain species had apparently migrated to the New World without leaving a trace in the Old World. This was a far more complicated riddle. Migration theory might explain the habitation of the continent, but how could these species be found *nowhere* but the Americas? It might well be, Acosta reasoned, that certain American species, including llamas, armadillos, and alpacas, migrated from Armenia, where Mount Ararat was believed to lie, but it was harder to comprehend their absence in other parts. Given that their migratory path must have traversed significant parts of the known world, why were there no remains or population groups of these animals along their migratory path?

At this point, Acosta put forth his most radical theory on the connection between natural environments and the existence of life, a theory that introduced the possibility of regional extinction. Recognizing that certain environments were more compatible than others to the needs of specific animals, Acosta rationalized the pattern of animal migration in geographical terms. He suggested that if an animal species was well suited to a region, it would flourish there. If not, that animal would need to migrate or face extinction. Acosta thus concluded that Noachian animals who had reached inhospitable destinations had perished from those parts. "We must then say that, even though all the animals came out of the Ark, by natural instinct and the providence of Heaven, different kinds [*géneros*] went to different regions and in some of those regions were so contented that they did not want to leave them; or that if they did leave they were not preserved, or in the course of time became extinct [*vinieron a fenecer*], as happens with many things."[66]

Acosta's environmental solution, as Thayne Ford has noted, predated Carl Linnaeus's biogeographical principle of climate "suitability," as proposed in the latter's *Politia naturae* (1760), by nearly two centuries.[67] What is really astonishing is that Acosta depicted bio-distribution and the perishing of populations in a nearly contingent fashion. To be clear, Acosta's solution pointed to regional rather than global extinction of fauna, in the sense that certain animal species perished in some places and not in others. Yet the implications of regional "disappearances" for global biodiversity are especially clear to us today, in light of the current threat of mass extinction as a result of human activity. While there are, for instance, elephants in both Asia and Africa, if one of the two populations were suddenly to disappear, an entire species would be lost.

Although Acosta's arguments might have been internally coherent and consistent, his theory still raised serious questions. Not only had Acosta refuted Augustine's notion of angelic rescue, but his zoological understanding also posed a challenge to the Catholic position on the order and sense of purpose in the universe. Acosta's causal framework, which linked environmental conditions, the physiological needs of animals, and possible local extinction, appeared to complicate certain conventions about the orderly working of the natural world. In order to grasp the importance of this challenge, we must briefly examine Aquinas's ideas on the subject, not only because of his authoritative standing in the consolidation of church theology but, as we shall see below, because of his centrality to the discourse on the fauna of the New World.

The doctrine of divine providence, in the Christian tradition, denies the arbitrary arrangement of the world. The idea that chance might play a role in creation was unthinkable in the premodern world; it was still highly problematic as late as the mid-nineteenth century, when Darwin proposed the mechanism of natural selection, which ultimately overturned the last vestiges of natural theology's argument for "perfect adaptation." In the Catholic tradition, the doctrine of providence, as articulated by Thomas Aquinas, refuted the idea that the universe emerged by chance.[68] In his *Summa Theologiae*, Aquinas cited the existence of purpose and order in the "governance of the world" as the fifth argument for God's existence. The world is goal-directed, he argued, just "as the arrow is shot to its mark by the archer. Therefore, some intelligent being exists by whom all natural things are directed to their end; and this being we call God."[69] Aquinas was clear that the arrangement of animals over the terrestrial realm was an essential manifestation of God's wisdom: "We must first consider the creation of things themselves; then the orderly distribution of the parts of the world; then we see how the different species of things are distributed in the various parts of the world: the stars in the heaven, birds in the air, fish in the waters, animals on the earth; and finally we see how abundantly Divine providence gives to each of them whatever it needs."[70]

According to Aquinas, the distribution of "different species" in various parts of the earth reflected God's divine plan, which created the environmental conditions for each species to thrive. In each part of the earth, God secured the existence of animal species by providing "to each of them whatever it needs." Animals did not come or go, did not thrive or die out, beyond God's gaze. When Aquinas was raised to the status of an official doctor of the church in 1567, his teachings on natural philosophy became "implicated in the new Catholic regime," as Peter Dear notes, and served for the church "as a means of demarcating admissible Catholic teaching from heresy."[71]

Aquinas's teaching had a long-lasting impact on natural philosophers and theologians alike, who agreed that God placed each living being in the region where the environmental conditions were best suited to it. The Mexican physician Juan de Cárdenas, who published his own reflections on American nature just a year after Acosta, wrote, "our Supreme Maker created and planted everything in the place that was most amiable and proper to its nature."[72] Using Hippocratic-Galenic humoral principles, Cárdenas ruled out preternatural explanations for the unique characteristics of America, emphasizing instead that divine providence generated natural law to arrange and order each aspect of nature. Such conventions on the harmonious work of providence framed early modern natural philosophy.[73] As historian Kevin Killeen has noted, the term "God's providence" was "much used in the natural history of the seventeenth century to talk about animals and the brilliant providential intricacy of their structures."[74] Animals were supposed to reflect the ingenuity of God's providential design as manifested in creation. The animal and plant kingdoms were testaments to God's design, for both their biological complexity and their geographical distribution.

To be sure, Acosta would never have suggested, either explicitly or implicitly, that God's providence had led to anything less than a perfectly ordered world. However, his explanation left the matter of the appearance and disappearance of various animals to environmental contingencies, and thus almost beyond God's attention. His solution for the perishing of animals in areas that did not suit their nature stood in striking contrast to Aquinas's view on God's placement of animals. Acosta depicted postdiluvian migrations as a process of "natural selection," in which contingencies and chance determined the fate of animals in a specific ecological environment. But why would God have created the world's animals only to eliminate them along the way?

Jesuits and Dominicans at a Crossroads

Acosta's legacy was felt well into the seventeenth century. Among his readers was the Dominican Gregorio García (ca. 1560–1627), who knew Acosta's work well and generally respected his opinions on matters of faith and natural science. García described him as "a very knowledgeable man, curious to investigate and search many things that he saw while living in the Indies."[75] But he was not satisfied with a number of Acosta's scriptural interpretations,[76] including some of his more daring speculations on the Amerindians and their natural environment. For example, García rejected Acosta's conclusion that the natives could not have come to the New World by boat on the grounds that they did not know the art of navigation. Instead, García countered that Noah himself had invented navigation. García even posited that the natives might have known about the lodestone, something that Adam, who knew about all things in nature, was certainly aware of and that Noah probably also knew. Although García did not explicitly refer to Acosta's thesis on the animal kingdom, he wrote that he was not satisfied with existing explanations of the mystery of exotic animals, a statement that implicitly rejected Acosta's ideas. This was a telling omission; after all, Acosta was the first thinker to explore flood zoology in the American context in depth, and he had certainly popularized this discussion. García stated numerous times how "exhausted" and "tired" he was from studying this perplexing question "for many years"—yet he persisted.[77] Driven to find a solution that would harmonize scripture and biblical commentaries with the lessons of nature, García enlisted angels and environmental adaptations to show that the geographical distribution of species was entirely within God's purview.

Theology aside, García's dissatisfaction with existing theories on New World fauna largely mirrored broader concerns over the reputation and self-representation of his order. The Dominicans "formed the first order in the Church with an academic mission, the first preaching order of perpetual students," as J. S. Cummins reminds us. While the order enjoyed great esteem and enduring authority, by the end of the fifteenth century its members believed that their intellectual tradition was nothing less than sacred; the "Dominican word-warriors, 'Masters of the Sacred Page,'" "saw themselves as guardians of an inviolable orthodoxy." The establishment of the Jesuit Order and its rapid success challenged the Dominicans' privileged position. Soon, the Jesuits began to enjoy significant influence, wealth, and prestige, which led to direct confrontations with members of the Dominican order, especially in Spain. So great was the rivalry between "these two, the Jacob and Esau of the Church . . . that, said Benedict XIV, they seemed almost to have forgotten that they had any common cause."[78]

These two powerful orders, founded by two Spanish priests, saw themselves in an ideal position to lead the Catholic world, and they fought over "patronage, influence and power both within the Church structures and society," in Piotr Stolarski's words. Significantly, the two orders also competed over intellectual leadership, including the right to interpret texts and traditions. The Dominicans were resentful that the newer order challenged and contested their long-standing privileged position. As a result of the Dominicans' identity as the guardians of orthodoxy, this competition was understood as a debate over the legitimacy of different interpretations of sacred texts and the authority to make them. The meteoric rise of the Jesuits notwithstanding, the Dominicans remained a powerful group within the church. Their strength was apparent in their numbers at the Council of Trent, in which two hundred Dominican bishops, theologians, and delegates took part, including the renowned Spanish Dominicans Dominic de Soto, Bartholomé Carranza, and Melchior Cano. The hostility between the two orders reached a climax in the early seventeenth century.[79]

García published his *Origen de los Indios* in 1607, coinciding with what scholars have characterized as a period of fierce "struggle for theological hegemony" within the church.[80] This struggle was plainly apparent in the Molinist controversy, which began in Spain when the Dominican Domingo Bañez (1528–1604) lodged a strong objection to the doctrine of salvation proposed in 1588 by the Jesuit Luis de Molina (1535–1600). This controversy over the nature of free will, grace, and predestination resulted in fierce disputes between the two orders (and not just their individual members) over the essence of God's foreknowledge. While the Jesuits stressed that human beings have the freedom to accept or reject Christ's grace, the Dominicans held that God knew who was elected and in fact determined each person's fate.[81] The Dominicans vigorously defended their view of the "absolute omnipotence of God vis-à-vis his creation."[82] In the final years of the sixteenth century, these doctrinal disagreements led the papacy to establish a special commission, the Congregatio de Auxiliis Gratiae, to examine the opposing ideas of each side.[83] While the debate was initially confined to Spain, over time the theological dispute sparked a profound division among Catholics beyond the Iberian Peninsula. Numerous congregations were held between 1598 and 1607, escalating the public confrontation and struggle for leadership between the two orders.[84] By 1607, Pope Paul V insisted that the Dominicans and Jesuits stop decrying each other as heretical and permitted each order to maintain its doctrinal stance.

The Dominicans' efforts, as Rivka Feldhay has observed, "were not dissociated from their traditional role as a small, privileged group which saw itself as guardian of true faith. They defended old principles of the division and organization of the universe, old boundaries between the celestial and the terrestrial, the intellectual and the practical, in order to support their traditional position as an authoritative elite."[85] Similarly, García was motivated to write his work in order to guard the proper interpretation of church doctrine. By writing about New World animals, he would protect the Dominican view on the order and purpose of the universe and emphasize God's omnipotence over the arrangement of species. In the context of a struggle for hegemony with the powerful Jesuits, García acted in accordance with the self-representation of the Dominicans and "corrected" Acosta's environmental solution. At a time when Scholasticism was losing ground to new philosophical methods, and experience was slowly replacing the authority of written texts, García applied church teachings to the existence of New World animals and positioned himself as the defender of Catholic orthodoxy.

The Scholastic and Exotic Animals

Gregorio García was born around 1560 in Cózar, Jaén, and died in 1627 in Baeza, Spain. We know little about his personal life. He joined the Order of Preachers in Andalusia and around the turn of the century spent twelve years in America—three in Mexico and nine in Peru—before returning to Spain. He was struck by the wonders of the new land: "unused waters, new air, a hitherto unseen sky, rare animals and birds; fruits, herbs and plants never before written about."[86] He published another work, *Predicación del evangelio en el Nuevo Mundo viviendo los apóstoles* (1625), which aimed to prove that the Gospel had already been preached around the world, including in America, during the time of the apostles. His commitment to a late Renaissance Dominican worldview emerges throughout his works, in which he synthesized Scholasticism with his personal experience in the West Indies.

On the surface, García's *Origen de los Indios* stands out as an anomaly among the many other eyewitness reports from America. The structure of the work followed a scholastic style in which the author discussed a topic through arguments and counterarguments. In each chapter, García presented a possible "solution" to the question of the origins of the native peoples, explored it in detail (mainly through the presentation of the opinions of ancient authorities), and noted both the weaknesses and the internal logic of each solution. In accordance with the church's view that "Indians are truly men," articulated in Pope Paul III's "Sublimis Deus," García determined in his first proposition that the Amerindians were descendants of Adam and survivors of the flood. He then deduced that the natives came from "one of the three parts of the known world, Europe, Asia, and Africa," since the origin of humankind was one. Ultimately, departing from the absolute authority of *Fé divina*, García declared that any hypothesis regarding the origins of the Amerindians was a matter of *opinion*, as long as the Catholic faith was not questioned.[87] The remarkable diversity of customs and languages among the native peoples seemed to indicate to García that the Amerindians were descended from a mixture of various peoples from the Old World. He concluded that there were many possible postdiluvian origins and that none of them posed a threat to sacred literature.

Dominicans based their understanding of nature and revelation on the philosophical system of one of their own, Thomas Aquinas (fig. 18). According to Aquinas, there was no conflict between reason, best articulated by Aristotelian philosophy, and scriptural revelation. Any apparent contradiction between the two was based not on the falsehood of either source but on mistaken interpretations.[88] García relied on scriptural interpretation as his methodological foundation. As he attempted to merge his observations of America with traditional commentaries on nature and the origins of men, García followed Aquinas's logic: "Holy scripture sets up no confusion, since all meanings are based on one, namely, the literal sense."[89] In keeping with

Fig. 18. Engraving of Thomas Aquinas kneeling before the crucifix at the front of "epistola dedicatoria." From Gregorio García, *Origen de los Indios de el Nuevo Mundo, e Indias Occidentales [. . .] segunda impresión* (Madrid: Francisco Martinez Abad, 1729). Photo: Biblioteca Histórica de la Universidad Complutense de Madrid. BH FG 2191.

the self-representation and charisma of the Order of Preachers,[90] García acted as a "watchdog," an arbiter of truth, making sense of America while defending the doctrines of the church, and especially those of Aquinas, to whom he dedicated his book.

Interestingly, García was also influenced by the work of Alejo Venegas, whose theory about the correspondence between God's three "books" was discussed in chapter 1; García called him "a very learned man" in both theology and natural philosophy.[91] Venegas, as we saw, suggested that a "book" was like the biblical ark, in the sense that it "was invented to save the treasures of knowledge" just as an ark was designed to "save corporal objects."[92] The ark and the book of nature, as we shall see, were fundamental in García's reconstruction of the natural history of American species.

Writing roughly fifteen years after Acosta, García was staunchly committed to the idea that the natural environment and people of America offered an opportunity to learn about scriptural revelation and divine providence. He expressed this commitment to the expansion of knowledge, distancing himself from the typical colonizer narrative: "Not everyone who goes to the West Indies goes in search of gold and silver; there are those who search for the treasure of science [*el tesoro de la ciencia*] and the understanding of all that has been found in the New World."[93] This insightful and very personal statement implicitly overturned colonizer views such as that famously put forth by Bernal Díaz del Castillo, who took part, alongside Hernán Cortés, in the conquest of Mexico and memorably stated, "[we came here] to serve God . . . and to get rich."[94] García's interest in intellectual engagement echoes the Dominican identity of the "perpetual student," whose academic inquiries were an essential part of the Dominican spiritual outlook. Dominicans strove to imprint their intellectual signature on the American colonies; significantly, they established one of the first universities in the Western Hemisphere, the Universidad Nacional Mayor de San Marcos in Lima, in 1551. This sort of commitment to "the treasure of science" rather than to material spoils also predated what Sarah Irving has identified as Francis Bacon's "non-colonial means" for the restoration of man's knowledge, entrenched in his utopian "New Atlantis."[95] Catholic missionaries were close to the Baconian ideal of the "merchants of light" who constantly brought news to Bensalem through their exploratory travels, and García described his own efforts in a similar way. However, unlike Bacon's visionary scheme for the restoration of Adamic knowledge, García saw America's anthropology and natural history, above all, as "proof texts" that could enrich religious understanding and invalidate unorthodox opinions.

To be sure, animals were not García's most pressing concern. While Dominican friars like Francisco Ximénez, presented in chapter 1, helped spread new zoological information, García's lengthy treatment of New World species mainly served evangelical ends.[96] Like Acosta, he attempted to (historically) link the native peoples to Adam's family in order to support the cause of the mission: "Indians held information on the creation of the world and the creation of Adam and Eve, the Universal Flood, and of Noah and his wife."[97] The Christian mission, from this perspective, was necessary to liberate the native people from their heresies and restore them to the family of humankind. In this context, animals became an important source of information. Before the Fall, Adam had full communion with God's knowledge. We saw in the previous chapter how the tradition regarding Adam's divine knowledge was exploited by José Antonio González de Salas in order to imbue the field of geography with religious significance. García, too, reiterated the biblical narrative, asserting that "Adam had awareness, understanding, and knowledge of all natural things that God had created; and he also knew all the sciences and liberal and mechanical arts."[98] According to the biblical story, Adam named the animals according to their essences; all were present before him. But the "nameless" animals in the West Indies were unfamiliar to ancient authorities, their very existence thus posing a puzzling enigma.

García insisted that the history of animals could not contradict sacred literature. If the Bible said that all animals perished in the flood except for those Noah saved, then this point had to be considered a fact no less true than the scriptural explanation of the origin of man: "The reason we must say that the people of the Indies originate from Europe or Asia is in order not to contradict sacred literature, which clearly teaches that man is descended from Adam: since we are not allowed to give another origin for man, the same divine literature tells us that all the beasts and land animals perished except those that were saved for the propagation of their kind [*géneros*] in Noah's Ark."[99] Taking this doctrinal certainty as his primary foundation, García addressed two central and related questions by focusing on the case of exotic animals: what was the nature of the animals in the New World, and how did they get there? García repeated Acosta's question regarding the origins of all the strange and exotic animals (*animales peregrinas*) in Peru, including the guanaco, vicuña, llama, and alpaca, who "were not known by philosophers and naturalists because they do not exist in Asia, Africa and Europe."[100] Like Acosta, he wondered why these species had left no trace in the known world.

Despite his reliance on Acosta's natural history, García did not mention Acosta's determinist biogeographical model, which made regional extinction a conceivable answer. From the beginning of his discussion, García lamented that there was no satisfying or definitive answer to the question of the origins of the rare animals. Agreeing with Acosta (and Aquinas), he averred that scripture did not offer the possibility of a second creation after the flood. Continuing his survey of possible solutions, García commented that animal species from the Old World might have come by land, as Acosta had argued, but noted that a land bridge did not explain why entire species migrated to separate parts of the world leaving no hint of their migration in the other parts.

These were far from idle speculations. Indeed, García did not specify his difficulty with Acosta's solution. However, we know that he saw himself as a follower of Aquinas and based his understanding of nature on the latter's philosophical system. While Aquinas stated that God did not care for animals as he did for rational creatures (since they are not free to control their actions and choose to follow God), they were not excluded from divine providence, as manifested in their geographical distribution.[101] God's providence ordered all things to their ends, a fact that extended to irrational animals. Aquinas further asserted, "For God's foreknowledge is infallible even regarding contingent future things, inasmuch as God in his eternity sees future things as actual in their existing."[102] What we can glean from García's writings suggests that he might have found it unreasonable that creatures would prosper or perish in seemingly random fashion. We can speculate that for a scholar like García, dedicated as he was to the belief that God had a plan for all creation, it was implausible that God would create certain species and command Noah to preserve these animals on the ark, only to eliminate them later as they moved across the world. Such a futile fate appeared to undermine the scholastic view that God had knowledge of all creation, its past and its future. As historian Neal Gillespie has noted, "Animals offered in their adaptations, structures, and instincts the best evidence anyone could want of God's benign foresight, protective providence, and infinite intelligence."[103] God's benign foresight seemed irreconcilable with environmental determinism, which potentially sentenced God's creatures to death in unsuitable natural conditions.

Taking an opposing position to that of Acosta, García offered an alternative and no less intricate explanation of biodiversity. His theory combined two main ideas from church exegetical tradition: Aquinas's views on crossbreeding and Augustinian ideas on angelic translocation, which Acosta had utterly rejected.

Critically, all of García's answers *denied* arbitrariness or chance in creation and, in particular, the placement of animals (and their geographical distribution after the flood) across the terrestrial globe. Biodiversity and the existence of different ecosystems were, García insisted, part of God's design and reflected the benevolence of creation. Through the observation of animal distribution, he believed, again echoing Aquinas, one could surmise a divine plan. "In the beginning of the world," he wrote, "God our Lord created in each province different species of herbs, plants, and animals, and even in different parts of the sea, various and diverse fish; and not without mystery, or without special providence, the Creator wanted to distribute across the world this variety and diversity of plants, animals, birds, and fish, bringing about more perfection in the universe and pointing to his wisdom."[104] Like Aquinas, García saw in the arrangement and distribution of species the hand of God. The biological and environmental diversity of creation, according to García, were not accidents of nature but reflections of God's divine wisdom. The question of the distribution of the animals and their dispersal across the globe, however, remained.

While Acosta's migration theory suggested that the natural conditions of a region determined the existence or "disappearance" of certain animals, García proffered the possibility that species could evolve and change over time in order to fit different habitats. His solution echoes Oviedo's remarks that American biodiversity was the result of varied localities and constellations. Developing this point even further, García suggested that the rare animals that he had encountered in Peru "proceeded from wild and domestic species that live in Africa, Asia and Europe, that passed to the Indies by water or land." Yet, he continued, "due to the disposition of the land, and the particular influences and constellation of the heavens . . . they acquired accidental differences."[105] According to García, climatic and terrestrial influences had a major impact on the development of species. In this way, García suggested that the llama in Peru might have evolved from camels, an idea with which Carl Linnaeus, the developer of modern biological taxonomy, would agree in the eighteenth century. Like Acosta, García modeled his solution within the framework of biogeography, but he suggested "proto-evolutionary" processes to explain the radical difference between the animals of both worlds. The American species adapted to the New World's environmental conditions.

To clarify his position, García dedicated much of his fourth chapter to the topic of monstrosity, employing the category of monsters as a halfway classification that explained how certain animals could evolve and become exotic.[106] The term "monster" was a liminal taxonomy that was frequently used to describe exceptions to regular patterns of nature. The literary tradition on this subject established that monsters were infrequent anomalies that were profoundly different in appearance from their progenitors. Monstrosity could signify several and often contradictory meanings, including the belief that monsters were "against nature" (*contra naturam*). Alternatively, other thinkers, including Augustine and Isidore of Seville, from whose writings García borrowed certain ideas, argued that a monster was part of God's plan, a means of communication with humankind through an adornment of his creation.[107] For example, Augustine argued that God could change "the natures of His own creation into whatever He pleases," thereby spreading "abroad a multitude of those marvels which are called monsters, portents, prodigies, phenomena." Augustine explained that the term "monster" referred to the fact that they show (*monstrant* in Latin) signs from God or "signify something."[108] From this perspective, monsters were not contrary to nature and did not stand outside God's providence, a key distinction for García.

Significantly, García generally avoided negative connotations associated with the term "monster" and instead employed the concept to speculate on the possibility of biological transformation. The monster provided a conceptual framework through which García could analyze models of animal speciation. He asserted that there were two types of "monstrosity." The first resulted from the union of two different species (for instance, mules), and the second was a consequence either of natural failure (*defecto de la naturaleza*) or of natural or stellar influences (at the moment of conception). García proposed that an individual might be a "monster" (read, mutant) with respect to its species or that an entire breed could be "monstrous" (read, divergent) in relation to its original biological group: "They acquired this monstrosity by reason of heavenly constellations, the character of the land, and other contingencies and factors in which they lived."[109]

Seen from this perspective, García did not understand monsters as supernatural, miraculous, or malicious phenomena that transgressed nature but rather as hybrids or the result of mutations. On the one hand, he agreed with Augustine and Isidore that monsters were not against nature. On the other, he did not repeat their belief that monsters were omens. The union of parents of different species could create, according to García, "a third species." By definition, this new species was not monstrous since it resembled its parents and continued over generations to reproduce. It instead represented a sort of hybrid animal (*animal mestizo*), a term that was very loaded in the Spanish colonies because of the preoccupation with crossbreeding and purity of blood (*limpieza de sangre*), which resulted in its employment to describe humans.[110] The category of monsters provided García with a conceptual tool to convey an identifiable model of the kinds of change already known and documented in literature, which came about owing to crossbreeding and environmental conditions. Critically, García doubted that the American species could or should be considered "monsters" in any negative sense, and instead maintained that such animals evolved over time and, in some cases, even formed new species. For García, this left open the possibility that these animals had been transformed into a separate species sometime after the first six days of creation and became substantially different from their progenitors. His solution to biodiversity made clear that change was divinely ordained and part of God's larger plan for creation. The survival of species could not be simply the result of circumstantial factors caused by a distant God.

However, García's line of argument risked replacing the idea of *creatio ex nihilo* by a divine creator with a longer and more complicated process of natural adaptation. Alteration and mutability among and within species might solve one problem for García, but it could raise other theological questions, such as those reflected in today's debates between Darwinists and creationists. Did God foresee or plan this process of change when he created the original species? If these animals came into existence after God's six days of work, should they not be understood as *contra naturam*?

To answer these questions, García again relied on commentaries that suggested that change might be part of God's greater plan. The discussion of the nature of crossbreeds found in these older interpretations offers a window into the concept of species. The Thomist position implied that even crossbreeds were part of God's initial plan, and Aquinas had no problem applying the term *species* to them (as did later Spanish theologians, such as the Jesuit Benito Pererius).[111] The innovation in García's zoological discussion lay in his readiness to apply Thomist reasoning and categories to the newly encountered animals; this provided an opportunity to make a case for mutability in animal species. From this perspective, García's ideas on animals' transformation across time and place maintained the basic "law" of providence over all creatures, including those who might have appeared after the act of creation depicted in the Bible.

But García still faced the question of how animals came to their current dwelling places after the universal flood. He suggested that angels had carried the animals both before and after the flood. Postcreation speciation might have explained how the animals changed in response to environmental conditions, but García felt that their geographical distribution must have a heavenly explanation. He stated that the "best" solution was that the "ministry of angels" was responsible for transporting them "to the different parts of the world, in which they had developed." This angelic operation was similar to how the animals were supposedly carried from their place of creation to Adam in order to be named, an idea that Augustine had already expounded and that was supported as well by "our father Saint Thomas." This explanation, García asserted, "is the best, and it solves all the difficulties and the objections raised, that so much fatigued us, surrounding the animals of Peru."[112]

We discussed in chapter 3 how angels revealed the secrets of nature to human beings, contributing to the emergence of new ways of understanding nature. García's ideas on angelic transportation are worth noting not for their zoological merits, obviously, but for revealing his doctrinal priorities. In essence, he rejected the randomness inherent in Acosta's migration hypothesis, whereby animals roamed the land until they settled in a suitable habitat. Animals returned to their *native environment* after the flood, according to García, meaning that they were indigenous (from the time of creation!) to the American continent: "Now with much satisfaction, I will say again that they returned with natural instinct, and natural and heavenly providence to the same land in which their progenitors initially created them."[113] It is fascinating that Acosta had previously used almost identical phrasing to conclude that the animals migrated through the land via "natural instinct" and "heavenly providence."[114] Whereas Acosta wrote, "por instinto natural y providencia del cielo, diversos géneros se fueron a diversas regiones," for García, the same animals "se volvieron con instincto natural, y providencia del cielo, y naturaleza, a la misma tierra donde primero fueron criados sus progenitores." Both authors thus appealed to laws of nature and providence, although each did so to justify quite different conclusions. García, for his part, ruled out any "random" selection in bio-distribution.

Nonetheless, there is the potential for confusion when examining García's ideas. If he ultimately relied on angels to explain bio-distribution, why did he dedicate so much energy to entertaining the possibility of biological mutation (via the category of monstrosity) in the first place? Angels obviated the need to account for postcreation speciation: all animals in their current form could have simply been created *ex nihilo* in the environment that best suited them. This apparent contradiction could be resolved by García's understanding of the perfection of nature as reflected in its diversity. García's angelic theory and his ideas about postcreation speciation did not have to be mutually exclusive. García did not specify when "evolution" began, how long the transformation process took, or what stage of development the animals had attained when they were transported to the West Indies and elsewhere. He was not a Darwinist but a Dominican friar. Mutation and angelic transportation can, in fact, be seen as compatible aspects of one divine plan to create and spread diversity in the universe.

Divine providence and God's foreknowledge were, for García, the most important factors in natural history (a consideration that propelled him to engage the topic in the first place). God did not move an animal from the ark (or from Eden) to a place that was "inimical" to its design and nature, as Acosta had implicitly suggested, but to a place where animals could reach their fullest potential by adapting to the environment. For García, the diversity of creatures pointed to God's creative power and his intricate plan. Angels carried the animals to the West Indies (and other parts across the world), where, thanks to divine foresight, they could evolve as a result of local environmental differences. It was one thing to create a camel, another thing entirely to create a camel that would one day become a llama. The resulting increase in the biodiversity of creation reflected God's wisdom, an idea that was reiterated by the German Jesuit Athanasius Kircher many years later (without reference, however, to a contingent of angels).

The recourse to angelic intervention in solving the zoological mystery was part of a broader Catholic interest in angels. As we have seen in the case of Sor María's cosmographic visions, angels played an important role in knowledge culture in the Hispanic world. Much later than García, the Jesuits Juan Eusebio Nieremberg and Barnabé Cobo, who speculated on the differences between animal populations in the Old and New Worlds, also preferred the angelic solution.[115] Historians have attributed Cobo's ideas on angels to Jesuit spirituality and way of proceeding, but García's earlier opinion in favor of angelic involvement points to the limits of Jesuit-centered historiography.[116] García incorporated angels (via Augustine) into his zoological thinking on American animals long before Cobo and Nieremberg wrote their treatises. Angels transcended monastic affiliations in seventeenth-century Catholicism.

But the most original argument in García's discussion was his readiness to consider the transformation of animal species in the intervening time since creation as a way to address the nature of the species found in America. This idea foreshadows Buffon's theory of human variety, which explained the "types" of humans in the world by their migrations into diverse climatic and environmental regions, which resulted in subsequent alterations.[117] While García wrote in a genre that was called into question by newer methodologies, his novel ideas on the formation of life and postcreation speciation were innovative and surprising. Nonetheless, the break between "traditional" and "modern" forms of knowledge—direct experience and the "new science," on one hand, and scholastic learning, on the other—has prevented historians from looking seriously at his zoological insights.

For all of their differences, García and Acosta both saw a reflection of God's omnipotence in the marvelous variety of species and objects in America; similarly, in creation, they both saw signs of God's providence. For García, God's omnipotence expressed itself in divine wisdom and generosity, which was reflected in the foresight that guided creation. Like other Dominican theologians, and especially Luis de Granada, introduced earlier, García believed that the world was written in the "fractioned and illuminated letters" of creatures that reflected God's providential design.[118] For Granada, every created thing in the universe, and the entire structure of nature and the patterns in it, could be read like a text that exhibited the traces of God's hand. The abundance of species—a diversity that García worked hard to explain—reflected God's infinite attributes. We have seen throughout this study that Dominicans were not alone in adopting a typological view of nature. Yet the Dominicans, who had since the thirteenth century fashioned their theology around Thomist-Aristotelian concepts, positioned themselves as guardians of the sacred word, responsible for defending the old principles regarding the division and organization of the universe. In a new world, García saw himself as an heir to the Dominican tradition that looked for signs of divine providence in the order in creation.

Proper interpretation of divine providence was thus a major point of contention between members of these two orders; disagreements resulted in a series of doctrinal disputes about the nature of God's foreknowledge, especially in the context of the Molinist debate. Though the Dominican-Jesuit debates centered squarely on God's foreknowledge of *human* fate, we can read into them larger perspectives on all of God's creatures. Of course, Catholic theology never extended free will to the animal kingdom. But if the book of creatures reflected the mind of God, then there was no sense in claiming that God would save animals through Noah only to allow them to die later, as a result of having arrived at the "wrong place." García aimed to justify the Catholic mission, and his ideas on variation in nature were included in this rationalization. God has a plan; contingency and dying off by chance, as Acosta's environmental solution might imply, did not conform to this school of thought, at least as the Dominicans understood it. One might suggest that the source of the disagreement stemmed from what, since the late thirteenth century, had been framed as a dialectic between God's "two powers" (*potentia Dei ordinata* and *potentia Dei absoluta*). While the two theologians affirmed the working of providential design, it might well be that García placed particular emphasis on God's absolute power (i.e., God's extraordinary power, which could operate apart from the ordinary course of things) to determine speciation.[119] Either way, García did not include Acosta's thesis in his survey and instead elaborated on explanations that stressed God's design of creation in one way or another.

Ultimately, the difference between Acosta's and García's ideas did not stem from modern zoological techniques or classifications but from theological positions that guided their distinctive interpretations of postdiluvian events. The animal kingdom reflected the mind of the creator, and the Bible was the ultimate reference work for natural knowledge. Nevertheless, the two Spanish theologians arrived at different conclusions about the origin of the New World's species (and, no less significantly, on God's foreknowledge and omnipotence). At the same time, as I have emphasized throughout this chapter, regardless of their distinct theological postures, there was a social context for the competition between the Dominican and the Jesuit orders that was no less important than any theological dilemma. In the midst of struggles for leadership over the Catholic Church, García employed new zoological data in order to correct Acosta's ideas and assert Dominican scriptural authority. Published in 1607, the same year in which the pope demanded that the Dominicans and the Jesuits stop decrying the other as heretical, New World fauna became another front in a continuous battle.

The Legacy of the Flood Zoology

S'il n'existoit point d'animaux, la nature de l'homme serait encore plus incompréhensible.
—Georges-Louis Buffon, 1843

The rare American species continued to puzzle European writers. Spanish clergymen's articulation of postdiluvian zoology had a lasting impact that transcended national boundaries. When, in 1615, Giovanni Ciampoli (ca. 1590–1643) warned Galileo Galilei about the dangers of his discovery of the cratered surfaces of the moon, he specifically raised the concern that some might assume an analogy between the earth and the moon. "Someone adds to this and says that you assume that the moon is inhabited by men. Then another starts discussing how they could be descended from Adam or how they could have gotten out of Noah's Ark, and many other extravagant ideas that you never even dreamed of."[120] Ciampoli's words point to the heated discussions in Europe surrounding the origins of people and animals, and the continuing importance of the biblical narrative in solving that mystery.

The parameters of zoological thinking set by Spanish missionaries delineated the nature of the discussion for years to come, even well into the eighteenth century.[121] The idea of divine providence remained a central concern for natural philosophers. We can see this influence in the writings of two well-known continental Jesuits, Juan Eusebio Nieremberg and Athanasius Kircher, who repeated the ideas of Acosta and García.[122]

Nieremberg's *Curiosa y oculta filosofía* reproduced the central feature of García's solution, namely, that the exotic American species had been miraculously carried by guardian angels to the continent. Having never left Spain, Nieremberg relied entirely on the writings of missionaries and travelers who investigated nature in America, including Acosta, Oviedo, and Hernández.[123] Nature was, in Nieremberg's view, an amalgam of letters and ciphers that offered a way to God's mind. For him, studying the history of animals was imperative, since Adam was charged with observing and naming the animals; perhaps in response to the Galileo affair, his task was "not to contemplate the gala of the stars."[124] Like García, Nieremberg suggested that angels had carried the animals twice: first, from their original place of birth to be named by Adam in Eden, and, second, from Noah's ark back to their natural environments. Luis Millones Figueroa has suggested that Nieremberg's ideas about the American species were rooted in his position on "the immutability of the natural world since Creation."[125] God had created an unalterable and perfect world, not monsters that were by definition against nature. The historiographical tendency to focus on the Jesuits has prevented scholars from noticing that Nieremberg actually developed García's ideas regarding the "indigenous" character of the animals on the newly discovered continent.[126] Like García before him, Nieremberg accepted the scholastic premise of God's protection over each species and stressed that God had placed each animal in the environment that best suited its nature. In so doing, Nieremberg sided with García and distanced himself from Acosta's ideas. The similarity between the zoological thoughts of these two writers is remarkable, yet historians have long neglected García's work. We might ask why. While Karl Enenkel praises Nieremberg for acknowledging "the strange animals *as species their own right* (!)," a development Enenkel understands as "a great achievement in the field of taxonomy," he ignores García (and also Acosta, who articulated the same idea years earlier).[127] I believe that this refusal to acknowledge the significance of García's ideas stems mainly from his scholastic style. Although it is deemed antiquated, García's scholastic method effectively hid a novel and radical solution to the origin of species. While García's style appears to have put off modern scholars, Nieremberg's writings suggest that the Dominican writer nevertheless had a significant influence on his contemporaries.

Athanasius Kircher, the German Jesuit polymath in Rome, was equally informed by the earlier debates among Spanish clergy, but he suggested his own solution to the question of providence. Kircher's *Arca Noe* (1675) was an attempt to deploy contemporary literature and natural history in order to rationalize the biblical story of the ark. Explaining how all the animals could fit on a moderate-size seagoing vessel, Kircher supported the possibility of species transformation and hybridization. He was "able to increase the amount of biodiversity after the flood on the basis of the animals becoming modified by environmental conditions,"[128] in part by pointing to the existence of hybrid animals who developed after the flood.[129] For instance, Kircher believed that the armadillo was a hybrid of the hedgehog and the turtle. He also suggested that animal species could be transformed to a considerable extent when they migrated between different climates. For Kircher, climatic and environmental influences that shaped animal characteristics were divinely ordained, and mutability was part of God's design.[130] That later Jesuits like Nieremberg and Kircher concurred with García (on certain points) only demonstrates how necessary the "correction" was (it also shows that García was much more influential than historians have so far noticed). In any event, the tensions between the Jesuits and the Dominicans slowly dissolved in the intervening years. When Nieremberg and Kircher wrote their treatises in the 1630s and 1670s, respectively, the long-running Dominican-Jesuit disputes over grace, free will, and predestination had dissipated (leaving other matters to fuel their contentious relationship).

These debates over the geographical distribution of species were not reserved to overseas missionaries or theologians but concerned intellectuals across the European continent.[131] The influential English jurist and prolific author Sir Matthew Hale (1609–1676) discussed the same topic in his study of the "primitive origination of mankind" (1677). Echoing Acosta's and García's ideas, Hale proposed three possible explanations for the variety of species after the flood: migration, an "anomalous Mixture of Species," or "some accidental Variations in the process of time."[132] Migration, mutation (through propagation), and environmental adaptation, which constituted the basis of postdiluvian zoology for missionaries in the Spanish colonies, became accepted explanations for the distribution of species around the world.

Debates over the origins of American species continued into the Enlightenment, but the idea that the ark could have carried all the animals to their rescue became highly implausible. By the time the French Comte de Buffon, Georges-Louis Leclerc, penned his monumental *Natural History* (1749–88), the biblical conundrum that had served as an impetus for these debates had become obsolete. Buffon, arguably the eighteenth century's most renowned naturalist, described natural phenomena without reference to supernatural causes. He entirely disregarded biblical chronology as he estimated that it took around seventy thousand years for the planet to cool sufficiently to sustain life.[133] And in explaining the unequal geographical distribution of species across continents and their evolution over time, he felt no need to evoke Noah's ark. Nevertheless, even as the biological variations of animal species across the globe came to be explained in largely secular terms, Buffon's conclusions regarding the alteration of American species (which he understood in terms of degradation from Old World species)[134] remained noticeably similar to those of religious thinkers of earlier centuries. Scripture might have been absent, but the conclusions remained, as did interest in the differences between the Old and New World animal populations that had been based on an earlier engagement with the biblical exegesis.[135]

Ultimately, in the early modern period, the gathering of new zoological information offered scholars an opportunity to test theoretical frameworks supported by centuries-old Scholasticism against their new ideas about the origin of species. Building their theories on the foundations established by Augustine and Aquinas, Spanish friars formulated innovative zoological understandings, including the very definition of species and the role of ecology in the development of life. Environment mattered, and Spanish friars foreshadowed two important innovations in life science: extinction and speciation as a result of environmental adaptation. The theory of evolution suggests that the species in our world have evolved over an extended time, which has led to all manner of biological adaptations as primitive life-forms developed into complex organisms. Acosta's speculation on the possibility of regional "selection" based on biological and geographical conditions resembles the environmental considerations of the modern theory. Acosta's most innovative zoological idea was the notion that local environmental contingencies explained the pattern of distribution of living species in our world. To Acosta's mind, adaptability to a specific region therefore determined animals' migration patterns, reproduction, and "disappearance." By contrast, García's ideas about the transformation of animals echo other aspects of the modern theory of evolution that would eventually replace the narrative of *creatio ex nihilo* with an account of a long process of natural adaptation. Of course, García saw divine providence as the driving force behind the diversity of creatures, an idea that Darwin would later strongly oppose because, as he explained, if "each variation has been providentially arranged," then "natural selection [becomes] entirely superfluous, & indeed takes the whole case of appearance of new species out of the range of science."[136] Yet García would probably agree with Pope Francis that "[God] created beings and allowed them to develop according to the internal laws that he gave to each one, so that they were able to develop and to arrive and [sic] their fullness of being."[137]

It is, of course, an exaggeration to present early modern Catholic clergy as proto-evolutionary thinkers. Nevertheless, we must recognize their willingness to entertain the idea that biological change occurred as a result of environmental factors. In the end, these two components together—Acosta's suggestion of regional selection and García's proposal of postcreation speciation as animals adapted to new environments—would revolutionize our understanding of the development of species in the nineteenth century. Naturally, this was not the priority of friars who were the product either of the Jesuit curriculum or of premodern Dominican Scholasticism. For them, as with Sor María's cosmographic visions or confessional geographers' writings, the real challenge was to incorporate natural facts from an expanding world into their spiritual lexicon. The production of natural knowledge across imperial Spain was affected by, and responded to, pressing religious concerns, as Catholicism encountered new worlds of knowledge. Participating in a broader process of creating worlds of meanings, natural history partook in making Catholicism a global religion. On this contentious subject, animals, too, could testify.

CONCLUSION

This study has shown that colonial scientific exploration had vital repercussions for Catholic religious culture and thought. Iberian expansion and global trading networks made it possible (and necessary) to gather geographical and biological information from the four corners of the world. New empirical tools and methods were devised at the central agencies of Spain's colonial enterprise, contributing to the scientific transformation of the premodern world. As Spain's imperial ventures facilitated a new scientific program, these channels were adapted and modified to remodel early modern Catholicism into a world religion. Examining case studies in the fields of natural history, cosmography, and geography, we have uncovered the multiple ways in which observing nature supported religious ideologies and worldviews, as Catholic actors participated as both consumers and producers of natural knowledge. While Iberian theologians deepened the correspondence between God's three books (revelation, nature, and church teachings), pious observers looked to nature to affirm their way of life, repackaging Catholic doctrines and narratives with a new sense of scientific wonder.

This historical development in the wake of European imperialism and the new science, I have argued, was made possible by a theology that presented nature as a divine ladder connecting humans, creation, and God. The vital intersection between Hispanic religion and science went two ways: on the one hand, religion legitimated the study of nature, providing its practitioners with approval and acceptance for their scholarship, which was much needed at a time of confessional strife; on the other hand, in an intellectual climate that considered experience the *madre de ciencia*, observing nature opened new ways to articulate Catholic visions and beliefs, precisely because nature, according to religious doctrine, reflected church priorities and the truth of faith.

At the heart of this book stands a fundamental question regarding the relationship between Iberian Catholicism and modernity. Knowledge production and scientific practices in the Western world are often perceived as benchmarks for including societies in the metanarrative of modernity. Regardless of major revisions in the history and philosophy of science, scholars still tend to identify science as a critical feature of modernity, often insinuating an inherent connection between political developments such as sovereignty and bureaucratic centralization and science's very progress. The "polemics of Spanish science" is a paradigmatic historiographical case that has pitted the Scientific Revolution, in the Atlantic and elsewhere, against the Black Legend in order to undermine centuries of shibboleths regarding alleged Spanish exceptionalism and backwardness. As historian Jorge Cañizares-Esguerra has commented, "But why do students and the general public think of the Iberian empires in terms of ignorant, zealot friars and plundering conquistadores rather than of savvy naturalists and learned cosmographers? The answer, to be sure, lies in age-old religious battles harking back to the Reformation."[1] Simply put, such polemics are the historical legacy of a long-standing confessional struggle that equated Catholicism with the retrograde defense of "traditional" orthodoxy and the Protestant Reformation with progress, rationalism, modern science, and the eventual Weberian *Entzauberung der Welt* (disenchantment of the world). Yet the implicit assumption of a "path to modernity," one that follows, along a Baconian model, the union of science and the state, is itself misleading. The revolution in early modern science, if a revolution happened at all, was deep and meaningful precisely because it affected many areas of society and culture, including elements that we perceive nowadays as traditional and therefore as seemingly resistant to, or in conflict with, modern values and norms.

This book has thus presented the ways in which scientific metaphors and imagery permeated religious writings, and has shown how cosmographies and geographies were used for confessional and sacramental purposes during a critical moment in the reshaping of Catholic orthodoxy. Adapting to a new epistemic culture, Hispanic geographers and naturalists in new worlds actively transformed the meaning of the Spanish state's information-gathering initiatives for their own ends. Bringing together the cases of

Carmelite, Franciscan, and Dominican writers, among others, I have shown that, unlike frequent depictions of mendicant orders as outmoded (certainly in comparison to the Jesuits), they too exhibited interest in natural scholarship as part of their religious outlook. The study of the earth provided a symbolic language in which to articulate the sacred and support distinct and diverse religious ideologies that have often remained unnoticed in historical accounts, overshadowed by the monolithic voice of Spanish imperialism.

For all the various reasons that religious protagonists turned to the study of nature, it is clear that they used natural knowledge to reaffirm the righteousness of Catholicism and to spread the faith. Moving beyond a center-periphery paradigm, historians have increasingly applied a global approach to the Catholic Reformation, one that considers the broader significance of local Catholic manifestations around the world. This book has joined that effort by emphasizing that the natural explorations in Spanish America played an integral part in Catholic renewal. Taking a cultural perspective on Atlantic knowledge production has allowed me to expand our understanding of early modern confessionalism, both geographically and thematically. Employing a Dominican "explanation" (in Aquinas's sense) for exotic American species, and re-creating a Carmelite drama by compiling geographical information, enables us to see the significance of overseas evangelization in the clarification of faith and the shaping of Catholic identities across the Atlantic.

Moreover, placing natural histories and cosmographical and geographical works within the "cultural field" of the Catholic Reformation reveals how scientific disciplines helped construct worlds of meanings for men and women. Aware of the propagandistic potential of studies of the earth, religious and lay savants integrated discussions of scriptural authority, the sacraments, the Virgin Mary, and various Catholic doctrines and values into their otherwise secular scholarship. Merging knowledge and faith, natural science became a means of broadcasting a clear and unifying Catholic message, providing what scholar Charles Long would call "orientation in the ultimate sense." The accumulation of natural knowledge was a rich source for the reconfiguration of global Catholicism, and not only, as the Jesuit-centered paradigm suggests, for a selective group of actors. Cosmographical knowledge was integrated into mystical and scholastic works; geographical writings and travel literature fostered imaginative forms of religious consciousness not just for *criollo* writers but also in Iberian convents and monasteries; confessional geographers and naturalists gave a particularly Catholic interpretation to the findings that were uncovered in a new ecological environment. In short, the history of the Catholic Reformation should not be circumscribed by Eurocentric cultural geography or by patterns of social control and Tridentine elucidation of doctrine. The world outside the Iberian Peninsula played an essential part in this production, participating in the circulation of ideas and knowledge and cementing a truly global religion that took advantage of new channels of imperial knowledge.

The impact of these developments on the study of the New World was particularly significant, since many of the written documents that examined the social and natural dimensions of the Western Hemisphere were written by Roman Catholic priests and missionaries. By the mid-sixteenth century, the ecological transformation of the Americas was well under way, with the explicit intention of the Spanish Crown to make the continent habitable and economically prosperous for Europeans. The change, however, was not restricted to the so-called Columbian exchange. From a Christian anthropocentric standpoint, making the continent "habitable" also involved a process of transferring Christian meanings to a new environment. The new landscapes, however, were not simply decoration or background against which history took its course. As spatial theorists have stressed, space is not merely an empty "container" in which things happen; the environment of the new continent set the conditions for the reconfiguration of faith, once again revealing the profound connection between human religion and the natural environment. The belief in a sacred planet, one that supported all the material and spiritual needs of humankind, constituted part of the epistemological framework that undergirded knowledge about the local environment. For historical actors who partook "in the process of mapping a symbolic landscape and constructing a symbolic dwelling in which they might have their own space and find their own place," studying the geography and natural history of the new continent was a tool for transmitting sacred meanings to a wider audience by restaging a physical relationship with the transcendent and reenacting elements of particular Catholic traditions.[2] As Catholic clergy brought space alive and infused their studies with Catholic consciousness, they conferred a quasi-theological status on ecology. They made new worlds an integral part of their sacred habitat.

Notes

Preface
1. Venegas, *Diferencias de libros* (1569), fol. 35r; Granada, *Símbolo de la fe*, 133.

Chapter 1
1. Compare figure 1 with the painting of Aquinas by Carlo Crivelli held at the National Gallery, at https://www.nationalgallery.org.uk/paintings/carlo-crivelli-saint-thomas-aquinas.
2. Instruction of Philip II to Dr. Hernández, January 11, 1570, in Hernández, *Mexican Treasury*, 46.
3. López Piñero and Pardo Tomás, "Contribution of Hernández."
4. García, *Origen de los Indios*, 6. All translations are my own unless otherwise noted.
5. Bacon, *Of the Advancement of Learning*, 208; Bacon, *New Organon*, 78. In Spain, consider Medina, *Libro de grandezas y cosas memorables*, 42–44. On Spain's role in establishing the viewpoint that the moderns had superseded the ancients, see Maravall, *Antiguos y modernos*.
6. Juanini, *Cartas escritas*, "Al lector."

7. See, for example, Livingstone, *Putting Science in Its Place*. See also Osler, "Canonical Imperative."
8. The literature on science and empire is extensive. See Schiebinger, "Forum Introduction"; MacLeod, "Introduction"; and the essays in Delbourgo and Dew, *Science and Empire*.
9. Bleichmar et al., *Science in the Spanish and Portuguese Empires*; Xavier and Županov, *Catholic Orientalism*; López Piñero, *Historia de la ciencia*.
10. Barrera Osorio, *Experiencing Nature*; Sánchez Martínez, *La espada, la cruz y el padrón*; Pimentel, "Iberian Vision"; Brendecke, *Empirical Empire*.
11. Portuondo, *Secret Science*.
12. Barrera Osorio, "Experts, Nature," 134; Segev, "'For the Sciences Migrate.'"
13. See, for instance, the essays in Schiebinger and Swan, *Colonial Botany*; Smith and Findlen, *Merchants and Marvels*.
14. Portuondo, *Secret Science*; Padrón, *Spacious Word*.
15. On the emergence of local "patriotic" epistemologies, see Cañizares-Esguerra, *How to Write the History*. On the

intellectual responses to the New World, see Grafton, with Shelford and Siraisi, *New Worlds, Ancient Texts*. For the impact on classical geographical knowledge, see Wey Gómez, *Tropics of Empire*. For the shaping of anthropological thinking, see Rubiés, *Travellers and Cosmographers*. On medicine and materia medica, see Cook, *Matters of Exchange*; Gómez, *Experiential Caribbean*.

16. Mancall, *Nature and Culture*.
17. Nieremberg, *Historia naturae maxime peregrinae*, 16.
18. Stroumsa, *New Science*, 80.
19. Badiano, *Aztec Herbal*. On Franciscans and the medicine *mechoacan*, see Barrera Osorio, "Knowledge and Empiricism," 228–29. The Colegio de Santa Cruz was also important for its part in the ethnographic work of the Franciscan Bernardino de Sahagún, who resided there periodically as he studied pre-Hispanic Aztec society. See Sahagún's *Florentine Codex*. On this topic, see Pardo Tomás, "Conversion Medicine."
20. On Spanish missionaries' contribution to the study of cultures, see Romano, "Iberian Missionaries in God's Vineyard"; to minerology and metallurgy, Salazar-Soler, "Obras más que de gigantes"; to the recording of astronomical constellations, Calancha, *Corónica moralizada*. See also Cañizares-Esguerra, "New Worlds, New Stars," 50–51.
21. Harris, "Jesuit Scientific Activity"; Harris, "Confession-Building, Long-Distance Networks"; Findlen, "How Information Travels." On the significance of scientific activities to Jesuit spirituality, see the essays in O'Malley et al., *Jesuits*; Millones Figueroa and Ledezma, *Saber de los Jesuitas*; Asúa, *Science in the Vanished Arcadia*; Alberts, *Conflict and Conversion*.
22. See Prieto, *Missionary Scientists*, especially Prieto's analysis of Barnabé Cobo's writings, 176–92.
23. On the notion of collective empiricism, see Daston and Galison, *Objectivity*, 19–27.
24. On the reappraisal of the so-called conflict thesis, see the essays in Lindberg and Numbers, *God and Nature*.
25. In the early Christian tradition, theologians emphasized that God intended nature to remain mysterious and unintelligible. For instance, Lactantius (ca. 250–ca. 325) pointed out that God deliberately made Adam the last of his creation so that he should not acquire any knowledge of the process of creation. Eamon, *Science and the Secrets of Nature*, 59–61. Ambrose of Milan explained the absence of scientific discussion in scripture, claiming that "there is no place in the words of the Holy Scripture for the vanity of perishable knowledge." Gaukroger, *Emergence of a Scientific Culture*, 58.
26. Gaukroger, *Emergence of a Scientific Culture*, 23, 47.
27. Hsia, *World of Catholic Renewal*, 47.
28. Walsham, "Reformation and the 'Disenchantment.'"
29. Kamen, *Spanish Inquisition*, 153. See also Pardo Tomás, *Ciencia y censura*, 265–339; López Piñero, *Ciencia y técnica en la sociedad española*, 393.
30. The term "Black Legend" describes anti-Spanish attitudes that resulted from propagandistic Protestant writings. Jorge Cañizares-Esguerra has pointed out that the sciences that the Iberian empires supported, including geography, botany, and cartography, were mostly ignored in the history of the Scientific Revolution. This has resulted in the portrayal of Spain as a backward country, the very antithesis of enlightened Europe. Cañizares-Esguerra, "Colonial Iberian Roots of the Scientific Revolution," in *Nature, Empire, and Nation*, 14–46. See also Navarro Brotons and Eamon, *Más allá de la Leyenda Negra*. On the historiographical term, see García Cárcel, *Leyenda Negra*.

31. Here I borrow Barrera-Osorio's terminology; see his *Experiencing Nature*, 59.
32. On the historiographical terms for the Catholic renewal, see Jedin, "Catholic Reformation or Counter-Reformation"; Olin, *Catholic Reform*, ix–xiii, 1–46; Bireley, *Refashioning of Catholicism*, 2; Mullett, *Catholic Reformation*, 1–6.
33. Ditchfield, "Catholic Reformation and Renewal," 163; see also Ditchfield, "Decentering the Catholic Reformation."
34. On the Crown rights of patronage, see Prien, *Christianity in Latin America*, 24–30.
35. García Oro, *Cisneros y la reforma*; Sainz Rodríguez, *Siembra mística del Cardenal Cisneros*.
36. O'Malley, *Trent*, 40–43; Mullett, *Catholic Reformation*, 22; Hsia, *World of Catholic Renewal*, 47; Mixson and Roest, *Companion to Observant Reform*.
37. Mullett, *Catholic Reformation*, 181.
38. Of the significance of long-distance intellectual networks, see Findlen's introduction in *Empires of Knowledge*, 1–16.
39. Merton, *Science, Technology, and Society*, 136. On the "Merton thesis," see Cohen, *Scientific Revolution*, 314–21.
40. Harrison, *Bible, Protestantism*, 114, 92.
41. Segev, "Science of Faith," 31–77; see also Portuondo, *Spanish Disquiet*.
42. See, for instance, Andrés Martín, *Historia de la mística*; McGinn, *Mysticism in the Golden Age*.
43. See Colin Thompson's prologue, xx–xxi, and Hilaire Kallendorf's "Introduction: Expanding the Mystical Canon," 1–12, both in Kallendorf, *New Companion to Hispanic Mysticism*.
44. Godínez, *Practica de la theologia mystica*, "Al lector," [i].
45. Consider the spiritual praxis of *recogimiento*, which entails "a series of stages of meditation on 'nothing,' and a total denial of one's self." Van Deusen, *Between the Sacred and the Worldly*, xi. Contemplating nature was a constant theme even among those who developed detached spiritual attitudes—for instance, Francisco de Osuna, Luis de León, and Juan de la Cruz. See Calvert, *Francisco de Osuna*; Cuevas, "Fray Luis de León"; Collings, *John of the Cross*, 44.
46. Manson, "Design Argument and Natural Theology," 295; Topham, "Natural Theology and the Sciences," 59.
47. On this topic, see Ritchey, *Holy Matter*, 4–18.
48. Bono, *Word of God*, 12.
49. Curtius, *European Literature*, 319–26; Harrison, *Bible, Protestantism*, 39–63. See also Meer and Mandelbrote, *Nature and Scripture*.
50. The notion of a consciously ordered world was certainly not new to Christianity and can be found in earlier Christian teachings, including Thomas Aquinas's articulation of the fifth argument on God's existence. Gaukroger, *Emergence of a Scientific Culture*, 132.
51. Berkel and Vanderjagt, *Book of Nature*, ix.
52. Campanella, *Defense of Galileo*, 54, 68–69.
53. Originally titled *Scientia libri creaturarum seu naturae et de homine*, the manuscript was written in 1436, shortly before Sabunde's death, and first printed in 1484. The second printed edition was published in 1485 under the title *Theologia naturalis*, as the work became known. See Bujanda, "Influence de Sebonde en Espagne."
54. Sabunde quoted in Hall, "Natural Theology in the Middle Ages," 69.
55. Bujanda, "Influence de Sebonde en Espagne." On Bonaventure's images describing creation, see Delio, "Theology, Spirituality, and Christ," 373; Glacken, *Traces on the Rhodian Shore*, 237–40.
56. At the turn of sixteenth century, Cardinal Jiménez de Cisneros commissioned translations of medieval mystical texts, including those by Gregory the Great,

Bernard Clairvaux, and Catherine of Siena, and a popularized version of Pseudo-Dionysius's mystical theology. Sainz Rodríguez, *Siembra mística del Cardenal Cisneros*, 33–56.

57. See Ares's note to the reader in his translation of Sabunde's *Dialogos de la naturaleza del hombre*, "Al lector," ¶¶5r.
58. Consider the *Second Alphabet* by Francisco de Osuna. Calvert, *Francisco de Osuna*, 80–84.
59. Oré, *Symbolo Catholico Indiano*, 82.
60. Ibid., 202.
61. Granada, *Símbolo de la fe*, 128.
62. On Granada's typological reading of nature, see Cañizares-Esguerra, "Typological Readings of Nature," 49–53.
63. Kamen, *Spanish Inquisition*, 97, 126–27. On Valdéz's Index of 1559, see Pinto Crespo, *Inquisición y control ideólogico*, 149–77.
64. Granada, *Símbolo de la fe*, 146.
65. See, for example, Pimentel, "Baroque Natures"; Hendrickson, *Jesuit Polymath of Madrid*.
66. Nieremberg, *Curiosa y oculta filosofía*, 2 (bk. 1, chap. 1), 300 (bk. 2).
67. Phillips, *Church and Culture*, 115.
68. On Venegas, see Daniel Eisenberg's introduction to the 1983 facsimile edition of Venegas's *Diferencias de libros*, 7–34; Adeva Martín, *Maestro Alejo Venegas*.
69. Venegas, *Diferencias de libros* (1569), fols. 5r–6r.
70. Ibid., fol. 35r. Luis Jerónimo de Oré similarly used the expression the "university of creatures," and Luis de Granada claimed that "the university" of nature was superior to the reputable university in Paris. Oré, *Symbolo Catholico Indiano*, 82; Granada, *Símbolo de la fe*, 146.
71. Walsham, "Reformation and the 'Disenchantment,'" 505.
72. Venegas, *Diferencias de libros* (1569), fols. 113r, 112v.
73. Bireley, *Refashioning of Catholicism*, 49.
74. Harrison, "Book of Nature," 2.
75. Feldhay, "Cultural Field of Jesuit Science."
76. Keitt, *Inventing the Sacred*, 4. See also Hsia, *Social Discipline in the Reformation*.
77. On the development of a *criollo* religious self-consciousness, see Rubial García, *Santidad controvertida*.
78. Diefendorf, *From Penitence to Charity*, 20.
79. See, for example, Cervantes and Redden, *Angels, Demons, and the New World*; Cervantes, *Devil in the New World*; Remensnyder, *Conquistadora*; Earle, *Body of the Conquistador*; and Davies, *Renaissance Ethnography*.
80. Smith, "Science on the Move."
81. Burke, *Social History of Knowledge*, esp. 1–17.
82. On "symbolic vocabulary," see Lawson and McCauley, *Rethinking Religion*, 37–41.
83. Durkheim, *Elementary Forms of the Religious Life*, 47.
84. Smith, *Map Is Not Territory*, 290–91.
85. Long, *Signification*, 7.
86. See, for example, García, *Origen de los Indios*, 17. Covarrubias, in his *Tesoro de la lengua castellana* (1611), defines science in Aristotelian terms as "certain knowledge of something through its causes" (bk. 2, "Physics").
87. For interest in the occult in the Hispanic world, see, for instance, Torquemada, *Jardin de flores curiosas* (1570), bk. 3, 264–65; and Fray Esteban Villa's astrological writings on the correspondences between the heavens and plants. On the New World and the occult, see Bauer, *Alchemy of Conquest*.
88. On this topic, see Biener and Schliesser, *Newton and Empiricism*, 18–52; Vanzo, "From Empirics to Empiricists."
89. O'Gorman, *Invención de América*.

Chapter 2

1. On Pedro de Medina, see Ursula Lamb's introduction to Medina, *Navigator's Universe*, 3–18. The first document to indicate that Medina was ordained

a priest is from 1538. Martín Merás, *Introducción y estudio a la "Suma,"* 8.
2. Medina, *Libro de la verdad*, 323–24.
3. On the medieval legacy, see discussion in Grant, *Foundations of Modern Science*, 86–152.
4. Funkenstein, *Theology and the Scientific Imagination*.
5. Mundy, *Mapping of New Spain*, 11.
6. Portuondo, *Secret Science*, 22–38.
7. Short, *Making Space*, 36.
8. See, for example, Pimentel, "Iberian Vision"; Portuondo, *Secret Science*; Brendecke, *Empirical Empire*.
9. Waters, *Iberian Bases*.
10. Feldhay, *Galileo and the Church*, 74; Delumeau, *Catholicism Between Luther and Voltaire*.
11. Ditchfield, "Catholic Reformation," 174–75. For a now classic study of the propagation of religious ideologies in post-Reformation Europe, see Scribner, *For the Sake of Simple Folk*. Consider also Soergel, *Wondrous in His Saints*; Delano-Smith, "Maps as Art and Science"; Taylor, "Funeral Sermons and Orations."
12. Mullett, *Catholic Reformation*, 196–214. For an overview, see Hall and Cooper, *Sensuous in the Counter-Reformation Church*; and the essays in part 3, "Ideas and Cultural Practices," in Bamji, Janssen, and Laven, *Ashgate Research Companion to the Counter-Reformation*, esp. 337–93.
13. Phillips, *Church and Culture*, 136.
14. Blair, "Mosaic Physics."
15. On the Iberian editions of *De sphaera*, see Crowther, "Sacrobosco's *Sphaera*."
16. Compare Pérez de Moya's *Arithmética práctica y speculativa* (1562) and John Dee's *Mathematicall Preface* (1570). Likewise, Juan de Herrera conceived of mathematics as the foundation of knowledge; see Taylor, *Arquitectura y magia*; Portuondo, *Secret Science*, 79–84; Harkness, *John Dee's Conversations with Angels*, 91–97.
17. Rocamora y Torrano, *Sphera del universo*, fol. 7r–v.
18. Aristotle, *De Anima*, 14–17.
19. Rocamora y Torrano, *Sphera del universo*, fol. 1r.
20. Ibid., fol. 1r–v.
21. Neuner and Dupuis, *Christian Faith*, 102. See also Howell, *God's Two Books*, 25.
22. Rocamora y Torrano, *Sphera del universo*, fol. 1r–v.
23. Kessler, "Medietas/Mediator," 40.
24. Morgan, *Sacred Gaze*, 33, 55.
25. Wandel, *Eucharist in the Reformation*, 230; on the council's sessions, see 215–31.
26. Olson, *Science and Religion*, 59–63.
27. Mullett, *Catholic Reformation*, 5.
28. Remensnyder, *Conquistadora*, 301–2; Warner, *Alone of All Her Sex*, 315.
29. On this topic, see Brading, *Mexican Phoenix*.
30. On Zamorano, see Portuondo, *Secret Science*, 96–100.
31. Isidoro de Sevilla, *Etimologías*, 1:676.
32. Twomey, *Sacred Space of the Virgin Mary*, 189, 191–92, 360.
33. Remensnyder, *Conquistadora*, 215–8. See also Phillips, "Visualizing Imperium," 819.
34. Wandel, *Eucharist in the Reformation*, 215.
35. Waterworth, *Canons and Decrees*, 35.
36. Donovan, *Catechism of the Council of Trent*, 150. See also Spinks, *Early and Medieval Rituals*, 151–56.
37. Syria, *Arte de la verdadera nauegacion*, 22–23.
38. Ibid., 23. This idea also appears in Jean Bodin's *Universae naturae theatrum* (1596); see Blair, *Theater of Nature*, 3.
39. Ferrer Maldonado, *Imagen del mundo*, "Al lector."
40. On Ferrer Maldonado's exploration (1588), see Williams, *Voyages of Delusion*, 375–80; Pimentel, *Testigos del mundo*, 125–28.
41. Ferrer Maldonado, *Imagen del mundo*, 80, 79.
42. Vermij, "Subterranean Fire."
43. Medina, *Libro de la verdad*, 481. On Medina's perception of hell, see Lamb's introduction to Medina, *Navigator's Universe*, 25.

44. Vermij, "Subterranean Fire," 326.
45. Bellarmino quoted in Shea, "Galileo and the Church," 125. Cardinal Bellarmino dedicated a chapter to the subterranean location of hell in his *Controversia generalis de Christo*.
46. Shea, "Galileo and the Church," 125.
47. Resta, *Meteorologia de igneis aereis*.
48. Council of Trent, session 6 (1547), "Decree Concerning Justification," chap. 8, quoted in Schroeder, *Canons and Decrees*, 34–35.
49. Kolb, *Martin Luther*, 81.
50. McGrath, *Iustitia Dei*, 330, 324–44.
51. Brosseder, "Reading the Peruvian Skies," 400–401.
52. Goodman, *Power and Penury*, 20. See also Clark, *Thinking with Demons*, 476–77.
53. Ryan, *Kingdom of Stargazers*, 121–24.
54. Goodman, *Power and Penury*, 20.
55. Ernst, "'Veritatis amor dulcissimus,'" 61.
56. Burdick, *Mathematical Works Printed in the Americas*, 116–27; Maza, *Enrico Martínez*.
57. Martínez, *Reportorio de los tiempos*, 4, "Prologo," [ix], 11.
58. Ibid., 31.
59. Kahn, "Machiavelli's Afterlife and Reputation," 245.
60. Botero, *Della ragion di stato*; Pagden, *Spanish Imperialism*, 2, 44–49.
61. Quevedo, *Politica de Dios y gobierno de Cristo*, 9.
62. Solórzano Pereira quoted in Brading, *First America*, 222 (see also 237–41).
63. Martínez, *Reportorio de los tiempos*, "Prologo," [viii], [ix].
64. Mayhew, "'Geography Is Twinned with Divinity,'" 29.

Chapter 3

1. See Colin Thompson's "Prologue," xx–xxi, and Hilaire Kallendorf's "Introduction: Expanding the Mystical Canon," 9, both in Kallendorf, *New Companion to Hispanic Mysticism*. For a theoretical overview, see McGinn, *Foundations of Mysticism*, 291–343.
2. For an overview, see Katz, *Occult Tradition*.
3. Pimentel, "Baroque Nature"; Harkness, *John Dee's Conversations with Angels*.
4. On bilocation in the Hispanic world, see Tar, "Flying Through the Empire."
5. María de Jesús, *Redondez de la tierra*, BNE, Cervantes MS 5513. I also consulted MS 9346 (1716).
6. On the date, see Fedewa, *María of Ágreda*, 280. Questions regarding the authorship of the *Redondez* are perennial. In the twentieth century, Manuel Serrano y Sanz contested Sor María's authorship (*Apunes para una biblioteca*, 37). We will probably never know for certain, but Sor María included the text in the list of her works in the prologue to her autobiography (Colahan, *Visions of Sor María*, 31). It was also recognized by her contemporaries as her work. Historian Thomas Kendrick commented, "for a long time there was no doubt that Mary was the author. The Minister-General of the Franciscans, Alonso de Salizanes, and Father Samaniego, who were both present at her death-bed, were certain of that, and Salizanes owned the original manuscript when he was Bishop of Córdoba (1675–85). Samaniego, who can be counted on to recognize Mary's handwriting, borrowed it in order to make a copy for himself. There are many other copies of the Mapa in the sets of Mary's unpublished writings compiled by a single scribe." Kendrick, *Mary of Agreda*, 23. For discussion of the authorship question, see Colahan, *Visions of Sor María*, 28–31. The association of the text with Sor María continued in the 1737 extended edition for the bibliographical catalogue of the West and East Indies (originally written in 1629 by the Spanish historian and jurist Antonio de León Pinelo, ca. 1595–1660; the original catalogue, however, does not contain an entry on Sor María). León Pinelo, *Epitome de la bibliotheca oriental* (1737), 612. In the eighteenth and nineteenth

centuries, scholars and clergymen expressed doubts as to whether Sor María wrote the *Redondez*, but modern scholars, including Thomas Kendrick, Clark Colahan, Marilyn Fedewa, Mónica Díaz, and Stephanie Kirck, among others, accept her as the author.
7. Colahan, *Visions of Sor María*, 21–23.
8. Kendrick, *Mary of Agreda*, 24. Kendrick titles the third chapter of his book, which focuses on the *Redondez*, "A Juvenile Book."
9. In "Theorizing Transatlantic Women's Writing," Mónica Díaz and Stephanie Kirck have demonstrated the importance of the work to the building of Sor María's authority. For examples of the earlier historiography, see Kessell, *Spain in the Southwest*; Hickerson, "Visits of 'the Lady in Blue'"; MacLean, "María de Ágreda."
10. Kendrick, *Mary of Agreda*, 24.
11. Smith, "Alchemy as a Language," 8–9, 4.
12. On the Franciscans' efforts to mediate between their contemplative spirituality and their missionary duties, see Turley, *Franciscan Spirituality*.
13. The literature on female religious writings and experiences in Spain is a rich and growing field. See Cruz and Hernández, *Women's Literacy in Early Modern Spain*; Lehfeldt, *Religious Women in Golden Age Spain*; Weber, "Literature by Women Religious"; Bilinkoff, *Avila of Saint Teresa*; Poutrin, *Le voile et la plume*; Haliczer, *Between Exaltation and Infamy*; Sánchez Lora, *Mujeres, conventos y formas*.
14. On women's engagement with cartographic and geographical materials, see the essays in Beck, "Feminine Subject in the History of Discovery."
15. Fedewa, *María of Ágreda*, 12.
16. Haliczer, *Between Exaltation and Infamy*, 150–51.
17. Kendrick, *Mary of Agreda*, 8, 148.
18. Haliczer, *Between Exaltation and Infamy*, 149; Kendrick, *Mary of Agreda*, 7–10.
19. Kendrick, *Mary of Agreda*, 8–9; Haliczer, *Between Exaltation and Infamy*, 149.
20. This choice meant that hers was the only discalced convent in the province. Kendrick, *Mary of Agreda*, 9–10; Fedewa, *María of Ágreda*, 32.
21. Tar, "Literature of Franciscan Nuns," 62–63, 226–27, 244.
22. Fedewa, *María of Ágreda*, 21.
23. The letters were published in several editions. See Seco Serrano's edition, *Cartas de Sor María de Jesús*.
24. For example, Kessell, *Spain in the Southwest*; Hickerson, *Jumanos*; MacLean, "María de Ágreda"; Nogar, *Quill and Cross*.
25. Nogar, *Quill and Cross*, 17. For an analysis of the five primary texts that established María as a "bilocating protomissionary," see 9–39.
26. Ibid., 38.
27. See Baker H. Morrow's introduction to Benavides, *Harvest of Reluctant Souls*, xiv.
28. In his second *memorial*, Benavides incorporated two paragraphs that had previously appeared in Zárate Salmerón's *Relaciones*. Anna Nogar suggests that Benavides was probably unaware of Sor María when he wrote the first *memorial* and that only after completing it, while in Mexico City, did he learn about the Castilian nun (18)—although Benavides claimed in the 1634 *memorial* that he had heard about Sor María in New Mexico. Unlike Benavides, Zárate Salmerón did not provide a detailed version of the "miraculous conversion" but only associated Sor María with the missionary project in the northern territories. Zárate Salmerón, *Relaciones de todas las cosas*, 55. On this point, see Nogar, *Quill and Cross*, 14–18.
29. Evangelisti, "Religious Women, Mystic Journeys," 16.
30. María de Jesús describes the elemental region (from the sphere of the moon to the center of earth) in *Redondez de la tierra*, fols. 47r–51v. On the rejection of Copernican heliocentric theory, see Navarro Brotóns, "Continuity and Change in Cosmological Ideas."
31. Colahan, *Visions of Sor María*, 21.

32. Short, *Making Space*, 34–40; McLean, *Cosmographia of Sebastian Münster*, 124.
33. Colahan, *Visions of Sor María*, 23.
34. María de Jesús, *Redondez de la tierra*, fol. 80r.
35. Ibid., fol. 71v.
36. Grant, *History of Natural Philosophy*, 172.
37. Colahan, *Visions of Sor María*, 21. Consider also the models of the cosmos in Chaves, *Chronographia o reportorio de tiempos* (1561), fols. 85r–86r; Figueroa, *Opusculo de astrologia*, fols. 4–14; and Pedro de Medina's works, discussed above.
38. María de Jesús, *Redondez de la tierra*, fols. 75v, 76v, 77v.
39. Ibid., fol. 71r–v.
40. Ibid., fol. 52r. In 1698, the Franciscan Agustín Vetancurt asserted that the circumference of the earth was 6,300 leagues, the diameter, 2,004 leagues, and that at the earth's center were hell and purgatory. *Teatro mexicano*, 42.
41. María de Jesús, *Redondez de la tierra*, fol. 6r–v.
42. Ibid., fol. 72r–v.
43. On Giorgio's (sometimes spelled Georgi or Zorzi) *De harmonia mundi*, see Schmidt-Biggemann, *Philosophia perennis*, 305–15; Yates, *Occult Philosophy*, 33–42.
44. María de Jesús, *Redondez de la tierra*, fol. 13r–v.
45. Ibid., fol. 1r.
46. Bellarmino wrote this text in 1614; it first appeared in print in 1615. In 1619, the Dominican friar Anders Gil Vicario translated it for the first time from Latin into Spanish; I have used this translation. See John O'Malley's preface to Donnelly and Teske edition of Bellarmino, *Spiritual Writings*.
47. Bellarmino, *Escala espiritual*, 20.
48. Ibid., 50. Granada explained the abundance of species by suggesting that because creatures were created to attest to God's greatness, God had to create countless numbers of them to represent his many attributes: "Y porque vuestras perfecciones, Señor, eran infinitas, y no podía haber una sola criatura que las representase todas, fue necesario criarse muchas." Granada, *Símbolo de la fe*, 146.
49. María de Jesús, *Redondez de la tierra*, fols. 11r–v, 1v.
50. Cañizares-Esguerra, *Puritan Conquistadores*, 110–11. See also Phelan, *Millennial Kingdom of the Franciscans*.
51. Lara, *City, Temple, Stage*, 111–48.
52. María de Jesús, *Redondez de la tierra*, fols. 35v–36v.
53. Quoted in Daston and Park, *Wonders and the Order of Nature*, 25. On exoticism and marvels in medieval literature, see 21–66.
54. Daston and Park note that preexisting catalogues of natural wonders were imbued with symbolic moral significance. In a fourteenth-century Franciscan compilation of the exotic, for instance, the enormous ears of the Scythians signified their "willingness to hear the word of God." Ibid., 45. It well may be that Sor María used this image of the ear to hint about natives' readiness for conversion.
55. María de Jesús, *Redondez de la tierra*, fol. 37r–v. According to Acosta, Satan spread among the Indians a distorted religion. See Pagden, *Fall of Natural Man*, 175–79.
56. Castañega, *Tratado de las supersticiones*, 13.
57. Cervantes, *Devil in the New World*, 25. See also Olmos, *Tratado de hechicerías*.
58. María de Jesús, *Redondez de la tierra*, fols. 37v, 41r.
59. Paul III, "Sublimis Deus."
60. María de Jesús, *Redondez de la tierra*, fol. 42v.
61. Francis Xavier, "Xavier to his companions residing in Rome. From Cochin, January 20, 1548" (EX I 375–96; FX III 335–37), in *Letters and Instructions of Francis Xavier*, 179; Županov, *Missionary Tropics*, 35–86.
62. María de Jesús, *Redondez de la tierra*, fol. 41r. On the significance of early modern martyrdom, see Gregory,

Salvation at Stake. On the trope of martyrdom expressed by female mystics in their spiritual journeys, see Evangelisti, "Religious Women, Mystic Journeys," 12, 18–19.
63. Jaffary, *False Mystics*, 28.
64. Keitt, *Inventing the Sacred*, 78–86; Haliczer, *Between Exaltation and Infamy*.
65. Jaffary, *False Mystics*, 3. On the *alumbrados*, see García Gutiérrez, *Herejía de los alumbrados*; Huerga, *Historia de los alumbrados*; Kamen, *Spanish Inquisition*, 94–97; McGinn, *Mysticism in the Golden Age*, 45–50.
66. Kamen, *Spanish Inquisition*, 102–5.
67. Colahan, *Visions of Sor María*, 26.
68. Roest, *History of Franciscan Education*, 207.
69. Consider the production of the Codex *badianus* (1552), discussed in chapter 1. See Badiano, *Aztec Herbal*.
70. See, for example, León-Portilla, *Bernardino de Sahagún*. For examples of later Franciscan regional knowledge compositions, see López de Cogolludo, *Historia de Yucathan*; Laureano de la Cruz, *Nuevo descubrimiento del río Marañón*; and Vetancurt, *Teatro mexicano*.
71. Thevet, *Cosmographie vniuerselle*, "Preface," [3].
72. See discussion in Campbell, *Wonder and Science*, 30–44; Lestringant, *Mapping the Renaissance*, 9–11.
73. Thevet, *Cosmographie vniuerselle*, "Preface" [3].
74. Sorrell, *St. Francis of Assisi and Nature*, esp. 39–69.
75. Valadés, *Rhetorica christiana* (1579). I have also used the 1989 Spanish-Latin edition translated by Tarsicio Herrera Zapién.
76. María de Jesús, *Redondez de la tierra*, fol. 3v. Her biographer Ximénez Samaniego added that Sor María experienced the world by "abstract means" (*la mostrò el Señor por especies abstractivas maravillosamente todo el mundo*). Ximénez Samaniego, *Vida de la V. Madre Sor María*, III; see also 168.
77. María de Jesús, *Redondez de la tierra*, fol. 3r-v.
78. Blair, *Theater of Nature*, 153–79, esp. 174–75, 154.
79. Fioravanti quoted in Lestringant, *Mapping the Renaissance*, 19.
80. Granada, *Obras del V. P. M. Fray Luis*, 1:198–99 (part 2, chap. 14). Compare with Francisco de Osuna; see McGinn, *Mysticism in the Golden Age*, 37.
81. María de Jesús, *Mística ciudad de Dios*, 349–87 (bk. 3, chaps. 1–9). On this point, see Colahan, "Mary of Agreda," 57.
82. Pérez de Moya, *Arithmética práctica y speculativa*, 644.
83. Granada, *Símbolo de la fe*, 146.
84. For instance, the Spanish cosmographer from Aragon, Martín Cortés de Albacar, divided God's creation into three categories: "corporales, como los elementos; spirituales, como los ángeles y compuestos de estos como el hombre." Cortés, *Breue compendio de la sphera*, ix.
85. Raymond, introduction to *Conversations with Angels*, 4.
86. Nieremberg, *De la hermosura de Dios*, 379.
87. Harkness, *John Dee's Conversations with Angels*, 103.
88. Giorgio quoted in ibid., 109.
89. Walsham, "Catholic Reformation"; and the essays in Marshall and Walsham, *Angels in the Early Modern World*.
90. Walsham, "Catholic Reformation," 273–74.
91. "Holy Guardian Angels," 289.
92. Walsham, "Catholic Reformation," 279; Johnson, "Guardian Angels," 193.
93. Poutrin, "'Livres extatiques,'" 59–60.
94. Johnson, "Guardian Angels," 193.
95. Von Henneberg, "Saint Francesca Romana," 467.
96. Kircher continued exploring the workings of the earth in his *Iter Exstaticum II* (1657). On these works, see Rowland, "Athanasius Kircher, Giordano Bruno"; Rowland, "Athanasius Kircher's Guardian Angel."
97. Morrow, introduction to Benavides, *Harvest of Reluctant Souls*, xii–xiv.

98. Nogar, *Quill and Cross*, 17.
99. Zárate Salmerón, *Relaciones de todas las cosas*, 55.
100. Benavides, *Tanto, que se sacó de una carta*, 7.
101. Smith, "Alchemy as a Language," 8–9.
102. Morrow, introduction to Benavides, *Harvest of Reluctant Souls*, xii–xiv.
103. Benavides, *Harvest of Reluctant Souls*, 70.
104. Colahan, *Visions of Sor María*, 120; MacLean, "María de Ágreda," 35–36; Nogar, *Quill and Cross*, 23–24.
105. María de Jesús to the Franciscan Order in New Mexico, May 15, 1631, quoted in Benavides, *Tanto, que se sacó de una carta*, 10, 12, 16.
106. Nogar, *Quill and Cross*, 45.
107. MacLean, "María de Ágreda," 32, 37.
108. Kessel, *Spain in the Southwest*, 103.
109. MacLean, "María de Ágreda," 38.
110. Rowe, *Saint and Nation*, 112, 110, 115; Escurial, *Sermon predicado*, fol. 16v.
111. Ameyugo, *Nueva maravilla de la gracia*, 382.
112. Benavides, *Tanto, que se sacó de una carta*, 3.
113. Morrow, introduction to Benavides, *Harvest of Reluctant Souls*, xi.
114. Kessell, *Kiva, Cross, and Crown*, 144 (Kessell's translation); Benavides, *Tanto, que se sacó de una carta*, 2; *Benavides' Revised Memorial of 1634*, 135–49.
115. Morrow, introduction to Benavides, *Harvest of Reluctant Souls*, xi.
116. Nogar, *Quill and Cross*, 28.
117. Benavides, *Tanto, que se sacó de una carta*, 6.
118. Ibid., 5. On the blue color of the habit, see Kessel, *Kiva, Cross, and Crown*, 150–51.
119. Benavides, *Tanto, que se sacó de una carta*, 5.
120. Walsham, "Catholic Reformation," 273–74; Evangelisti, "Religious Women, Mystic Journeys."
121. Niño, *A la sereníssima Señora Infanta*, 108–11.
122. *Benavides' Revised Memorial of 1634*, 140; Benavides, *Tanto, que se sacó de una carta*, 5.
123. Keck, *Angels and Angelology*, 142–43.
124. Kessel, *Kiva, Cross and Crown*, 146.

Chapter 4

1. For biographical notes, see López Rueda, *González de Salas*, 21–31; on the *Compendio geográphico i histórico*, 141–82.
2. Mela, *Compendio geográphico*, A3v.
3. Harrison, *Fall of Man*, 17–28.
4. Mela, *Compendio geográphico*, A4v.
5. That González de Salas turned a classical writer into a great "Spaniard" (*el grande Español*) reflects an intriguing process of appropriation at a time when the Spanish Empire was asserting its own greatness. Ibid., A3r.
6. Smet, "Some Unpublished Documents," 156, 154.
7. Consider Kircher's use of missionary networks. See Gorman, "The Angel and the Compass."
8. Portuondo, *Secret Science*, 6–7. See also Sandman, "Controlling Knowledge."
9. On the Catholic mission and ethnography, see Rubiés, "Ethnography and Cultural Translation"; Romano, "Iberian Missionaries in God's Vineyard."
10. Lach, *Century of Discovery*, bk. 2, 709–10.
11. González de Mendoza, *Historia de las cosas más notables*; Sola, *Cronista de China*. Also consider Jesuit works, including that of the founder of the Jesuit mission in China, Matteo Ricci (1552–1610). In 1615 at Augsberg, Nicolas Trigault (1577–1628) translated Ricci's Italian manuscript into Latin as *De Christiana expeditione apud Sinas suscepta ab Societate Jesus* (On the Christian mission among the Chinese by the Society of Jesus); see also the work of the Italian Jesuit missionary Martino Martini (1614–1661).
12. Xavier and Županov, *Catholic Orientalism*, 45.
13. Parry, *Age of Reconnaissance*, 3.
14. Livingstone, *Geographical Tradition*, 33.
15. On Africa, consider the writings of the traveler al-Hasan ibn Muhammad

al-Wazzan (Leo Africanus), *Historiale description de l'Afrique*.
16. On the tripartite division of early modern geography, see Cormack, "Good Fences Make Good Neighbors," 641–42.
17. There are countless works on this theme. See, for example, ibid.; Cormack, *Charting an Empire*; Withers, "Reporting, Mapping, Trusting"; Godlewska and Smith, *Geography and Empire*; Carey, "Compiling Nature's History"; Buisseret, *Monarchs, Ministers, and Maps*; Kivelson, *Cartographies of Tsardom*.
18. Branch, *Cartographic State*, esp. 100–120.
19. Goodman, *Power and Penury*; Mundy, *Mapping of New Spain*; Portuondo, *Secret Science*; Padrón, *Spacious Word*; Prieto, "Alexander and the Geographer's Eye"; Reguera Rodríguez, *Geógrafos del rey*; Sánchez Martínez, *La espada, la cruz y el padrón*; Sánchez Martínez, "Official Image of the World"; Cerezo Martínez, *Cartografía náutica española*; Fernandez-Armesto, "Maps and Exploration"; Kagan and Schmidt, "Maps and the Early Modern State"; Martín Merás, *Cartografía marítima hispana*.
20. See Lefebvre, *Production of Space*. On the deployment of geography for national and colonial objectives, consider the case of India, addressed in Edney, *Mapping an Empire*, and Zionists' transformation of Palestine into a modern Jewish state. Benvenisti, *Sacred Landscape*. See also the discussion in Kaplan and Herb, "How Geography Shapes National Identities."
21. Durkheim, *Elementary Forms of the Religious Life*, 47.
22. Eliade, *Patterns in Comparative Religion*, 28.
23. Tweed, *Crossing and Dwelling*, 74–75.
24. Christian, *Local Religion in Sixteenth-Century Spain*, 70–146.
25. For example, consider Mundy, *Mapping of New Spain*, esp. 1–12, and Goodman, *Power and Penury*.
26. On the Padrón Real, see Sánchez Martínez, *La espada, la cruz y el padrón*.
27. The English writer Peter Heylyn commented that geography, which emerged from cosmology, required that scholars "look not on the Earth simply as an Element, for so it belongeth to philosophy; but as a *spherical* body proportionably composed of Earth and Water." Heylyn, *Cosmographie in four bookes*, 22 (an enlarged version of the author's *Microcosmos* of 1621). See also Headley, "Geography and Empire."
28. The manuscript of Ptolemy's work arrived in Florence from Constantinople in 1406 and was soon translated into Latin. Historians used to describe a fundamental shift in the field of geography beginning with this development, but a more nuanced view is now accepted. See Portuondo, *Secret Science*, 34; Padrón, *Spacious Word*, 69.
29. Padrón, *Spacious Word*, 71.
30. On Bernhard Varenius, see Bowen, *Empiricism and Geographical Thought*, 77–90. For analysis of medieval geographical narratives, see Daston and Park, *Wonders and the Order of Nature*, 21–66; Lozovsky, "Earth Is Our Book."
31. See Rubiés, "Instructions for Travellers"; Stagl, *History of Curiosity*.
32. On the formation of natural history, see Ogilvie, *Science of Describing*, 1–23.
33. Beginning in the late eighteenth century, the description of peoples was gradually separated from the study of geography, and the term *ethnographie* was coined after *geographie*. Hans Vermuelen credits the German Enlightenment, and especially Leibniz's historical-linguistic program, with this development. See Vermuelen, *Before Boas*, 275–83 (on August Ludwig Schlözer) and 302–6 (on historian Johann Christoph Gatterer's classification of geographical sciences).
34. Venegas, *Diferencias de libros* (1983 facsimile ed.), bk. 2., chap. 16, fol. 53r. The subtle differences between topography and chorography are not immediately clear. The number of geographical subdisciplines changed

from author to author. For example, see Syria, *Arte de la verdadera nauegacion*, 63.
35. Venegas, *Diferencias de libros* (1983 facsimile ed.), bk. 2, chap. 16, fol. 53r.
36. Girava, *Dos libros de cosmographia*, 55–56.
37. The section on the Indies appears in the first part of the book and includes Mexico, Florida, and California, the coasts of Central and South America, the Straits of Magellan, Peru, and various Pacific islands, including Japan. Botero, *Relaciones vniuersales del mundo*, fols. 134–204.
38. Headley, "Geography and Empire," 1134.
39. See Maravall, *Antiguos y modernos*, 561–62.
40. Harley, *New Nature of Maps*, 57.
41. Ramírez, "Descripción del reino del Perú"; Lizárraga, *Descripción del Perú*; Padrón, *Spacious Word*, 45–91, esp. 78–79.
42. Consider the writings of the Spanish missionary and traveler Pedro Cubero Sebastián, who described cities in Europe, Asia, New Spain, and the Philippines. Cubero Sebastián, *Peregrinacion del mundo*.
43. "Real Cédula al Arzobispo de México pidiendo informes sobre las características de la Tierra," November 27, 1548, Valladolid, in Solano, *Cuestionarios para la formación*, 5–7.
44. For instance, writing to Charles V from Conchin, India, in 1525, the Dominican Juan Caro, who was knowledgeable in navigation, offered to teach this art in the Casa's school for pilots. Fray Juan Caro al Emperador, December 29, 1526, in Fernández de Navarrete, *Colección de documentos y manuscriptos*, 16:282–84. See also Fray Caro a su cuñado (Dr. Porras, en Sevilla), December 19, 1525, ibid., 278–80.
45. Spate, *Spanish Lake*, 100–110.
46. On Spain's growing interest in Asia, and its "Chinese enterprise," see Ollé, *Empresa de China*.
47. Mathes, "Early California Propaganda"; Antonio de la Ascensión, "Relación breve," 572.
48. Mathes, "Early Exploration of the Pacific Coast," 424.
49. Consider Pope Gregory XIII's request from the Augustinian Juan González de Mendoza to publish his description of China, which resulted in his *Historia de las cosas más notables* (1585), fol. 4r (dedication).
50. Shalev, *Sacred Words and Worlds*, 7–8. See also Larner, "The Church and the Quattrocento Renaissance," 38.
51. Larner, "The Church and the Quattrocento Renaissance," 38.
52. I am using the term coined by Ricardo Padrón to describe "a specific type of geographical writing designed to assist its reader in forming a cartographic image." Padrón, *Spacious Word*, 92.
53. Altuna, *Discurso colonialista de los caminantes*, 115–18.
54. The original manuscript of Ocaña's *Relación* is held by the Biblioteca de la Universidad de Oviedo (M-215), also available online at https://digibuo.uniovi.es/dspace/handle/10651/27859. The manuscript has been printed in several critical editions. I have consulted Blanca López de Mariscal and Abraham Madroñal's 2010 edition, *Viaje por el Nuevo Mundo*.
55. "La gradución de todos los puertos de la costa del Peru desde Panama hasta el estrecho de Magallenes." Ocaña, *Relación*, fols. 110r–111r. The descriptive section on Chile is between fols. 78r and 107v; "Descripción de la tierra del Paraguay, y de Buenos Aires y del Tucumán," ibid., fols. 119r–140v.
56. Prior to the sixteenth century, the four doctors of the Western church were Saint Gregory the Great, Saint Ambrose, Saint Augustine, and Saint Jerome.
57. Starr-LeBeau, *Shadow of the Virgin*, 12; Hernández, *Virgin of Guadalupe and the Conversos*, 44–47.
58. Peña Núñez, *Imágenes contra el olvido*, 46–48.
59. On Ocaña's efforts to promote the Guadalupan cult, see Mills, "Diego de Ocaña's Hagiography."

60. Mills, "Mission and Narrative," 116, 119.
61. On Enciso's *Suma de geographía*, see Padrón, *Spacious Word*, 84–91; Prieto, "Alexander and the Geographer's Eye."
62. On this project, see Barrera Osorio, *Experiencing Nature*, 81–100; Alvarez Peláez, *Conquista de la naturaleza americana*, 170–232.
63. Alonso de Santa Cruz's new navigational charts and the appointment of Gonzalo Fernández de Oviedo to the position of chronicler of the Indies (*cronista de Indias*) are but two illustrative examples of this process before Ovando's appointment. For analysis of Ovando's cosmographical reforms, see Portuondo, *Secret Science*, 115–36.
64. The use of questionnaires continued; under the presidency of the Count of Lemos, the council dispatched a questionnaire with 355 questions, published in Solano, *Cuestionarios para la formación*, 97–111.
65. Consejo de las Indias, *Ordenanzas reales del Consejo de Indias*, fol. 2r. This section, titled "Título del Consejo," was printed in 1585. I consulted the facsimile edition, Muro Orejón, "Ordenanzas de 1571," 371. The provision that details the specific way in which cosmographical information should be collected is titled "Instrucciones para hacer las descripciones" (or "Título de las descripciones"). This section was probably written and approved by the council in 1571; it received royal approval on July 3, 1573. Portuondo, *Secret Science*, 118. The provisions were edited in Sánchez Bella, "Título de las descripciones." See also Solano, *Cuestionarios para la formación*, 16–74.
66. See articles 5 and 6 in Solano, *Cuestionarios para la formación*, 19. See also article 40 on p. 28 and article 55 on p. 55.
67. "Descripción del arzobispado de Antequera de la Nueva España hecha por el obispo del dicho opispado," Antequera, ca. 1570. The manuscript is conserved in the Benson Latin American Collection, University of Texas at Austin, UTX JGI-XXIII-7. It is published in García Pimentel, *Relación de los obispados*, 59–68. María Portuondo offers a detailed analysis of Velasco's use of these types of documents in *Secret Science*, 172–83.
68. Consider Richard Hakluyt's *Principal Navigations, Voyages, Traffiques* (first edition 1589, expanded 1598–1600) and Robert Boyle's "General Heads for a Natural History" (published in the *Philosophical Transactions* in 1666), two major works in the development of geographical methodology. On the Royal Society's geographical program, see Hunter, "Robert Boyle and the Early Royal Society"; Carey, "Hakluyt's Instructions."
69. Brendecke, *Empirical Empire*, 68–86.
70. Ocaña, *Viaje por el Nuevo Mundo*, 183 (fol. 107r). Citations of Ocaña's work give the page number in López de Mariscal and Madroñal's 2010 edition, followed, in parentheses, by the folio number in the manuscript held by the Biblioteca de la Universidad de Oviedo.
71. Ibid., 163 (fol. 78r).
72. Ibid., 165 (fols. 79v, 82r), 171 (fol. 88v). On deserted cities, see fol. 82v (Angol); and Peña Núñez, *Fray Diego de Ocaña*, 141–47.
73. Ocaña, *Viaje por el Nuevo Mundo*, 163 (fol. 78r).
74. Ibid., 171–72 (fol. 90r).
75. Harley, *New Nature of Maps*, 57. For the case of Imperial Spain, see Sánchez Martínez and Pardo Tomás, "Between Imperial Design and Colonial Appropriation."
76. Scott, *Contested Territory*, 2, 36.
77. Peña Núñez, *Fray Diego de Ocaña*, 169.
78. Ocaña, *Viaje por el Nuevo Mundo*, 87–89 (fols. 16r, 14v–15r).
79. See Talavera, *Historia de Nuestra Señora de Guadalupe*.
80. Ocaña, *Viaje por el Nuevo Mundo*, 484–85 (fol. 346v). Compare the known passage from Jerome's "Letter to Eustochium" (letter no. 22), which describes Jerome's

suffering in "the solitude of the desert" and his longing for Rome. Rice, *Saint Jerome in the Renaissance*, 7. Kenneth Mills, in "Mission and Narrative," places Ocaña's passing of Pariacaca within the apostolic narrative tradition.
81. On the long history of the sacred image, see Hernández, *Virgin of Guadalupe and the Conversos*, 21–30.
82. Ibid., 25; Starr-LeBeau, *Shadow of the Virgin*, 15.
83. Phillips and Phillips, *Worlds of Christopher Columbus*, 193.
84. Remensnyder, *Conquistadora*, 9.
85. Pedro del Puerto, "Viaje de un monje gerónimo," 140, 147–48, 151.
86. Philip Soergel made this argument in the context of the printing of pilgrimage books on local shrines in Bavaria. *Wondrous in His Saints*, 36.
87. Vázquez de Espinosa, *Compendio y descripción*, 807.
88. Ibid., 562–63. Espinosa noted the representations of human feet that Saint Thomas was said to have left in the same area. On the cross of Carabuco, see Brosseder, *Power of Huacas*, 33–35.
89. Vázquez de Espinosa, *Compendio y descripción*, 807.
90. On the genre of compendia, see Stagl, *History of Curiosity*, 115–21.
91. On the history of the Carmelites, see Friedman, *Latin Hermits of Mount Carmel*; Jotischky, *Carmelites and Antiquity*, 8–44.
92. Bedouelle, *Reform of Catholicism*, 103–4.
93. Bilinkoff, *Avila of Saint Teresa*, 116–52.
94. Vázquez de Espinosa, *Compendio y descripción*, 681.
95. For a good treatment of this development, see Rowe, *Saint and Nation*.
96. Velasco Bayon, "Obispos Carmelitas en América," 415–16; Serrano Espinosa, "Cofradías del Carmelo Descalzo." However, few Carmelites arrived as individuals outside monastic community; see Velasco, "Antonio Vázquez de Espinosa en América," 171.
97. Velasco Bayon, "Obispos Carmelitas en América," 416.
98. Rosales, "Provincia de San Alberto de Indias." Consider also other Carmelite projects in Newfoundland and California, on which see Luca Codignola, *Coldest Harbour in the Land*; Mathes, "Early California Propaganda."
99. Bireley, *Refashioning of Catholicism*, 172–73. See also Padden, "Ordenaza del Patronazgo of 1574."
100. Bireley, *Refashioning of Catholicism*, 173.
101. Tomás de Jesús, *De procuranda salute omnium gentium*, bk. 2, chap. 1, "De erigenda Congregatione pro fide propaganda" (On the creation of a congregation for the propagation of the faith); see also Salaville, "Théoricien de l'apostolat catholique."
102. Tomás de Jesús, *De procuranda salute omnium gentium*, bk. 1, chap. 3; Guilday, "Sacred Congregation de Propaganda Fide," 481.
103. Rohrbach, *Journey to Carith*, 268.
104. Velasco, "Antonio Vázquez de Espinosa en América," 186; Smet, "Some Unpublished Documents," 155.
105. Smet, "Some Unpublished Documents," 157.
106. Vargas Ugarte, *Biblioteca Peruna I*, 115.
107. Velasco, "Antonio Vázquez de Espinosa en América," 213–17.
108. Ibid., 184; Smet, "Some Unpublished Documents," 153.
109. Velasco, "Antonio Vázquez de Espinosa en América," 185–86; Lohmann Villena, "Unos datos inéditos."
110. Vázquez de Espinosa, *Compendio y descripción*, 691.
111. León Pinelo, *Question moral*, fol. 91v.
112. Vázquez de Espinosa, *Compendio y descripción*, 54.
113. See the discussion in Pimentel, "Baroque Natures," and Prieto, *Missionary Scientists*, 195–220, for example, on the contrasting cases of Juan Esubio Niermeberg and Alonso de Ovalle.
114. Vázquez de Espinosa, *Compendio y descripción*, 359.

115. Salinas y Córdoba, *Memorial, informe, y manifiesto*, fol. 17v; León Pinelo, *Paraíso en el Nuevo Mundo*, bk. 5, chap. 6. On this topic, see Earle, *Body of the Conquistador*, 93–103.
116. Antonio de la Ascensión, "Relación breve," 550; the English translation is in Antonio de la Ascensión, "Brief Report of the Discovery," 114.
117. The Carmelites were no different from other mendicant friars who used similar language to sanctify colonial territories. See the discussion in Rubial García, *Paraíso de los elegidos*, 210–30.
118. Vázquez de Espinosa, *Compendio y descripción*, 57–58.
119. Huddleston, *Origins of the American Indians*.
120. Vázquez de Espinosa, *Compendio y descripción*, 74. On this topic, see Segev, *Sephardic Conquistadores*, 132–33.
121. Vázquez de Espinosa, *Compendio y descripción*, 56.
122. Vázquez de Espinosa, *Confesionario general*, "Prologo."
123. For instance, in Florida. Vázquez de Espinosa, *Compendio y descripción*, 186.
124. On the function of typological thinking in Spanish colonialism, see Cañizares-Esguerra, "Typology in the Atlantic World." On the reference to the Bible, see MacCormack, *On the Wings of Time*, 245–74. The Carmelites' own narrative of the origins of monasticism is intimately bound up with typological thinking; see Jotischky, *Carmelites and Antiquity*, 317–24.
125. Pallas, *Missión a las Indias*, 45 (bk. 1, chap. 1, fols. 1–2).
126. Vázquez de Espinosa, *Compendio y descripción*, 257, 249.
127. Ibid., 190.
128. Ackerman, *Elijah, Prophet of Carmel*, 35–74, 81–82, 87–89.
129. Vázquez de Espinosa, *Compendio y descripción*, 728–29.
130. Dean, *Culture of Stone*, 1–3.
131. Ditchfield, "Thinking with Saints," 579; see also Bilinkoff, *Colonial Saints*, xiv–xxii.
132. Verástique, *Michoacán and Eden*, 45–49.
133. Graziano, *Millennial New World*, 24–25.
134. Bilinkoff, *Avila of Saint Teresa*, 134. Teresa de Ávila states in *The Way of Perfection*, "Human forces are not sufficient to stop the spread of this fire caused by these heretics" (1.2).
135. Nicholas Gallicus quoted in Tyler, *Teresa of Avila*, 57.
136. Johnson, "Gardening for God"; Flor, *Península metafísica*.
137. In 1585, Tomás de Jesús joined the Discalced Carmelites in Granada, where Juan de la Cruz was prior. Toft, "Tomás de Jesús."
138. Horn, *Postconquest Coyoacan*, 198–200. Horn claims that the Carmelites' disputes with their neighbors began a year after the order was granted the possession of the slopes (in 1605) and continued into the eighteenth century (200). Such repeated disputes over resources might be background to Espinosa's efforts to present the Carmelites' project in a positive light.
139. Vázquez de Espinosa, *Compendio y descripción*, 249.
140. Ibid., 186.
141. Eliade, *Patterns in Comparative Religion*, 28.
142. Outside Spain, consider the Italian Jesuit Francesco Bressani (1612–1672), who was sent as a missionary to the Huron (Wendat) Indians. In addition to publishing in Italy an account based on his experiences in New France, a map ascribed to the Italian friar provided an accurate representation of the St. Lawrence Seaway and Great Lakes region, along with features that promoted the Jesuit mission to the Hurons. Bressani, *Breve relatione d'alcune missioni*. For Bressani's map of New France, see his "Accurate Picture of New France."
143. See, for example, Gascoigne, "Royal Society, Natural History," 547.

Chapter 5

1. Beatty, "Chance and Natural Selection"; Johnson, *Darwin's Dice*, 2.
2. Román y Zamora, *Republicas del mundo*. On Saint Ambrose's *Hexameron*, see Harrison, *Bible, Protestantism*, 22.
3. Ferrer de Valdecebro, *Hallado en las aves mas generosas* and *Hallado en las fieras, y animales silvestres*. Consider also Luis de Granada's *Símbolo de la fe*.
4. For instance, the behavioral patterns of dolphins, livestock, and birds were seen as indicators of a coming storm. Syria, *Arte de la verdadera nauegacion*, 31. Likewise, animals were believed to "testify" to supernatural events. In the mid-seventeenth century, the Dominican Narciso Camós noted that of the 182 Marian shrines he had visited in Catalonia, more than sixty fundamental legends involved animals' (including oxen, bulls, sheep, dogs) discovering an image of the Virgin Mary. Christian, *Apparitions in Late Medieval and Renaissance Spain*, 15–19; Camós, *Jardín de María*.
5. Grafton, with Shelford and Siraisi, *New Worlds, Ancient Texts*; Millones Figueroa, "Historia natural del padre Bernabé Cobo."
6. Wey Gómez, *Tropics of Empire*, 162–63; for objections to the theory, see 233–34.
7. The phrase is ascribed to Amerigo Vespucci in his 1503 letter *Mundus Novus: Letter to Lorenzo Pietro di Medici*, 1. For a reprint of the Latin, see Wallisch's translation of Vespucci, *Mundus Novus des Amerigo Vespucci*, 16.
8. "Carta de Alonso de Zauzo al emperador Carlos V, Santo Domingo, 22 January, 1518," in Jiménez de la Espada and Martínez Carreras, *Relaciones geográficas de Indias: Perú*, 1:11.
9. This is Peter Martyr's description of Hispaniola; see Peter Martyr, *De Orbe Novo*, 1:364 (decade 3, bk. 7, 235). Citations of Peter Martyr's work give the volume and page number in Francis Augustus MacNutt's English translation, followed, in parentheses, by the citation from Joaquín Torres Asensio's 1892 edition.
10. Cieza de León, *Chronica del Peru*, fol. 189r–v.
11. Lafaye, *Quetzalcóatl and Guadalupe*, 39.
12. Magner, *History of Life Sciences*, 300; Ogilvie, *Science of Describing*, 268–71.
13. Alvarez Peláez, *Conquista de la naturaleza americana*. On animals, see 469–524.
14. Asúa and French, *New World of Animals*; Few and Totorici, *Centering Animals in Latin American History*; Barrera Osorio, *Experiencing Nature*, 102–3; López Piñero, *Ciencia y técnica en la sociedad española*, 279–96; Bleichmar, "Books, Bodies, and Fields," 98–99.
15. Asúa and French's *New World of Animals* devotes a chapter to the writings of friars regarding American species. In chapter 5, they focus on the Jesuits (Cobo, Kircher, and Nieremberg), but their conclusions are somewhat ambivalent. They claim that the friars' accounts were not exceptionally different from the common contemporary view and thus reject an exclusive or unique religious consideration (142). At the same time, they acknowledge the religious significance of zoology, calling Nieremberg's work "mystical zoology" (170).
16. Brian Ogilvie asserts, for example, that Iberian authors "played little role in elaborating the Renaissance science of describing." *Science of Describing*, 24. In Magner's *History of Life Sciences*, there is no mention of Spanish naturalists. Nor does Enenkel and Smith's *Zoology in Early Modern Culture* include essays about Spanish zoology.
17. See Parrish, *American Curiosity*; Jardine, Secord, and Spary, *Cultures of Natural History*; Freedberg, *Eye of the Lynx*; Findlen, *Possessing Nature*.
18. Freedberg, *Eye of the Lynx*, 6–7. See also the illustrations in Conrad Gessner's monumental *Historiae animalium* (1551–

58); Ashworth, "Remarkable Humans and Singular Beasts"; Harrison, "Reading Vital Science."
19. Enenkel, "Species and Beyond," 58. Likewise, Peter Harrison had argued that "the most direct challenge to the powerful symbolic universe was to come not from new discoveries in the empirical world, but from a new approach to the interpretation of texts." Harrison, *Bible, Protestantism*, 92.
20. Magasich-Airola and de Beer, *America Magica*, 149. On scriptural commentaries and natural science, see Kevin Killeen's analysis of Thomas Browne's zoological ideas in Killeen, *Biblical Scholarship*, chap. 5. See also Harrison, *Bible, Protestantism*; Killeen and Forshaw, *The Word and the World*; Howell, *God's Two Books*; Oosterhoff and Meer "God, Scripture."
21. Bono, *Word of God*, 12.
22. Vespucci, *Mundus Novus: Letter to Lorenzo Pietro di Medici*, 8, and *Mundus Novus des Amerigo Vespucci*, 30.
23. Vespucci, *Cartas de viaje*, 76.
24. On Peter Martyr's work, see O'Gorman, *Cuatro historiadores de indias*, 11–44.
25. Peter Martyr, *De Orbe Novo*, 1:179 (decade 1, bk. 10, 121).
26. On the perception of American plenty, see Worster, *Shrinking the Earth*, 3–25.
27. Peter Martyr, *De Orbe Novo*, 1:263 (decade 2, bk. 9, 172).
28. Ibid., 1:164 (decade 1, bk. 10, 111).
29. MacCormack, "Limits of Understanding," 79.
30. López de Gómara, *Historia general de las Indias*, fol. iiv.
31. Paden, "The Iguana and the Barrel of Mud," 203–5.
32. On Oviedo, see Gerbi, *Nature in the New World*, 129–200.
33. Fernández de Oviedo, *Oviedo dela natural hystoria delas Indias*, fol. 19v.
34. Alvarez Peláez, *Conquista de la naturaleza americana*, 44.
35. Fernández de Oviedo, *Oviedo dela natural hystoria delas Indias*, fol. 19r.
36. Asúa and French, *New World of Animals*, 192.
37. Fernández de Oviedo, *Oviedo dela natural hystoria delas Indias*, fol. 2v.
38. Barrera Osorio, *Experiencing Nature*, 86–87.
39. See López Piñero and Pardo Tomás, *Influencia de Francisco Hernández*.
40. Sánchez Bella, "Título de las descripciones," 147.
41. "Instrucción y memoria de las relaciones que se han de hacer para la descripción de las indias" (1577), in Solano, *Cuestionarios para la formación*, 84. For analysis of the responses, see Alvarez Peláez, *Conquista de la naturaleza americana*, 474–524. On Velasco's questionnaire, see Barrera Osorio, *Experiencing Nature*, 94–97; Portuondo, *Secret Science*, 213–18.
42. Writing in 1594, Jerónimo Cortés, the mathematician and naturalist from Valencia, claimed that there were 20,167 "known animals" in the world and 25,000 plants, adding that the actual numbers could be four or five times greater. Cortés, *Nuevo lunario perpetuo y pronóstico*, 317.
43. On Acosta's anthropological ideas, see Pagden, *Fall of Natural Man*; Valle, "From José de Acosta to the Enlightenment."
44. Acosta, *Historia natural y moral*, 131. All citations of the *Historia* are to Francisco Mateos's 1954 edition of Acosta's works unless otherwise noted.
45. Harris, "Confession-Building, Long-Distance Networks," 305. See also Findlen, "How Information Travels," 58–61.
46. Acosta, *Historia natural y moral*, 131.
47. Ibid., 130.
48. Prieto, *Missionary Scientists*, 19.
49. Portuondo, *Spanish Disquiet*, 2.
50. Acosta, *Historia natural y moral*, 47.
51. The first English translation appeared in 1604. Acosta's writings are known to have influenced such English thinkers as Francis Bacon and John Locke. Carey, *Locke, Shaftesbury, and Hutcheson*, 20.

52. Acosta, *Historia natural y moral*, 3.
53. Acosta's *Historia* included parts of his *Natura novi orbis*, to which Acosta added two books that examined the history and culture of the Amerindians. Prieto, *Missionary Scientists*, 147.
54. Ibid., 143–68.
55. On this topic, see Barrera Osorio, *Experiencing Nature*, 116–19; Grant, *History of Natural Philosophy*, 284.
56. Acosta, *Historia natural y moral*, 89.
57. On the evangelical nature of Acosta's work, see Prieto, *Missionary Scientists*, 13–36.
58. Augustine, *City of God*, 530. Citations of this work are to Marcus Dods's translation.
59. Acosta, *Historia natural y moral*, 131.
60. For example, on the church's exegetical tradition, consider Aquinas's position that nothing was created after the six days of creation; see Ruler, *Crisis of Causality*, 42–43.
61. Acosta, *Historia natural y moral*, 32.
62. Ibid., 26.
63. Contessa, "Noah's Ark and the Ark of the Covenant."
64. Augustine, *City of God*, 530.
65. Acosta, *Historia natural y moral*, 32.
66. Ibid., 131. Here I am using the translation by Frances López-Morillas: Acosta, *Natural and Moral History*, 236.
67. Ford, "Stranger in a Foreign Land," 29.
68. Pasulka, *Heaven Can Wait*, 136.
69. Aquinas, *Summa Theologiae* 1.2.3; Gaukroger, *Emergence of a Scientific Culture*, 132.
70. Aquinas, *Political Writings*, 38 (from Aquinas's treatises *De regimine principum* and *De regno*).
71. Dear, "The Church and the New Philosophy," 123.
72. Cárdenas, *Problemas, y secretos marauillosos*, fol. 150r–v. See also Segev, "Problem Solver."
73. Compare to Vetancurt, *Teatro mexicano*, 4; Román y Zamora, *Republicas del mundo*, fol. 21r–v; Ray, *Wisdom of God Manifested*.
74. Killeen, *Biblical Scholarship*, 177–78.
75. García, *Origen de los Indios*, 63.
76. Huddleston, *Origins of the American Indians*, 65.
77. García, *Origen de los Indios*, 110, 141, 148.
78. Cummins, *Question of Rites*, 16, 18–19, 27.
79. Stolarski, *Friars on the Frontier*, 18 (quotation), 16. Stolarski has noted that "the Dominican-Jesuit confrontation centered on the Nominalist tendencies of the Jesuits, who used Aquinas, but did not always agree with him when approaching Aristotle's philosophy" (39).
80. See Feldhay, *Galileo and the Church*, chap. 9, "Dominicans and Jesuits: A Struggle for Theological Hegemony," 171–200.
81. Campbell, *Religion of the Heart*, 9.
82. Feldhay, *Galileo and the Church*, 176.
83. Jensen, *Divine Providence and Human Agency*, 91–95.
84. Feldhay, *Galileo and the Church*, 172–73.
85. Ibid., 176.
86. García, *Origen de los Indios*, 5–6.
87. Ibid., 13, 15, 17–18.
88. Olson, *Science and Religion*, 61.
89. Aquinas, *Summa Theologiae*, 1.2.3.
90. Cummins, *Question of Rites*, 16.
91. García, *Origen de los Indios*, 84.
92. Venegas, *Diferencias de libros* (1569), fol. 5r.
93. García, *Origen de los Indios*, 6.
94. Díaz del Castillo, *Historia verdadera de la conquista*, 2:394.
95. Irving, *Natural Science and the Origins*, 23–24; on the New World in Bacon's thought, see 37–38.
96. Chapters 1–27 in the fourth book of Ximénez's *Quatro libros de la naturaleza* are devoted to animals and their therapeutic value.
97. García, *Origen de los Indios*, 534–35.
98. Ibid., 24.
99. Ibid., 69–70.
100. Ibid., 110.
101. Attfield, "Christian Attitudes to Nature," 379.
102. Aquinas, "Article 140: Many Things Are Contingent, with Divine Providence Abiding," in Aquinas, *Compendium of Theology*, 109.

103. Gillespie, "Natural History, Natural Theology," 28.
104. García, *Origen de los Indios*, 144.
105. Ibid., 116.
106. Ibid.
107. On this topic, see Davies, "The Unlucky, the Bad, and the Ugly," esp. 74–75; Van Duzer, "*Hic sunt dracones*," 387–88; Verner, *Epistemology of the Monstrous*, 2–7.
108. Augustine, *City of God*, 778. On human monstrosity, see 530–32. See also Isidoro de Sevilla, *Etimologías*, 11.3.1.
109. García, *Origen de los Indios*, 136–37, 134.
110. Ibid., 135, 137–38; Martínez, *Genealogical Fictions*, 165.
111. Pererius (1535–1610) used "the more perfect animal species" to refer to the animals that God created on the sixth day, arguing that "the 'less perfect' were produced later." On the question whether crossbreeds were created with the other animals on the sixth day, see Ruler, *Crisis of Causality*, 44–45.
112. García, *Origen de los Indios*, 147–48.
113. Ibid., 147.
114. Compare García, *Origen de los Indios*, 147, with Acosta, *Historia natural y moral*, 131.
115. Nieremberg, *Curiosa y oculta filosofía*, 9 (bk. 1, chap. 11); Cobo, *Historia del Nuevo Mundo* (Jiménez de la Espada ed.), 3:67–72 (bk. 1, chap. 8).
116. See, for example, Prieto, *Missionary Scientists*, 187–88.
117. Buffon, *Histoire naturelle*, 14:311.
118. Granada, *Símbolo de la fe*, 146.
119. On this topic, see Oakley, "Absolute and Ordained Power of God."
120. Ciampoli quoted in Lindberg and Numbers, *God and Nature*, 124.
121. For instance, in *Teatro crítico universal* (1726–39), the Benedictine Benito Jerónimo Feijóo rejected ideas of mutability and decadence in the world, for such ideas would presuppose that creation was not perfect. For this reason, Feijóo also rejected the idea that animal or vegetable species could disappear. Capel, "Religious Beliefs, Philosophy, and Scientific Theory," 225; see also Capel, *Física sagrada*, 72–77.
122. On Kircher's and Nieremberg's zoological ideas, see Enenkel, "Species and Beyond," 99–110; Breidbach and Ghiselin, "Athanasius Kircher (1602–1680)"; Ledezma, "Legitimación imaginativa del Nuevo Mundo"; Millones Figueroa, "Intelligentsia jesuita"; Pimentel, "Baroque Natures"; Kircher, *Arca de Noe*; Hendrickson, *Jesuit Polymath of Madrid*.
123. Pimentel, "Baroque Natures," 105.
124. Hendrickson, *Jesuit Polymath of Madrid*, 107–8.
125. Millones Figueroa, "Intelligentsia jesuita," 39.
126. See, for example, Pimentel, "Baroque Natures," 109; Enenkel, "Species and Beyond," 99–104.
127. Enenkel, "Species and Beyond," 101 (emphasis in original).
128. Breidbach and Ghiselin, "Athanasius Kircher (1602–1680)," 999.
129. Enenkel, "Species and Beyond," 108.
130. Millones Figueroa, "Intelligentsia jesuita."
131. Browne, "Noah's Flood, the Ark."
132. Hale, *Primitive Origination of Mankind*, 201.
133. Roger, *Buffon*, 93–105.
134. On Buffon's "degeneration" hypothesis, see Dugatkin, *Mr. Jefferson and the Giant Moose*, 10–30; Gerbi, *Dispute of the New World*, 3–34.
135. Buffon, *Barr's Buffon*, 184.
136. Charles Darwin, August 1, 1861, quoted in Johnson, *Darwin's Dice*, xx.
137. See https://www.catholicnewsagency.com/news/30810/francis-inaugurates-bust-of-benedict-emphasizes-unity-of-faith-science.

Conclusion
1. See Cañizares-Esguerra's introduction to *Science in the Spanish and Portuguese Empires*, 2.
2. Tweed, *Crossing and Dwelling*, 74.

Bibliography

Ackerman, Jane. *Elijah, Prophet of Carmel.* Washington, DC: Institute of Carmelite Studies Publications, 2003.

Acosta, José de. *De procuranda Indorum salute.* In *Obras del P. José de Acosta,* edited by Francisco Mateos, 390–608. Madrid: Ediciones Atlas, 1954.

———. *Historia natural y moral de las Indias.* In *Obras del P. José de Acosta,* edited by Francisco Mateos, 3–244. Madrid: Ediciones Atlas, 1954.

———. *Historia natural y moral de las Indias, en que se tratan de las cosas notables del cielo, y elementos, metales, plantas y animales dellas: Y los ritos, y ceremonias, leyes y gobierno, y guerras de los Indios.* Seville: Juan de León, 1590.

———. *Natural and Moral History of the Indies.* Edited by Jane E. Mangan. Translated by Frances López-Morillas. Durham: Duke University Press, 2002.

Acuña, René, ed. *Relaciones geográficas del siglo XVI: México.* 3 vols. Mexico City: UNAM, 1986.

Adeva Martín, Alejo. *El maestro Alejo Venegas de Busto: Su vida y sus obras.* Toledo: Instituto Provincial de Investigaciones y Estudios Toledanos, 1987.

Alberts, Tara. *Conflict and Conversion: Catholicism in South East Asia.* Oxford: Oxford University Press, 2013.

Altuna, Elena. *El discurso colonialista de los caminantes, siglos XVII–XVIII.* Ann Arbor: CELACP, 2002.

Alvarez Peláez, Raquel. *La conquista de la naturaleza americana.* Madrid: CSIC, 1993.

Alver, Abel A. *Animals of Spain: An Introduction to Imperial Perceptions and Human Interaction with Other Animals, 1492–1826.* Leiden: Brill, 2011.

Ameyugo, Francisco de. *Nueva maravilla de la gracia, descubierta en la vida de la Venerable Madre Sor Juana de Jesús María [. . .].* Madrid: Bernardo de Villadiego, 1673.

Andrés Martín, Melquiades. *Historia de la mística de la Edad de Oro en España y América.* Madrid: Biblioteca de Autores Cristianos, 1994.

———. *La teología española en el siglo XVI.* 2 vols. Madrid: Editorial Católica, 1976.

Antonio de la Ascensión. "A Brief Report of the Discovery in the South Sea." In *Spanish Exploration in the Southwest, 1542–1706,* edited and translated by

Herbert E. Bolton, 104–34. New York: Charles Scribner's Sons, 1916.

———. "Relación breve en que se da noticia del descubrimiento que se hizo en la Nueva España, en la Mar del Sur." 1602. In *Colección de documentos inéditos relativos al descubrimiento, conquista y colonización de las antiguas posesiones españolas en América y Oceanía*, vol. 8, edited by Juaquín Pacheco, Francisco de Cárdenas, and Luis Torres de Mendoza, 537–74. Madrid: Imprenta de M. Bernaldo de Quirós, 1867.

Aquinas, Thomas. *Aquinas: Political Writings*. Edited and translated by R. W. Dyson. Cambridge: Cambridge University Press, 2002.

———. *Compendium of Theology*. Translated by Richard J. Regan. Oxford: Oxford University Press, 2009.

———. *Summa Theologiae*. Vol. 1. Translated by Thomas Gilby. Cambridge: Cambridge University Press, 2006.

Aristotle. *De Anima: Books II and III*. Translated by D. W. Hamlyn. Oxford: Clarendon Press, 1968.

Ashworth, William, Jr. "Natural History and the Emblematic Worldview." In *The Scientific Revolution: The Essential Readings*, edited by Marcus Hellyer, 132–56. Malden, MA: Blackwell, 2003.

———. "Remarkable Humans and Singular Beasts." In *The Age of the Marvelous*, edited by Joy Kenseth, 113–44. Hanover: Hood Museum of Art, Dartmouth College, 1992.

Asúa, Miguel de. *Science in the Vanished Arcadia: Knowledge of Nature in the Jesuit Missions of Paraguay and Río de la Plata*. Leiden: Brill, 2014.

Asúa, Miguel de, and Roger French. *A New World of Animals: Early Modern Europeans on the Creatures of Iberian America*. Burlington, VT: Ashgate, 2005.

Attfield, Robin. "Christian Attitudes to Nature." *Journal of the History of Ideas* 44, no. 3 (1983): 369–86.

Augustine. *The City of God*. Translated by Marcus Dods. New York: Modern Library, 1993.

———. *The Works of Saint Augustine: A Translation for the 21st Century*. Translated by Edmund Hill. Edited by John E. Rotelle. Hyde Park, NY: New City Press, 1991.

Bacon, Francis. *The Advancement of Learning and New Atlantis*. Edited by Arthur Johnson. Oxford: Oxford University Press, 1974.

———. *The New Organon*. Edited by Lisa Jardine and Michael Silverthorne. Cambridge: Cambridge University Press, 2000.

———. *Of the Advancement of Learning*. Edited by George William Kitchin. London: J. M. Dent, 1915.

Badiano, Juan. *An Aztec Herbal: The Classic Codex of 1552*. Translated by William Gates Dover. Mineola, NY: Dover Publications, 2000.

Bamji, Alexandra, Geert H. Janssen, and Mary Laven, eds. *The Ashgate Research Companion to the Counter-Reformation*. Burlington, VT: Ashgate, 2013.

Barrera Osorio, Antonio. *Experiencing Nature: The Spanish American Empire and the Early Scientific Revolution*. Austin: University of Texas Press, 2006.

———. "Experts, Nature, and the Making of Atlantic Empiricism." *Osiris* 25, no. 1 (2010): 129–48.

———. "Knowledge and Empiricism in the Sixteenth-Century Spanish Atlantic World." In *Science in the Spanish and Portuguese Empires, 1500–1800*, edited by Daniela Bleichmar, Paula De Vos, Kristin Huffine, and Kevin Sheehan, 219–32. Stanford: Stanford University Press, 2009.

Bauer, Ralph. *The Alchemy of Conquest: Science, Religion, and the Secrets of the New World*. Charlottesville: University of Virginia Press, 2019.

Beatty, John. "Chance and Natural Selection." *Philosophy of Science* 51, no. 2 (1984): 183–211.

Beck, Lauren, ed. "The Feminine Subject in the History of Discovery and Exploration." Special issue, *Terrae Incognitae: The Journal of the Society* for the History of Discoveries 48, no. 1 (2016).

Bedouelle, Guy. *The Reform of Catholicism, 1480–1620*. Translated by James K. Farge. Toronto: Pontifical Institute of Mediaeval Studies, 2008.

Bellarmino, Roberto. *Escala espiritual, para subir, y ascender a conocer a Dios por los leuantamientos, y ascensiones del alma*. Translated by Anders Gil Vicario. Barcelona: Sebastian de Cormellas, 1619.

———. *Robert Bellarmine: Spiritual Writings*. Edited and translated by John Patrick Donnelly and Roland J. Teske. New York: Paulist Press, 1989.

Benavides, Alonso de. *Fray Alonso de Benavides' Revised Memorial of 1634*. Edited and translated by Frederick Webb Hodge, George P. Hammond, and Agapito Rey. Albuquerque: University of New Mexico Press, 1945.

———. *A Harvest of Reluctant Souls: Fray Alonso de Benavides's History of New Mexico*. Translated and edited by Baker H. Morrow. Albuquerque: University of New Mexico Press, 1996.

———. *Memorial a la sanctidad de Urbano 8 n[uest]ro señor acerca delas conuerciones del Nuevo Mexico: Hechas en el felicisso t[iem]po del gouierno de su pontificado, y presentado a Su Sd. por el Pe. Fr. Alonso de Benavides dela orden de n[uest]ro pe*. 1634. Newberry Library, Chicago, Special Collections, Ayer MS 1044.

———. *The Memorial of Fray Alonso de Benavides, 1630*. Annotated by Frederick Webb Hodge and Charles Fletcher Lummis. Translated by Mrs. Edward E. Ayer. Albuquerque: Horn and Wallace, 1965.

———. *Memorial [. . .] tratase en el de los tesoros espirituales, y temporales, que la Diuina Magestad ha manifestado en aquellas conuersiones, y nueuos descubrimientos, por medio de los padres desta serafica religion*. Madrid: Imprenta Real, 1630.

———. *Tanto, que se sacó de una carta, que el R.P. Fr. Alonso de Benavides, custodia, que fue del Nuevo Mexico, embió à los religiosos de la Santa Custodia de la conversion de San Pablo de dicho reyno, desde Madrid, el año de 1631*. Ca. 1760. Reprint, San Marino, CA: n.p., 1924.

Benvenisti, Meron. *Sacred Landscape: The Buried History of the Holy Land Since 1948*. Berkeley: University of California Press, 2000.

Berkel, Klaas van, and Arjo Vanderjagt, eds. *The Book of Nature in Early Modern and Modern History*. Louvain: Peeters, 2006.

Biener, Zvi, and Eric Schliesser, eds. *Newton and Empiricism*. Oxford: Oxford University Press, 2014.

Bilinkoff, Jodi. *The Avila of Saint Teresa: Religious Reform in a Sixteenth-Century City*. Ithaca: Cornell University Press, 1992.

Bireley, Robert S. J. *The Counter-Reformation Prince: Anti-Machiavellianism or Catholic Statecraft in Early Modern Europe*. Chapel Hill: University of North Carolina Press, 1990.

———. *The Refashioning of Catholicism, 1450–1700: A Reassessment of the Counter Reformation*. Washington DC: Catholic University of America Press, 1999.

Blair, Ann. "Mosaic Physics and the Search for a Pious Natural Philosophy in the Late Renaissance." *Isis* 91, no. 1 (2000): 32–58.

———. *The Theater of Nature: Jean Bodin and Renaissance Science*. Princeton: Princeton University Press, 1997.

Bleichmar, Daniela. "Books, Bodies, and Fields: Sixteenth-Century Transatlantic Encounters with New World *Materia Medica*." In *Colonial Botany: Science, Commerce, and Politics in the Early Modern World*, edited by Londa Schiebinger and Claudia Swan, 83–99. Philadelphia: University of Pennsylvania Press, 2004.

Bleichmar, Daniela, Paula De Vos, Kristin Huffine, and Kevin Sheehan, eds. *Science in the Spanish and Portuguese Empires, 1500–1800*. Stanford: Stanford University Press, 2009.

Bono, James J. *The Word of God and the Language of Men: Interpreting Nature* in *Early Modern Science and Medicine*. Madison: University of Wisconsin Press, 1995.

Botero, Giovanni. *Della ragion di stato*. Venice: Appresso i Gioliti, 1589.

———. *Relaciones vniuersales del mundo, de Iuan Botero benes, primera, y segunda parte; traduzidas a instancia de don Antonio Lopez de Calatayud*. Valladolid: Por los Herederos de Diego Fernandez de Cordoua, 1603.

Bowen, Margarita. *Empiricism and Geographical Thought: From Francis Bacon to Alexander von Humboldt*. Cambridge: Cambridge University Press, 1981.

Boyle, Robert. "General Heads for a Natural History of a Country, Great or Small." *Philosophical Transactions* 1, no. 11 (1666): 186–89.

Brading, David A. *The First America: The Spanish Monarchy, Creole Patriots, and the Liberal State, 1492–1867*. New York: Cambridge University Press, 1993.

———. *Mexican Phoenix: Our Lady of Guadalupe; Image and Tradition Across Five Centuries*. Cambridge: Cambridge University Press, 2001.

Branch, Jordan. *The Cartographic State: Maps, Territory, and the Origins of Sovereignty*. Cambridge: Cambridge University Press, 2013.

Breidbach, Olaf, and Michael T. Ghiselin. "Athanasius Kircher (1602–1680) on Noah's Ark: Baroque 'Intelligent Design' Theory." *Proceedings of the California Academy of Sciences* 57, no. 36 (2006): 991–1002.

Brendecke, Arndt. *The Empirical Empire: Spanish Colonial Rule and the Politics of Knowledge*. Berlin: De Gruyter, 2016.

Bressani, Francesco Giussepe. "An Accurate Picture of New France, 1657 (*Novae Franciae Accurata Delineatio*, 1657)." National Library of France. Library of Congress online catalog, https://www.wdl.org/en/item/15494/.

———. *Breve relatione d'alcune missioni de' PP. della Compagnia di Giesù nella Nuova Francia*. Macerata: Per gli Heredi d'Agostino Grisei, 1653.

Brosseder, Claudia. *The Power of Huacas: Change and Resistance in the Andean World of Colonial Peru*. Austin: University of Texas Press, 2014.

———. "Reading the Peruvian Skies." In *A Companion to Astrology in the Renaissance*, edited by Brendan Dooley, 399–428. Leiden: Brill, 2014.

Browne, Janet. "Noah's Flood, the Ark, and the Shaping of Early Modern Natural History." In *When Science and Christianity Meet*, edited by David C. Lindberg and Ronald L. Numbers, 111–38. Chicago: University of Chicago Press, 2003.

———. *The Secular Ark: Studies in the History of Biogeography*. New Haven: Yale University Press, 1983.

Buffon, Georges-Louis Leclerc, Comte de. *Barr's Buffon: Buffon's Natural History, Containing a Theory of the Earth, a General History of Man, of the Brute Creation, and of Vegetables, Minerals, &c.* London: J. S. Barr, 1797.

———. *Histoire naturelle, générale et particulière [. . .]*. 36 vols. Paris: Imprimerie Royale, 1749–88.

Buisseret, David, ed. *Monarchs, Ministers, and Maps: The Emergence of Cartography as a Tool of Government in Early Modern Europe*. Chicago: University of Chicago Press, 1992.

Bujanda, J. M. de. "L'influence de Sebonde en Espagne au XVIe siècle." *Renaissance and Reformation* 10 (1974): 78–84.

Burdick, Bruce Stanley. *Mathematical Works Printed in the Americas, 1554–1700*. Baltimore: Johns Hopkins University Press, 2009.

Burgoa, Francisco de. *Geográfica descripción de la parte septentrional del Polo Artico de la América y nueva iglesia de las Indias Occidentales*. 1674. 2 vols. Mexico City: Tall. Graf. de la Nación, 1934.

Burke, Peter. *A Social History of Knowledge: From Gutenberg to Diderot*. Cambridge: Polity Press, 2000.

Calancha, Antonio de la. *Corónica moralizada del Orden de San Augustín en el Perú*. Barcelona: Pedro Lacavalleria, 1638.

Calvert, Laura. *Francisco de Osuna and the Spirit of the Letter*. Chapel Hill: University of North Carolina Press, 1973.

Camós, Narciso. *Jardín de María plantado en el principado de Cataluña*. 1657. Reprint, Barcelona: Editorial Orbis, 1949.

Campanella, Thomas. *A Defense of Galileo, the Mathematician from Florence*. Edited and translated by R. J. Blackwell. Notre Dame: University of Notre Dame Press, 1994.

Campbell, Mary Baine. *Wonder and Science: Imagining Worlds in Early Modern Europe*. Ithaca: Cornell University Press, 1999.

Campbell, Ted A. *The Religion of the Heart: A Study of European Religious Life in the Seventeenth and Eighteenth Centuries*. Columbia: University of South Carolina Press, 1991.

Cañizares-Esguerra, Jorge. *How to Write the History of the New World: Histories, Epistemologies, and Identities in the Eighteenth-Century Atlantic World*. Stanford: Stanford University Press, 2001.

———. Introduction to *Science in the Spanish and Portuguese Empires, 1500–1800*, edited by Daniela Bleichmar, Paula De Vos, Kristin Huffine, and Kevin Sheehan, 1–7. Stanford: Stanford University Press, 2009.

———. *Nature, Empire, and Nation: Explorations of the History of Science in the Iberian World*. Stanford: Stanford University Press, 2006.

———. "New Worlds, New Stars: Patriotic Astrology and the Invention of Indian and Creole Bodies in Colonial Spanish America, 1600–1650." *American Historical Review* 104 (1999): 33–68.

———. *Puritan Conquistadores: Iberianizing the Atlantic, 1550–1700*. Stanford: Stanford University Press, 2006.

———. "Typological Readings of Nature: The Book of Nature in Lastanosa's Age." In *The Gentleman, the Virtuoso, the Inquirer: Vencencio Juan de Lastanosa and the Art of Collecting in Early Modern Spain*, edited by Mar Rey-Bueno and Miguel López Pérez, 47–63. Newcastle: Cambridge Scholars, 2008.

———. "Typology in the Atlantic World: Early Modern Readings of Colonization." In *Soundings in Atlantic History: Latent Structures and Intellectual Currents, 1500–1830*, edited by Bernard Bailyn and Patricia L. Denault, 237–64. Cambridge: Harvard University Press, 2009.

Capel, Horacio. *La física sagrada: Creencias religiosas y teorías científicas en los orígenes de la geomorfología española, siglos XVII–XVIII*. Barcelona: Ediciones del Serbal, 1985.

———. "Religious Beliefs, Philosophy, and Scientific Theory in the Origins of Spanish Geomorphology, XVII–XVIII Centuries." *Organon* 20–21 (1984–85): 219–29.

Cárdenas, Juan de. *Primera parte de los problemas, y secretos marauillosos de las Indias*. Mexico City: Pedro Ocharte, 1591.

Carey, Daniel. "Compiling Nature's History: Travellers and Travel Narratives in the Early Royal Society." *Annals of Science* 54, no. 3 (1997): 269–92.

———. "Hakluyt's Instructions: The Principal Navigations and Sixteenth-Century Travel Advice." *Studies in Travel Writing* 13, no. 2 (2009): 167–85.

———. *Locke, Shaftesbury, and Hutcheson: Contesting Diversity in the Enlightenment and Beyond*. Cambridge: Cambridge University Press, 2006.

Castañega, Martín de. *Tratado de las supersticiones y hechizerias y de la possibilidad y remedio dellas*. 1529. Edited by Juan Robert Muro Abad. Logroño, La Rioja: Instituto de Estudios Riojanos, 1994.

Cerezo Martínez, Ricardo. *La cartografía náutica española en los siglos XIV, XV y XVI*. Madrid: CSIC, 1994.

Cervantes, Fernando. *The Devil in the New World: The Impact of Diabolism in New*

Spain. New Haven: Yale University Press, 1999.
Cervantes, Fernando, and Andrew Redden, eds. *Angels, Demons, and the New World.* Cambridge: Cambridge University Press, 2013.
Chaves, Jerónimo de. *Chronographia o reportorio de tiempos.* Seville: Juan Gutierrez, 1561.
Christian, William A. *Apparitions in Late Medieval and Renaissance Spain.* Princeton: Princeton University Press, 1981.
———. *Local Religion in Sixteenth-Century Spain.* Princeton: Princeton University Press, 1989.
Cieza de León, Pedro de. *La chronica del Peru, nuevamente escrita.* Antwerp: Martín Nucio, 1554.
Clark, Stuart. *Thinking with Demons: The Idea of Witchcraft in Early Modern Europe.* Oxford: Oxford University Press, 1999.
Cobo, Bernabé. *Historia del Nuevo Mundo.* 1653. Edited by Marcos Jiménez de la Espada. 4 vols. Seville: E. Rasco, 1890–93.
———. *Historia del Nuevo Mundo.* 1653. In *Obras del P. Bernabé Cobo de la compañía de Jesús.* Edited by P. Francisco Mateos. 2 vols. Biblioteca de autores españoles 91–92. Madrid: Ediciones Atlas, 1964.
Codignola, Luca. *Coldest Harbour in the Land: Simon Stock and Lord Baltimore's Colony in Newfoundland, 1621–1649.* Montreal: McGill-Queen's University Press, 1988.
Cohen, H. Floris. *The Scientific Revolution: A Historiographical Inquiry.* Chicago: University of Chicago Press, 1994.
Colahan, Clark. "María de Jesús de Agreda: The Sweetheart of the Holy Office." In *Women in the Inquisition: Spain and the New World,* edited by Mary E. Giles, 155–70. Baltimore: Johns Hopkins University Press, 1999.
———. "Mary of Agreda, the Virgin Mary, and Mystical Knowing." *Studia Mystica* 3 (1988): 53–65.
———. *The Visions of Sor María de Agreda.* Tucson: University of Arizona Press, 1994.
Collings, Ross. *John of the Cross.* Collegeville, MN: Liturgical Press, 1990.
Consejo de las Indias. *Ordenanzas reales del Consejo de Indias: Gobernación y estado temporal.* Madrid: Francisco Sanchez, 1585.
Contessa, Andreina. "Noah's Ark and the Ark of the Covenant in Spanish and Sephardic Medieval Manuscripts." In *Between Judaism and Christianity: Art Historical Essays in Honor of Elisheva (Elisabeth) Revel-Neher,* edited by Katrin Kogman-Appel and Mati Meyer, 171–90. Leiden: Brill, 2009.
Cook, Harold J. *Matters of Exchange: Commerce, Medicine, and Science in the Dutch Golden Age.* New Haven: Yale University Press, 2007.
Cormack, Lesley B. *Charting an Empire: Geography at the English Universities, 1580–1620.* Chicago: University of Chicago Press, 1997.
———. "Good Fences Make Good Neighbors: Geography as Self-Definition in Early Modern England." *Isis* 82, no. 4 (1991): 639–61.
Cortés, Jerónimo. *El nuevo lunario perpetuo y pronóstico general y particular para cada reino y provincia.* 1594. Barcelona: Manuel Sauri, 1848.
Cortés, Martín. *Breue compendio de la sphera y de la arte de nauegar, con nueuos instrumentos y reglas, exemplificado con muy subtiles demonstraciones.* Seville: Casa de Anton Aluarez, [1551].
Covarrubias Horozco, Sebastián de. *Tesoro de la lengua castellana o española.* 1611. Madrid: Iberoamericana, 2006.
Crowther, Kathleen M. "Sacrobosco's *Sphaera* in Spain and Portugal." In *De Sphaera of Johannes de Sacrobosco in the Early Modern Period,* edited by Matteo Valleriani, 161–84. Cham, Switzerland: Springer, 2020.
Cruz, Anne J., and Rosilie Hernández, eds. *Women's Literacy in Early Modern Spain and the New World.* London: Routledge, 2011.
Cubero Sebastián, Pedro. *Peregrinacion del mundo.* Naples: Carlos Porsile, 1682.

Cuevas, Cristóbal. "Fray Luis de León renacentista de la naturaleza: Estética y apologética." In *Fray Luis de Leon: Historia, humanismo y letras*, edited by Víctor García de la Concha and Javier San José Lera, 367–80. Salamanca: Ediciones Universidad de Salamanca, 2006.

Cummins, J. S. *A Question of Rites: Friar Domingo Navarrete and the Jesuits in China*. Aldershot: Scolar Press, 1993.

Curtius, Ernst Robert. *European Literature and the Latin Middle Ages*. 1953. Translated by Willard R. Trask. Princeton: Princeton University Press, 1990.

Daston, Lorraine, and Peter Galison. *Objectivity*. New York: Zone Books, 2007.

Daston, Lorraine, and Katharine Park. *Wonders and the Order of Nature, 1150–1750*. New York: Zone Books, 1998.

Davies, Surekha. *Renaissance Ethnography and the Invention of the Human*. Cambridge: Cambridge University Press, 2016.

———. "The Unlucky, the Bad, and the Ugly: Categories of Monstrosity from the Renaissance to the Enlightenment." In *The Ashgate Research Companion to Monsters and the Monstrous*, edited by Asa Simon Mittman and Peter J. Dendle, 49–76. London: Routledge, 2012.

Dean, Carolyn. *A Culture of Stone: Inka Perspectives on Rock*. Durham: Duke University Press, 2010.

Dear, Peter. "The Church and the New Philosophy." In *Science, Culture, and Popular Belief in Renaissance Europe*, edited by Stephan Pumfrey, Paolo L. Rossi, and Maurice Slawinski, 119–39. Manchester: Manchester University Press, 1991.

Dee, John. *The Mathematicall Preface to the Elements of Geometrie of Euclid of Megara*. 1570. New York: Neale Watson, Science History Publications, 1975.

Delano-Smith, Catherine. "Maps as Art and Science: Maps in Sixteenth-Century Bibles." *Imago Mundi* 42 (1990): 65–83.

Delbourgo, James, and Nicholas Dew, eds. *Science and Empire in the Atlantic World*. New York: Routledge, 2008.

Delio, Ilia. "Theology, Spirituality, and Christ the Center: Bonaventure's Synthesis." In *A Companion to Bonaventure*, edited by Jay M. Hammond, J. A. Wayne Hellmann, and Jared Goff, 359–402. Leiden: Brill, 2014.

Delumeau, Jean. *Catholicism Between Luther and Voltaire: A New View of the Counter-Reformation*. London: Burns & Oates, 1977.

Díaz, Mónica, and Stephanie Kirck. "Theorizing Transatlantic Women's Writing: Imperial Crossings and the Production of Knowledge." *Early Modern Women: An Interdisciplinary Journal* 8 (2013): 53–84.

Díaz del Castillo, Bernal. *Historia verdadera de la conquista de la Nueva España*. Edited by Ramón Iglesia. 2 vols. Mexico City: Secretaría de Educación Popular, 1943.

Diefendorf, Barbara. *From Penitence to Charity: Pious Women and the Catholic Reformation in Paris*. Oxford: Oxford University Press, 2004.

Ditchfield, Simon. "Catholic Reformation and Renewal." In *The Oxford Illustrated History of the Reformation*, edited by Peter Marshall, 152–85. Oxford: Oxford University Press, 2015.

———. "Decentering the Catholic Reformation: Papacy and Peoples in the Early Modern World." *Archiv für Reformationsgeschichte* 101 (2010): 186–208.

———. "Thinking with Saints: Sanctity and Society in the Early Modern World." *Critical Inquiry* 35, no. 3 (2009): 552–84.

Donovan, Rev. J., ed. and trans. *Catechism of the Council of Trent*. Baltimore: J. Myres, 1833.

Dugatkin, Lee Alan. *Mr. Jefferson and the Giant Moose: Natural History in Early America*. Chicago: University of Chicago Press, 2015.

Durkheim, Émile. *The Elementary Forms of the Religious Life*. 1912. Translated by Joseph Ward Swain. London: George Allen, 1915.

Eamon, William. *Science and the Secrets of Nature: Books of Secrets in Medieval*

and *Early Modern Culture*. Princeton: Princeton University Press, 2006.
Earle, Rebecca. *The Body of the Conquistador: Food, Race, and the Colonial Experience in Spanish America, 1492–1700*. Cambridge: Cambridge University Press, 2014.
Edney, Matthew H. *Mapping an Empire: The Geographical Construction of British India, 1765–1843*. Chicago: University of Chicago Press, 1997.
Eliade, Mircea. *Patterns in Comparative Religion*. Translated by Rosemary Sheed. Cleveland: Meridian Books, 1963.
Enenkel, Karl A. E. "The Species and Beyond: Classification and the Place of Hybrids in Early Modern Zoology." In *Zoology in Early Modern Culture: Intersections of Science, Theology, Philology, and Political and Religious Education*, edited by Karl A. E. Enenkel and Paul J. Smith, 57–149. Leiden: Brill, 2014.
Enenkel, Karl A. E., and Paul J. Smith, eds. *Early Modern Zoology: The Construction of Animals in Science, Literature, and the Visual Arts*. 2 vols. Leiden: Brill, 2007.
———, eds. *Zoology in Early Modern Culture: Intersections of Science, Theology, Philology, and Political and Religious Education*. Leiden: Brill, 2014.
Ernst, Germana. "'Veritatis amor dulcissimus': Aspects of Cardano's Astrology." In *Secrets of Nature: Astrology and Alchemy in Early Modern Europe*, edited by William R. Newman and Anthony Grafton, 39–68. Cambridge: MIT Press, 2001.
Escurial, Diego del. *Sermon predicado en el convento de las Carmelitas Descalças de Madrid*. Madrid: La Viuda de Alonso Martín, 1627.
Evangelisti, Silvia. "Religious Women, Mystic Journeys, and Agency in Early Modern Spain." *Journal of Early Modern History* 22 (2018): 9–27.
Fedewa, Marilyn H. *María of Ágreda: Mystical Lady in Blue*. Albuquerque: University of New Mexico Press, 2009.
Feldhay, Rivka. "The Cultural Field of Jesuit Science." In *The Jesuits: Cultures, Sciences, and the Arts, 1540–1773*, edited by John W. O'Malley, Gauvin Alexander Bailey, Steven J. Harris, and T. Frank Kennedy, 107–30. Toronto: University of Toronto Press, 1999.
———. *Galileo and the Church: Political Inquisition or Critical Dialogue?* Cambridge: Cambridge University Press, 1995.
Fernandez-Armesto, Felipe. "Maps and Exploration in the Sixteenth and Early Seventeenth Century." In *The History of Cartography. Vol. 3, Cartography in the European Renaissance*, edited by David Woodward, 738–59. Chicago: University of Chicago Press, 2007.
Fernández de Enciso, Martín. *Suma de geographía q[ue] trata de todas las partidas y provincias del mundo, en especial de las Indias*. Seville: Jacobo Cromberger Aleman, 1519.
Fernández de Navarrete, Martín, ed. *Colección de documentos y manuscritos compilados por Fernández de Navarrete*. 32 vols. Madrid: Impr. de la Viuda de Calero, 1842–95. Reprint, Nendeln: Kraus-Thomson Organization, 1971.
Fernández de Oviedo y Valdés, Gonzalo. *La historia general delas Indias*. Seville: Iuam Cromberger, 1535.
———. *Oviedo dela natural hystoria delas Indias*. Toledo: Remon de Petras, 1526.
Ferrer de Valdecebro, Andrés. *Gobierno general, moral, y político: Hallado en las aves mas generosas y nobles; Sacado de sus naturales virtudes y propiedades*. 1668. Madrid: Bernardo de Villa-Diego, 1683.
———. *Gobierno general, moral y politico: Hallado en las fieras, y animales silvestres; Sacado de sus naturales virtudes, y propiedades*. 1658. Barcelona: Casa de Cormellas, por Thomàs Loriente, 1696.
Ferrer Maldonado, Lorenzo. *Imagen del mundo, sobre la esfera, cosmografia, y geografia, teorica de planetas, y arte de nauegar*. Alcala: Iuan Garcia y Antonio Duplastre, 1626.
Few, Martha, and Zeb Tortorici, eds. *Centering Animals in Latin American History*. Durham: Duke University Press, 2013.

Figueroa, Juan de. *Opusculo de astrologia en medecina y de los terminos, y partes de la astronomia necessarias para el uso della*. Lima, 1660.

Findlen, Paula, ed. *Empires of Knowledge: Scientific Networks in the Early Modern World*. London: Routledge, 2018.

———. "How Information Travels: Jesuit Networks, Scientific Knowledge, and the Early Modern Republic of Letters, 1540–1640." In *Empires of Knowledge: Scientific Networks in the Early Modern World*, edited by Paula Findlen, 57–105. New York: Routledge, 2018.

———. *Possessing Nature: Museums, Collecting, and Scientific Culture in Early Modern Italy*. Berkeley: University of California Press, 1994.

Flor, Fernando R. de la. *La península metafísica: Arte, literatura y pensamiento en la España de la Contrarreforma*. Madrid: Biblioteca Nueva, 1999.

Ford, Thayne R. "Stranger in a Foreign Land: José de Acosta's Scientific Realizations in Sixteenth-Century Peru." *Sixteenth Century Journal* 29, no 1 (1998): 19–33.

Freedberg, David. *The Eye of the Lynx: Galileo, His Friends, and the Beginnings of Modern Natural History*. Chicago: University of Chicago Press, 2002.

Friedman, Elias. *The Latin Hermits of Mount Carmel: A Study in Carmelite Origins*. Rome: Edizioni del Teresianum, 1979.

Funkenstein, Amos. *Theology and the Scientific Imagination: From the Middle Ages to the Seventeenth Century*. Princeton: Princeton University Press, 1986.

García, Gregorio. *Origen de los Indios de el Nuevo Mundo, e Indias Occidentales*. Valencia: Pedro Patricio Mey, 1607.

———. *Origen de los Indios del Nuevo Mundo e Indias Occidentales*. Edited by C. Baciero, A. M. Barrero, P. Borges, J. M. García Añoveros, and J. M. Soto Rábanos. Madrid: CSIC, 2005.

———. *Predicación del evangelio en el Nuevo Mundo viviendo los apóstoles*. Baeza: Pedro de la Cuesta, 1625.

García Cárcel, Ricardo. *La Leyenda Negra: Historia y opinión*. Madrid: Alianza Editorial, 1998.

García Gutiérrez, José María. *La herejía de los alumbrados: Del iluminismo castellano a los solicitantes extremeños*. Madrid: Mileto Ensayo, 1999.

García Oro, José. *Cisneros y la reforma del clero español en tiempo de los Reyes Católicos*. Madrid: CSIC, 1971.

García Pimentel, Luis, ed. *Relación de los obispados de Tlaxcala, Michoacán, Oaxaca y otros lugares en el siglo XVI: Manuscrito de la colección del señor don Joaquín García Icazbalceta*. 2 vols. Mexico City: García Pimentel, 1904.

Gascoigne, John. "The Royal Society, Natural History, and the Peoples of the 'New World(s),' 1660–1800." *British Journal for the History of Science* 42, no. 4 (2009): 539–62.

Gaukroger, Stephen. *The Emergence of a Scientific Culture: Science and the Shaping of Modernity, 1210–1685*. Oxford: Oxford University Press, 2006.

Gerbi, Antonello. *The Dispute of the New World: The History of a Polemic, 1750–1900*. Translated by Jeremy Moyle. Pittsburgh: University of Pittsburgh Press, 2010.

———. *Nature in the New World: From Christopher Columbus to Gonzalo Fernández de Oviedo*. Translated by Jeremy Moyle. Pittsburgh: University of Pittsburgh Press, 2010.

Gillespie, Neal C. "Natural History, Natural Theology, and Social Order: John Ray and the 'Newtonian Ideology.'" *Journal of the History of Biology* 20, no. 1 (1987): 1–49.

Giorgio, Francesco. *De harmonia mundi totius cantica tria*. 1525. Paris: André Berthelin, Roland Guillaume, 1545.

Girava, Gerónimo. *Dos libros de cosmographia: Compuestos nueuamente por Hieronymo Giraua Tarragones*. Milan: Iuan Antonio Castellon y Christoval Caron, 1556.

Glacken, Clarence J. *Traces on the Rhodian Shore: Nature and Culture in Western Thought from Ancient Times to the End* of the Eighteenth Century. Berkeley: University of California Press, 1967.

Godínez, Miguel. Practica de la theologia mystica. Seville: Juan Vejarano à Costa de Lucas Martin de Hermosilla, 1682.

Godlewska, Anne, and Neil Smith, eds. Geography and Empire. Oxford: Blackwell, 1994.

Gómez, Pablo F. The Experiential Caribbean: Creating Knowledge and Healing in the Early Modern Atlantic. Chapel Hill: University of North Carolina Press, 2017.

González de Mendoza, Juan. Historia de las cosas más notables, ritos y costumbres del gran reyno de la China. Rome: Vincentio Accolti, a Costa de Bartholome Grassi, 1585.

Goodman, David C. Power and Penury: Government, Technology, and Science in Philip II's Spain. Cambridge: Cambridge University Press, 1988.

Gorman, Michael John. "The Angel and the Compass: Athanasius Kircher's Geographical Project." In Athanasius Kircher: The Last Man Who Knew Everything, edited by Paula Findlen, 229–49. New York: Routledge, 2004.

Grafton, Anthony, with the collaboration of April Shelford and Nancy Siraisi. New Worlds, Ancient Texts: The Power of Tradition and the Shock of Discovery. Cambridge: Cambridge University Press, 1992.

Granada, Luis de. Introducción del símbolo de la fe. 1583. Edited by José María Balcells. Madrid: Cátedra, 1989.

———. Obras del V. P. M. Fray Luis de Granada: La guía de pecadores. 2 vols. Madrid: Antonio de Sancha, 1781.

Grant, Edward. The Foundations of Modern Science in the Middle Ages: Their Religious, Institutional, and Intellectual Contexts. Cambridge: Cambridge University Press, 1996.

———. History of Natural Philosophy: From the Ancient World to the Nineteenth Century. Cambridge: Cambridge University Press, 2007.

Graziano, Frank. The Millennial New World. Oxford: Oxford University Press, 1999.

Greer, Allan, and Jodi Bilinkoff, eds. Colonial Saints: Discovering the Holy in the Americas, 1500–1800. New York: Routledge, 2003.

Gregory, Brad S. Salvation at Stake: Christian Martyrdom in Early Modern Europe. Cambridge: Harvard University Press, 1999.

Guilday, Peter. "The Sacred Congregation de Propaganda Fide (1622–1922)." Catholic Historical Review 6 (1921): 478–94.

Hakluyt, Richard. The Principal Navigations, Voyages, Traffiques, and Discoveries of the English Nation. 1598–1600. 12 vols. Glasgow: MacLehose and Sons, 1903–5.

Hale, Matthew. The Primitive Origination of Mankind: Considered and Examined According to the Light of Nature. London: William Godbid, 1677.

Haliczer, Stephen. Between Exaltation and Infamy: Female Mystics in the Golden Age of Spain. New York: Oxford University Press, 2002.

Hall, Alexander W. "Natural Theology in the Middle Ages." In The Oxford Handbook of Natural Theology, edited by Russell Re Manning, John Hedley Brooke, and Fraser Watts, 57–74. Oxford: Oxford University Press, 2013.

Hall, Marcia B., and Tracy E. Cooper, eds. The Sensuous in the Counter-Reformation Church. New York: Cambridge University Press, 2013.

Harkness, Deborah. John Dee's Conversations with Angels: Cabala, Alchemy, and the End of Nature. Cambridge: Cambridge University Press, 1999.

Harley, John Brian. The New Nature of Maps: Essays in the History of Cartography. Baltimore: Johns Hopkins University Press, 2002.

Harris, Steven T. "Confession-Building, Long-Distance Networks, and the Organization of Jesuit Science." Early Science and Medicine 1 (1996): 287–318.

———. "Jesuit Scientific Activity in the Overseas Missions, 1540–1773." Isis 96, no. 1 (2005): 71–79.

Harrison, Edward. Masks of the Universe: Changing Ideas on the Nature of the

Cosmos. 2nd ed. Cambridge: Cambridge University Press, 2003.
Harrison, Peter. *The Bible, Protestantism, and the Rise of Natural Science.* Cambridge: Cambridge University Press, 1998.
———. "The Book of Nature and Early Modern Science." In *The Book of Nature in Early Modern and Modern History*, edited by Klass van Berkel and Arjo Vanderjagt, 1–26. Louvain: Peeters, 2006.
———. *The Fall of Man and the Foundation of Science.* Cambridge: Cambridge University Press, 2007.
———. "Reading Vital Science: Animals and the Experimental Philosophy." In *Renaissance Beasts: Of Animals, Humans, and Other Wonderful Creatures*, edited by Erica Fudge, 186–207. Urbana: University of Illinois Press, 2004.
Headley, John M. "Geography and Empire in the Late Renaissance: Botero's Assignment, Western Universalism, and the Civilizing Process." *Renaissance Quarterly* 53, no. 4 (2000): 1119–55.
Hendrickson, Scott D. *Jesuit Polymath of Madrid: The Literary Enterprise of Juan Eusebio Nieremberg.* Leiden: Brill, 2015.
Hernández, Francisco. *The Mexican Treasury: The Writings of Dr. Francisco Hernández.* Edited by Simon Varey. Translated by Rafael Cabran, Cynthia L. Chamberlin, and Simon Varey. Stanford: Stanford University Press, 2002.
Hernández, Marie Theresa. *The Virgin of Guadalupe and the Conversos: Uncovering Hidden Influences from Spain to Mexico.* New Brunswick: Rutgers University Press, 2014.
Heylyn, Peter. *Cosmographie in four bookes: Containing the chorographie and historie of the whole world.* Oxford: Henry Seile, 1652.
Hickerson, Nancy P. *The Jumanos: Hunters and Traders of the South Plains.* Austin: University of Texas Press, 1994.
———. "The Visits of 'the Lady in Blue': An Episode in the History of the South Plains, 1629." *Journal of Anthropological Research* 46, no. 1 (1990): 67–90.

"The Holy Guardian Angels." *Franciscan Annals* 9, no. 106 (1885): 289–94.
Horn, Rebecca. *Postconquest Coyoacan: Nahau-Spanish Relations in Central Mexico, 1519–1650.* Stanford: Stanford University Press, 1997.
Howell, Kenneth J. *God's Two Books: Copernican Cosmology and Biblical Interpretation in Early Modern Science.* Notre Dame: University of Notre Dame Press, 2002.
Hsia, Ronnie Po-chia. *Social Discipline in the Reformation: Central Europe, 1550–1750.* London: Routledge, 1989.
———. *The World of Catholic Renewal, 1540–1770.* Cambridge: Cambridge University Press, 2005.
Huddleston, Lee E. *The Origins of the American Indians: European Perspectives.* Austin: University of Texas Press, 1967.
Huerga, Álvaro. *Historia de los alumbrados, 1570–1630.* 6 vols. Madrid: Fundación Universitaria Española, Seminario Cisneros, 1978–94.
Hunter, Michael. "Robert Boyle and the Early Royal Society: A Reciprocal Exchange in the Making of Baconian Science." *British Journal for the History of Science* 40, no. 1 (2007): 1–23.
Ingoli, Francesco. *Relazione delle quatro parti del mundo.* Edited by Fabio Tosi. Rome: Urbaniana University Press, 1999.
Irving, Sarah. *Natural Science and the Origins of the British Empire.* London: Routledge, 2008.
Isidoro de Sevilla. *Etimologías: Edicion Bilingüe.* 2nd ed. Edited by José Oroz Reta and Manuel A. Marcos Casquero. 2 vols. Madrid: Biblioteca de Autores Cristianos, 1994.
Jaffary, Nora E. *False Mystics: Deviant Orthodoxy in Colonial Mexico.* Lincoln: University of Nebraska Press, 2004.
Jardine, Nicholas, James A. Secord, and Emma C. Spary, eds. *Cultures of Natural History.* Cambridge: Cambridge University Press, 1996.
Jedin, Hubert. "Catholic Reformation or Counter-Reformation?" In *The Counter-Reformation: The Essential Reading,*

edited by David Martin Luebke, 19–46. Malden, MA: Blackwell, 1999.

Jensen, Alexander S. *Divine Providence and Human Agency: Trinity, Creation, and Freedom*. Burlington, VT: Ashgate, 2014.

Jiménez de la Espada, Marcos, and José Urbano Martínez Carreras, eds. *Relaciones geográficas de Indias: Perú*. 3 vols. Biblioteca de autores españoles 183–85. Madrid: Ediciones Atlas, 1965.

Johnson, Curtis N. *Darwin's Dice: The Idea of Chance in the Thought of Charles Darwin*. Oxford: Oxford University Press, 2015.

Johnson, Trevor. "Gardening for God: Carmelite Deserts and the Sacralisation of Natural Space in Counter-Reformation Spain." In *Sacred Space in Early Modern Europe*, edited by Will Coster and Andrew Spice, 193–210. Cambridge: Cambridge University Press, 2005.

———. "Guardian Angels and the Society of Jesus." In *Angels in the Early Modern World*, edited by Peter Marshall and Alexandra Walsham, 191–213. Cambridge: Cambridge University Press, 2006.

Jotischky, Andrew. *The Carmelites and Antiquity: Mendicants and Their Pasts in the Middle Ages*. Oxford: Oxford University Press, 2002.

Juan de la Cruz. *Obras de San Juan de la Cruz, Doctor de la Iglesia*. Edited by Silverio de Santa Teresa. 5 vols. Burgos: El Monte Carmelo, 1929–31.

Juanini, Juan Bautista. *Cartas escritas a los muy nobles doctores Don Francisco Redi y D. Jvan Mathias de Lucas [. . .]*. Madrid: Imprenta Real, 1691.

Kagan, Richard L., and Benjamin Schmidt. "Maps and the Early Modern State: Official Cartography." In *The History of Cartography. Vol. 3, Cartography in the European Renaissance*, edited by David Woodward, 661–79. Chicago: University of Chicago Press, 2007.

Kahn, Victoria. "Machiavelli's Afterlife and Reputation to the Eighteenth Century." In *The Cambridge Companion to Machiavelli*, edited by John Najemy, 239–54. Cambridge: Cambridge University Press, 2010.

Kallendorf, Hilaire, ed. *A New Companion to Hispanic Mysticism*. Leiden: Brill, 2010.

Kamen, Henry. *The Spanish Inquisition: A Historical Revision*. New Haven: Yale University Press, 2014.

Kaplan, David H., and Guntram H. Herb. "How Geography Shapes National Identities." *National Identities* 13, no. 4 (2011): 349–60.

Katz, David. *The Occult Tradition from the Renaissance to the Present Day*. London: Jonathan Cape, 2005.

Keck, David. *Angels and Angelology in the Middle Ages*. Oxford: Oxford University Press, 1998.

Keitt, Andrew W. *Inventing the Sacred: Imposture, Inquisition, and the Boundaries of the Supernatural in Golden Age Spain*. Leiden: Brill, 2005.

Kendrick, Thomas D. *Mary of Agreda: The Life and Legend of a Spanish Nun*. London: Routledge and Kegan Paul, 1967.

Kessell, John L. *Kiva, Cross, and Crown: The Pecos Indians and New Mexico, 1540–1840*. Albuquerque: University of New Mexico Press, 1987.

———. *Spain in the Southwest: A Narrative History of Colonial New Mexico, Arizona, Texas, and California*. Norman: University of Oklahoma Press, 2002.

Kessler, Herbert L. "Medietas/Mediator and the Geometry of Incarnation." In *Image and Incarnation: The Early Modern Doctrine of the Pictorial Image*, edited by Walter Melion and Lee Palmer Wandel, 17–75. Leiden: Brill, 2015.

Killeen, Kevin. *Biblical Scholarship, Science, and Politics in Early Modern England: Thomas Browne and the Thorny Place of Knowledge*. Burlington, VT: Ashgate, 2009.

Killeen, Kevin, and Peter Forshaw, eds. *The Word and the World: Biblical Exegesis and Early Modern Science*. New York: Palgrave Macmillan, 2007.

Kircher, Athanasius. *El arca de Noe: El mito, la naturaleza y el siglo XVII*. Edited and translated by Atilano Martínez Tomé. Madrid: Ediciones OCTO, 1989.

———. *Arca Noe, in tres libros digesta*. Amsterdam: Apud J. Janssonium a Waesberge, 1675.

———. *Itinerarium exstaticum, quo mundi opificium, id est coelestis expansi, siderumque [. . .] compositio et structura ab infimo telluris globo, usque ad ultima mundi confinia*. Rome: Typis Vitalis Mascardi, 1656.

Kivelson, Valerie. *Cartographies of Tsardom: The Land and Its Meanings in Seventeenth-Century Russia*. Ithaca: Cornell University Press, 2006.

Kolb, Robert. *Martin Luther: Confessor of the Faith*. Oxford: Oxford University Press, 2009.

Lach, Donald F. *The Century of Discovery*. Vol. 1 of *Asia in the Making of Europe*. Chicago: University of Chicago Press, 2008.

Lafaye, Jacques. *Quetzalcóatl and Guadalupe: The Formation of Mexican National Consciousness, 1531–1813*. Chicago: University of Chicago Press, 1987.

Lara, Jaime. *City, Temple, Stage: Eschatological Architecture and Liturgical Theatrics in New Spain*. Notre Dame: University of Notre Dame Press, 2004.

Larner, John. "The Church and the Quattrocento Renaissance in Geography." *Renaissance Studies* 12, no. 1 (1998): 26–39.

Laureano de la Cruz. *Nuevo descubrimiento del río Marañón llamado de las Amazonas*. Reproduction of 1653 Madrid edition. Madrid: Biblioteca de la Irradiación, 1900.

Lawson, Thomas E., and Robert N. McCauley. *Rethinking Religion: Connecting Cognition and Culture*. Cambridge: Cambridge University Press, 1993.

Ledezma, Domingo. "Una legitimación imaginativa del Nuevo Mundo: La *Historia naturae, maxime peregrinae* del Jesuita Juan Eusebio Nieremberg." In *El saber de los Jesuitas, historias naturales y el Nuevo Mundo*, edited by Luis Millones Figueroa and Domingo Ledezma, 53–85. Madrid: Iberoamericana, 2005.

Lefebvre, Henri. *The Production of Space*. 1974. Oxford: Blackwell, 1991.

Lehfeldt, Elizabeth. *Religious Women in Golden Age Spain: The Permeable Cloister, Women, and Gender in the Early Modern World*. Burlington, VT: Ashgate, 2005.

Leo Africanus. *Historiale description de l'Afrique*. Antwerp: Christophe Plantin, 1556.

León Pinelo, Antonio de. *Epitome de la bibliotheca oriental y occidental, náutica, y geográfica de Don Antonio de León Pinelo*. Madrid: Francisco Martínez Abad, 1737.

———. *El paraíso en el Nuevo Mundo: Comentario apologético, historia natural y peregrina de las Indias Occidentales, islas de tierra firme del mar oceano*. Ca. 1656. Edited by Raul Porras Barenéchea. 2 vols. Lima: Imprenta Torres Aguirre, 1943.

———. *Question moral: Si el chocolate quebranta el ayuno eclesiástico*. Madrid: La Viuda de Iuan Gonçalez, 1636.

León-Portilla, Miguel. *Bernardino de Sahagún: First Anthropologist*. Translated by Mauricio J. Mixco. Norman: University of Oklahoma Press, 2002.

Lestringant, Frank. *Mapping the Renaissance: The Geographical Imagination in the Age of Discovery*. Translated by David Fausett. Cambridge: Polity Press, 1994.

Lindberg, David C., and Ronald L. Numbers, eds. *God and Nature: Historical Essays on the Encounter Between Christianity and Science*. Berkeley: University of California Press, 1986.

———, eds. *When Science and Christianity Meet*. Chicago: University of Chicago Press, 2003.

Livingstone, David N. *The Geographical Tradition: Episodes in the History of a Contested Enterprise*. Oxford: Blackwell, 1992.

———. *Putting Science in Its Place: Geographies of Scientific Knowledge*. Chicago: University of Chicago Press, 2003.

Lizárraga, Reginaldo de. *Descripción del Perú, Tucumán, Río de la Plata y Chile*. Ca. 1609. Edited by Ignacio Ballesteros. Madrid: Historia 16, 1987.

Lohmann Villena, Guillermo. "Unos datos inéditos sobre fray Antonio Vázquez de Espinosa." *Boletin bibliografica de la Biblioteca Central de la Universidad Nacional de San Marcos* 26, nos. 1–4 (1956): 43–44.

Long, Charles H. *Signification: Signs, Symbols, and Images in the Interpretation of Religion*. Philadelphia: Fortress Press, 1986.

López de Cogolludo, Diego. *Historia de Yucathan*. Madrid: J. Garcia Infanzon, 1688.

López de Gómara, Francisco. *Primera y segunda parte dela historia general de las Indias: Con todo el descubrimiento y cosas notables que han acaecido dende que se ganaron ata el año de 1551; Con la conquista de Mexico y de la Nueua España*. Zaragoza: A Costa de Miguel Capila, 1553.

López de Velasco, Juan. *Geografía y descripción universal de las Indias*. Compiled 1574. Edited by Justo Zaragoza. Madrid: Real Academia de Historia, 1894.

López Piñero, José María. *Ciencia y técnica en la sociedad española de los siglos XVI y XVII*. Barcelona: Labor Universitaria, 1979.

———, ed. *Historia de la ciencia y de la técnica en la Corona de Castilla*. Vol. 3, *Siglos XVI y XVII*. Salamanca: Junta de Castilla y León, Consejería de Educación y Cultura, 2002.

López Piñero, José María, and María Luz López Terrada. *La influencia española en la introducción en Europa de las plantas Americanas (1493–1623)*. Valencia: Instituto de Estudios Documentales e Históricos Sobre la Ciencia, Universitat de València–CSIC, 1997.

López Piñero, José María, and José Pardo Tomás. "The Contribution of Hernández to European Botany and *Materia Medica*." In *Searching for the Secrets of Nature: The Life and Works of Dr. Francisco Hernández*, edited by Simon Varey, Rafael Chabrán, and Dora Weiner, 122–37. Stanford: Stanford University Press, 2000.

———. *La influencia de Francisco Hernández (1515–1587) en la constitución de la botánica y la materia médica modernas*. Valencia: Instituto de Estudios Documentales e Históricos sobre la Ciencia, Universitat de València–CSIC, 1996.

López Rueda, José. *González de Salas, humanista barroco y editor de Quevedo*. Madrid: Fundación Universitaria Española, 2003.

Lozovsky, Natalia. *"The Earth Is Our Book": Geographical Knowledge in the Latin West ca. 400–1000*. Ann Arbor: University of Michigan Press, 2000.

MacCormack, Sabine. "Limits of Understanding: Perceptions of Greco-Roman and Amerindian Paganism in Early Modern Europe." In *America in European Consciousness, 1493–1750*, edited by Karen Ordahl Kupperman, 79–127. Chapel Hill: University of North Carolina Press, 1995.

———. *On the Wings of Time: Rome, the Incas, Spain, and Peru*. Princeton: Princeton University Press, 2007.

MacLean, Katie. "María de Ágreda, Spanish Mysticism, and the Work of Spiritual Conquest." *Colonial Latin American Review* 17, no. 1 (2008): 29–48.

MacLeod, Roy. "Introduction." In "Nature and Empire: Science and the Colonial Enterprise," edited by Roy MacLeod. Special issue, *Osiris* 15 (2000): 1–13.

Magasich-Airola, Jorge, and Jean-Marc de Beer. *America Magica: When Renaissance Europe Thought It Had Conquered Paradise*. London: Anthem Press, 2007.

Magner, Lois N. *A History of the Life Sciences*. Rev. and exp. ed. New York: CRC Press, 2002.

Mancall, Peter C. *Nature and Culture in the Early Modern Atlantic*. Philadelphia: University of Pennsylvania Press, 2018.

Manson, Neil A. "The Design Argument and Natural Theology." In *The Oxford Handbook of Natural Theology*, edited by Russell Re Manning, 295–309. Oxford: Oxford University Press, 2013.

Maravall, José Antonio. *Antiguos y modernos: La idea de progreso en el desarrollo inicial de una sociedad*. Madrid: Sociedad de Estudios y Publicaciones, 1966.

María de Jesús de Ágreda. *Cartas de Sor María de Jesús de Ágreda y de Felipe IV*. Edited by Carlos Seco Serrano. 2 vols. *Biblioteca de autores españoles 108–9*. Madrid: Ediciones Atlas, 1958.

———. *Mística ciudad de Dios: Vida de María; Texto conforme al autógrafo original*. Edited by Celestino Solaguren. Madrid: Fareso, 1970.

———. *Tratado del grado de luz y conocimiento de la ciencia infusa: Trata de toda la redondez de la tierra, de los habitadores de ella y algunos secretos que en sí contiene*. Biblioteca Nacional de España, Sala Cervantes, Cervantes MS 5513 and MS 9346 (1716).

Marshall, Peter, and Alexandra Walsham, eds. *Angels in the Early Modern World*. Cambridge: Cambridge University Press, 2006.

Martínez, Enrico. *Reportorio de los tiempos y historia natural desta Nueua España*. Mexico City: En la Emprenta del Mesmo Autor, 1606.

Martínez, María Elena. *Genealogical Fictions: Limpieza de Sangre, Religion, and Gender in Colonial Mexico*. Stanford: Stanford University Press, 2008.

Martín Merás, María Luisa. *Cartografía marítima hispana: La imagen de América*. Barcelona: Lunwerg, 1993.

———. *Introducción y estudio a la "Suma de cosmographia" de Pedro de Medina*. Valencia: Grial, 1999.

Mathes, W. Michael. "Early California Propaganda: The Works of Fray Antonio de la Ascencion." *California Historical Quarterly* 50, no. 2 (1971): 195–205.

———. "The Early Exploration of the Pacific Coast." In *A New World Disclosed*. Vol. 1 of *The North American Exploration*, edited by John Logan Allen, 400–452. Lincoln: University of Nebraska Press, 1997.

Mayhew, Robert. "'Geography Is Twinned with Divinity': The Laudian Geography of Peter Heylyn." *Geographical Review* 90 (2000): 18–34.

Maza, Francisco de la. *Enrico Martínez: Cosmógrafo e impresor de Nueva España*. Mexico City: Sociedad Mexicana de Geografía y Estadística, 1943.

McGinn, Bernard. *The Foundations of Mysticism: Origins to the Fifth Century*. Vol. 1 of *The Presence of God: A History of Western Christian Mysticism*. New York: Crossroads, 1994.

———. *Mysticism in the Golden Age of Spain (1500–1650)*. Vol. 6 of *The Presence of God: A History of Western Christian Mysticism*. New York: Crossroads, 2017.

McGrath, Alister E. *Iustitia Dei: A History of the Christian Doctrine of Justification*. 3rd ed. Cambridge: Cambridge University Press, 2005.

McLean, Matthew. *The Cosmographia of Sebastian Münster: Describing the World in the Reformation*. Aldershot: Ashgate, 2007.

Medina, Pedro de. *Arte de navegar en que se contienen todas las reglas, declaraciones, secretos y avisos q a la buena navagacio*. Valladolid: Francisco Fernández de Córdoba, 1545.

———. *A Navigator's Universe: The "Libro of Cosmographía" of 1538 by Pedro de Medina*. Translated by Ursula Lamb. Chicago: University of Chicago Press, 1972.

———. *Obras de Pedro de Medina: "Libro de grandezas y cosas memorables de España" [1548] y "Libro de la verdad" [1555]*. Edited by Ángel Gonzáles Palencia. Madrid: CSIC, 1944.

Meer, Jitse M. van der, and Scott Mandelbrote, eds. *Nature and Scripture in the Abrahamic Religions: Up to 1700*. 2 vols. Leiden: Brill, 2008.

Mela, Pomponio. *Compendio geográphico, i histórico de el orbe antiguo i descripción de el sitio de la Tierra, escrita por Pomponio Mela, español antiguamente en la Republica Romana; i ahora, con nueva i varia ilustración, restituido a la suia española, de la Librería de don Iusepe Antonio Gonzalez de Salas*. Madrid: Diego Díaz de la Carrera, 1644.

Merton, Robert K. *Science, Technology, and Society in Seventeenth-Century England*. New York: Howard Fertig, 1970.

Millones Figueroa, Luis. "La historia natural del padre Bernabé Cobo: Algunas claves para su lectura." *Colonial Latin American Review* 12, no. 1 (2003): 85–97.

———. "La intelligentsia jesuíta y la naturaleza del Nuevo Mundo en el siglo XVII." In *El saber de los Jesuitas, historias naturales y el Nuevo Mundo*, edited by Luis Millones Figueroa and Domingo Ledezma, 27–52. Madrid: Iberoamericana, 2005.

Millones Figueroa, Luis, and Domingo Ledezma, eds. *El saber de los Jesuitas, historias naturales y el Nuevo Mundo*. Madrid: Iberoamericana, 2005.

Mills, Kenneth. "Diego de Ocaña's Hagiography of New and Renewed Devotion in Colonial Peru." In *Colonial Saints: Discovering the Holy in the Americas, 1500–1800*, edited by Allan Greer and Jodi Bilinkoff, 51–75. New York: Routledge, 2003.

———. "Mission and Narrative in the Early Modern Spanish World: Diego de Ocaña's Desert in Passing." In *Faithful Narratives: Historians, Religion, and the Challenge of Objectivity*, edited by Andrea Sterk and Nina Caputo, 115–31. Ithaca: Cornell University Press, 2014.

Mixson, James D., and Bert Roest, eds. *A Companion to Observant Reform in the Late Middle Ages and Beyond*. Leiden: Brill, 2015.

Morgan, David. *The Sacred Gaze: Religious Visual Culture in Theory and Practice*. Berkeley: University of California Press, 2005.

Mullett, Michael A. *The Catholic Reformation*. London: Routledge, 1999.

Mundy, Barbara E. *The Mapping of New Spain: Indigenous Cartography and the Maps of the Relaciones Geográficas*. Chicago: University of Chicago Press, 2000.

Muñoz Camargo, Diego. "*Historia de Tlaxcala* [Descripción de la ciudad y provincia de Tlaxcala]." Ca. 1585. University of Glasgow Archives and Special Collections, MS Hunter 242 (U.3.15).

Muñoz de San Pedro, Miguel de. "La 'Relación' de las Indias de fray Antonio Vázquez de Espinosa." *Revista de Indias* 9, nos. 33–34 (1948): 837–87. Includes reprints of "Relación de todas las audiencias," by Antonio Vázquez de Espinosa.

Muro Orejón, Antonio. "Las ordenanzas de 1571 del Real y Supremo Consejo de las Indias: Texto facsimiliar de la edición de 1585; Notas de Antonio Muro Orejón." *Anuario de estudios americanos* 14 (1957): 367–423.

Navarro Brotóns, Victor. "Continuity and Change in Cosmological Ideas in Spain Between the Sixteenth and Seventeenth Centuries: The Impact of Celestial Novelties." In *Change and Continuity in Early Modern Cosmology*, edited by Patrick Bonner, 33–50. Dordrecht: Springer, 2012.

Navarro Brotóns, Victor, and William Eamon, eds. *Más allá de la Leyenda Negra: España y la revolución científica*. Valencia: Instituto de Historia de la Ciencia y Documentación López Piñero, 2007.

Neuner, Josef, and Jacques Dupuis, eds. *The Christian Faith in the Doctrinal Documents of the Catholic Church*. New York: Alba House, 2001.

Nieremberg, Juan Eusebio. *Curiosa y oculta filosofía: Primera y segunda parte de las maravillas de la naturaleza, examinadas en varias questiones naturales*. Madrid: En la Imprenta Real, 1643.

———. *De la hermosura de Dios y su amabilidad por las infinitas perfecciones del ser divino*. In *Obras escogidas del R. P. Juan Eusebio Nieremberg*, edited by D. Eduardo Zepeda-Henríquez, 2 vols., 2:295–480. Madrid: Ediciones Atlas, 1957.

———. *Historia naturae maxime peregrinae*. Antwerp: Officina Plantiniana, 1635.

Niño, Juanetin. *A la sereníssima Señora Infanta Sor Margarita De La Crvz, Religiosa Descalça de su Real Convento De Descalças Franciscas de Madrid*. Salamanca: Iacinto Taberniel, 1632.

Nogar, Anna. *Quill and Cross in the Borderlands: Sor María de Ágreda and the Lady in Blue, 1628 to the Present*. Notre

Dame: University of Notre Dame Press, 2018.
Oakley, Francis. "The Absolute and Ordained Power of God in Sixteenth- and Seventeenth-Century Theology." *Journal of the History of Ideas* 59, no. 3 (1998): 437–61.
Ocaña, Diego de. *Relación del viaje de Fray Diego de Ocaña por el Nuevo Mundo*. Biblioteca de la Universidad de Oviedo, M-215.
——. *Viaje por el Nuevo Mundo: De Guadalupe a Potosí, 1599–1605*. Edited by Blanca López de Mariscal and Abraham Madroñal. Madrid: Iberoamericana, 2010.
Ogilvie, Brian W. *The Science of Describing: Natural History in Renaissance Europe*. Chicago: University of Chicago Press, 2006.
O'Gorman, Edmundo. *Cuatro historiadores de indias, siglo XVI: Pedro Mártir de Anglería, Gonzalo Fernández de Oviedo y Valdés, Fray Bartolomé de las Casas, Joseph de Acosta*. Mexico City: Secretaría de Educación Pública, 1972.
——. *La invención de América: Investigación acerca de la estructura histórica del Nuevo Mundo y del sentido de su devenir*. 2nd ed. Mexico City: Fondo de Cultura Económica, 1977.
Olin, John. *Catholic Reform: From Cardinal Ximenes to the Council of Trent, 1495–1563; An Essay with Illustrative Documents and a Brief Study of St. Ignatius Loyola*. New York: Fordham University Press, 1990.
Ollé, Manel. *La empresa de China: De la armada invencible al galeón de Manila*. Barcelona: Acantilado, 2002.
Olmos, Andrés de. *Tratado de hechicerías y sortilegios*. Edited by Georges Baudot. Mexico City: UNAM, 1990.
Olson, Richard. *Science and Religion: From Copernicus to Darwin*. Baltimore: Johns Hopkins University Press, 2006.
O'Malley, John W. *Trent: What Happened at the Council*. Cambridge: Harvard University Press, 2013.
O'Malley, John W., Gauvin Alexander Bailey, Steven J. Harris, and T. Frank Kennedy, eds. *The Jesuits: Cultures, Sciences, and the Arts, 1540–1773*. Toronto: University of Toronto Press, 1999.
Oosterhoff, Richard J., and Jitse M. van der Meer. "God, Scripture, and the Rise of Modern Science (1200–1700): Notes in the Margin of Harrison's Hypothesis." In *Nature and Scripture in the Abrahamic Religions: Up to 1700*, edited by Jitse M. van der Meer and Scott Mandelbrote, 2 vols., 2:363–96. Leiden: Brill, 2008.
Oré, Luis Jerónimo de. *Symbolo Catholico Indiano*. Lima: Antonio Ricardo, 1598. Facsimile edition. Edited by Antonine Tibesar. Lima: Australis, 1992.
Osler, Margaret J. "The Canonical Imperative: Rethinking the Scientific Revolution." In *Rethinking the Scientific Revolution*, edited by Margaret J. Osler, 3–22. Cambridge: Cambridge University Press, 2000.
Padden, Robert C. "The Ordenaza del Patronazgo of 1574: An Interpretative Essay." In *The Church in Colonial Latin America*, edited by John F. Schwaller, 27–47. Wilmington, DE: Scholarly Resources, 2000.
Paden, Jeremy. "The Iguana and the Barrel of Mud: Memory, Natural History, and Hermeneutics in Oviedo's *Sumario de la natural historia de las Indias*." *Colonial Latin American Review* 16, no. 2 (2007): 203–26.
Padrón, Ricardo. *The Spacious Word: Cartography, Literature, and Empire in Early Modern Spain*. Chicago: University of Chicago Press, 2004.
Pagden, Anthony. *The Fall of Natural Man: The American Indians and the Origins of Comparative Ethnology*. New York: Cambridge University Press, 1982.
——. *Spanish Imperialism and the Political Imagination*. New Haven: Yale University Press, 1990.
Pallas, Gerónymo. *Missión a las Indias por el Pe Gerónymo Pallas: De Roma a Lima; La "Misión a las Indias" (1619) (razón y visión de una peregrinación sin retorno)*. Edited by José J. Hernández Palomo. Madrid: CSIC, 2006.

Pardo Tomás, José. *Ciencia y censura: La inquisición española y los libros científicos en los siglos XVI y XVII*. Madrid: CSIC, 1991.

———. "Conversion Medicine: Communication and Circulation of Knowledge in the Franciscan Convent and College of Tlatelolco, 1527–1577." *Quaderni storici* 48 (2013): 21–42.

Parel, Anthony J. *The Machiavellian Cosmos*. New Haven: Yale University Press, 1992.

Parrish, Susan Scott. *American Curiosity: Cultures of Natural History in the Colonial British Atlantic World*. Chapel Hill: University of North Carolina Press, 2006.

Parry, John Horace. *The Age of Reconnaissance*. Berkeley: University of California Press, 1981.

Pasulka, Diana Walsh. *Heaven Can Wait: Purgatory in Catholic Devotional and Popular Culture*. Oxford: Oxford University Press, 2015.

Paul III. "Sublimis Deus: On the Enslavement and Evangelization of Indians." 1537. Papal Encyclicals Online. http://www.papalencyclicals.net/Paul03/p3subli.htm.

Pedro del Puerto. "Viaje de un monje gerónimo al virreinato del Perú en el siglo XVII." 1624. Edited by Francisco V. Silva. *Boletín de la Real Academia de la Historia* 81 (1922): 433–60; 82 (1923): 132–64, 201–14.

Peña Núñez, Beatriz Carolina. *Fray Diego de Ocaña: Olvido, mentira y memoria*. Alicante: Publicaciones de la Universidad de Alicante, 2016.

———. *Imágenes contra el olvido: El Perú colonial en las ilustraciones de fray Diego de Ocaña*. Lima: Fondo Editorial, Pontificia Universidad Católica del Perú, 2011.

Pérez de Moya, Juan. *Arithmética práctica y speculativa (1562) and Varia historia de sanctas e illustres mujeres (1583)*. Both in vol. 2 of *Obras de Juan Pérez de Moya*, edited by Consolación Baranda. Madrid: Biblioteca Castro, 1998.

Peter Martyr d'Anghera. *De orbe novo Petri Martyris Anglerii, quas scripsit ab anno 1493 ad 1526*. Edited by Joaquín Torres Asensio. Madrid: Gomez Fuentenebro, 1892.

———. *De Orbe Novo: The Eight Decades of Peter Martyr d'Anghera*. Edited and translated from the Latin by Francis Augustus MacNutt. 2 vols. New York: G. P. Putnam's Sons, 1912.

Phelan, John Leddy. *The Millennial Kingdom of the Franciscans in the New World*. Berkeley: University of California Press, 1970.

Phillips, Carla Rahn. "Visualizing Imperium: The Virgin of the Seafarers and Spain's Self-Image in the Early Sixteenth Century." *Renaissance Quarterly* 58, no. 3 (2005): 815–56.

Phillips, Henry. *Church and Culture in Seventeenth-Century France*. New York: Cambridge University Press, 1997.

Phillips, William D., Jr. and Carla Rahn Phillips. *The Worlds of Christopher Columbus*. Cambridge: Cambridge University Press, 1993.

Pimentel, Juan. "Baroque Natures: Juan E. Nieremberg, American Wonders, and Preterimperial Natural History." In *Science in the Spanish and Portuguese Empires, 1500–1800*, edited by Daniela Bleichmar, Paula De Vos, Kristin Huffine, and Kevin Sheehan, 93–113. Stanford: Stanford University Press, 2009.

———. "The Iberian Vision: Science and Empire in the Framework of a Universal Monarchy, 1500–1800." In "Nature and Empire: Science and the Colonial Enterprise," edited by Roy MacLeod. Special issue, *Osiris* 15 (2000): 17–30.

———. *Testigos del mundo: Ciencia, literatura y viajes en la ilustración*. Madrid: Marcial Pons Historia, 2003.

Pinto Crespo, Virgilio. *Inquisición y control ideólogico en la España del siglo XVI*. Madrid: Taurus, 1983.

Plasencia, Juan de. *Doctrina christiana en lengua española y tagala*. Manila:

S. Gabriel, de la Orden de S. Domingo, 1593.
Ponce de León, Francisco. *Descripción del reyno de Chile, de sus puertos, caletas, y sitio de Valdiuia, con algunos discursos para su mayor defensa*. Madrid, 1644.
Portuondo, María M. *Secret Science: Spanish Cosmography and the New World*. Chicago: University of Chicago Press, 2009.
———. *The Spanish Disquiet: The Biblical Natural Philosophy of Benito Arias Montano*. Chicago: University of Chicago Press, 2019.
Poutrin, Isabelle. "Des 'livres extatiques,' venus d'Espagne: Thérèse d'Avila et Jeanne de la Croix, modèles de sainteté féminine." In *Confessional Sanctity*, edited by Jürgen Beyer, 49–63. Göttingen: Vandenhoeck & Ruprecht, 2009.
———. *Le voile et la plume: Autobiographie et sainteté féminine dans l'Espagne moderne*. Madrid: Casa de Velázquez, 1995.
Prien, Hans-Jürgen. *Christianity in Latin America*. Rev. and exp. ed. Leiden: Brill, 2013.
Prieto, Andrés. "Alexander and the Geographer's Eye: Allegories of Knowledge in Martín Fernández de Enciso's Suma de geographía (1519)." *Hispanic Review* 78 (2010): 169–88.
———. *Missionary Scientists: Jesuit Science in Spanish South America, 1570–1810*. Nashville: Vanderbilt University Press, 2011.
Pseudo-Dionysius. *Pseudo-Dionysius: The Complete Works*. Translated by Colm Luibhéid and Paul Rorem. New York: Paulist Press, 1987.
Quevedo, Francisco de. *Política de Dios y gobierno de Cristo*. Madrid: Espasa-Calpe, 1930.
Ramírez, Baltasar. "Descripción del reino del Perú, del sitio, temple, provincias, obispados y ciudades de los naturales, de sus lenguas y trajes." 1597. Biblioteca Nacional de España, Madrid, MS 19668.
Ray, John. *The Wisdom of God Manifested in the Works of the Creation*. London: Samuel Smith, 1691.

Raymond, Joad, ed. *Conversations with Angels: Essays Towards a History of Spiritual Communication, 1100–1700*. New York: Palgrave Macmillan, 2011.
Reguera Rodríguez, Antonio T. *Los geógrafos del rey*. Leon: Imprenta Kadmos, Universidad de León, 2010.
Re Manning, Russell, ed. *The Oxford Handbook of Natural Theology*. Oxford: Oxford University Press, 2013.
Remensnyder, Amy G. *La Conquistadora: The Virgin Mary at War and Peace in the Old and New Worlds*. Oxford: Oxford University Press, 2014.
Resta, Francisco. *Meteorologia de igneis aereis aqueisque corporibus*. Rome: Apud F. Monetam, 1644.
Rice, Eugene F., Jr. *Saint Jerome in the Renaissance*. Baltimore: Johns Hopkins University Press, 1985.
Ritchey, Sara. *Holy Matter: Changing Perceptions of the Material World in Late Medieval Christianity*. Ithaca: Cornell University Press, 2014.
Rocamora y Torrano, Ginés. *Sphera del universo*. Madrid: Iuan de Herrera, 1599.
Rodríguez de León, Juan. *El predicador de las gentes, san Pablo: Ciencia, preceptos, avisos y obligaciones de los predicadores evangelicas con doctrina del apóstol*. Madrid: Maria de Quiñones, 1638.
Roest, Bert. *A History of Franciscan Education, c. 1210–1517*. Leiden: Brill, 2000.
———. *Order and Disorder: The Poor Clares Between Foundation and Reform*. Leiden: Brill, 2013.
Roger, Jacques. *Buffon: A Life in Natural History*. Ithaca: Cornell University Press, 1997.
Rohrbach, Peter-Thomas. *Journey to Carith: The Sources and Story of the Discalced Carmelites*. Washington, DC: Institute of Carmelite Studies Publications, 2007.
Romano, Antonella. "Iberian Missionaries in God's Vineyard: Enlarging Humankind and Encompassing the Globe in the Renaissance." *History of the Human Sciences* 32, no. 4 (2019): 8–27.

Román y Zamora, Hieronymo. *Republicas del mundo: Divididas en tres partes.* Salamanca: Juan Fernández, 1595.

Rosales, Alfonso Martínez. "La provincia de San Alberto de Indias de Carmelitas descalzos." *Historia mexicana* 31, no. 4 (1982): 471–543.

Rowe, Erin Kathleen. *Saint and Nation: Santiago, Teresa of Avila, and Plural Identities in Early Modern Spain.* University Park: Penn State University Press, 2011.

Rowland, Ingrid D. "Athanasius Kircher, Giordano Bruno, and the Panspermia of the Infinite Universe." In *Athanasius Kircher: The Last Man Who Knew Everything*, edited by Paula Findlen, 191–205. New York: Routledge, 2004.

———. "Athanasius Kircher's Guardian Angel." In *Conversations with Angels: Essays Towards a History of Spiritual Communication, 1100–1700*, edited by Joad Raymond, 250–72. New York: Palgrave Macmillan, 2011.

Rubial García, Antonio. *El paraíso de los elegidos: Una lectura de la historia cultural de Nueva España (1521–1804).* Mexico City: Fondo de Cultura Económica, 2010.

———. *La santidad controvertida: Hagiografía y conciencia criolla alrededor de los venerables no canonizados de Nueva España.* Mexico City: Fondo de Cultura Económica, 1999.

Rubiés, Joan-Pau. "Ethnography and Cultural Translation in the Early Modern Missions." *Studies in Church History* 53 (2017): 272–310.

———. "Instructions for Travellers: Teaching the Eye to See." *History and Anthropology* 9, nos. 2–3 (1996): 139–90.

———. *Travellers and Cosmographers: Studies in the History of Early Modern Travel and Ethnology.* Aldershot: Ashgate, 2007.

Ruler, J. A. van. *The Crisis of Causality: Voeticus and Descartes on God, Nature, and Change.* Leiden: Brill, 1995.

Ryan, Michael A. *A Kingdom of Stargazers: Astrology and Authority in the Late Medieval Crown of Aragon.* Ithaca: Cornell University Press, 2011.

Sabunde, Ramón. *Dialogos de la naturaleza del hombre, de su principio y su fin.* Translated by Antonio Ares. Madrid: Iuan de la Cuesta, 1616.

———. *Violeta del anima: Que es suma de la theologia natural [. . .] nueuame[n]te traduzido d[e] latin en romançe castellano.* Valladolid: Francisco Fernández de Cordova, 1549.

Sacro Bosco, Joannes de. *Tractado de la sphera: Que compuso el doctor Ioannes de Sacrobusto con muchas additions.* Translated by Jerónimo de Chaves. Seville: Iuan de Leon, 1545.

Sahagún, Bernardino de. *Florentine Codex: General History of the Things of New Spain.* Translated and edited by Arthur J. O. Anderson and Charles E. Dibble. 13 vols. Santa Fe, NM: School of American Research and the University of Utah, 1950–82.

Sainz Rodríguez, Pedro. *La siembra mística del Cardenal Cisneros y las reformas en la Iglesia.* Madrid: Fundación Universitaria Española, 1979.

Salaville, Sévérien. "Un théoricien de l'apostolat catholique au XVIIe siècle: Le Carme Thomas de Jésus ou Didace Sanchez d'Avila." *Échoes d'Orient* 19, no. 118 (1920): 129–52.

Salazar-Soler, Carmen. "Obras más que de gigantes: Los Jesuitas y las ciencias de la tierra en el Virreinato del Perú (siglos XVI y XVII)." In *El saber de los Jesuitas, historias naturales y el Nuevo Mundo*, edited by Luis Millones Figueroa and Domingo Ledezma, 147–72. Madrid: Iberoamericana, 2005.

Salinas y Córdoba, Buenaventura de. *Memorial, informe, y manifiesto del p.f. Buenauentura de Salinas y Cordoua, de la orden de S. Francisco [. . .].* [Madrid], ca. 1646.

Samaniego, José Ximénez. *Relacion de la vida de la V. Madre Sor Maria de Jesus, abadesa, que fue del Convento de la Purisima Concepcion de la villa de Agreda.*

Ca. 1670. Madrid: La Imprenta de la Causa de la V. Madre, 1762.

Sánchez Bella, Ismael. "El título de las descripciones del Código de Ovando." In *Dos estudios sobre el Código de Ovando*, 91–217. Pamplona: Ediciones Universidad de Navarra, 1987.

Sánchez Lora, José Luis. *Mujeres, conventos y formas de la religiosidad barroca*. Madrid: Fundación Universitaria Española, 1988.

Sánchez Martínez, Antonio. *La espada, la cruz y el padrón: Soberanía, fe y representación cartográfica en el mundo ibérico bajo la monarquía hispánica, 1503–1598*. Madrid: CSIC, 2013.

———. "An Official Image of the World for the Hispanic Monarchy: The Padrón Real of the Casa de la Contratación in Seville, 1508–1606." *Nuncius* 29 (2014): 389–438.

Sánchez Martínez, Antonio, and José Pardo Tomás. "Between Imperial Design and Colonial Appropriation: The *Relaciones Geográficas de Indias* and Their *Pinturas* as Cartographic Practices in New Spain." *Bulletin for Spanish and Portuguese Historical Studies* 39, no. 1 (2014): 1–20.

Sandman, Alison. "Controlling Knowledge: Navigation, Cartography, and Secrecy in the Early Modern Spanish Atlantic." In *Science and Empire in the Atlantic World, 1500–1800*, edited by Nicholas Dew and James Delbourgo, 31–51. New York: Routledge, 2008.

Schiebinger, Londa. "Forum Introduction: The European Colonial Science Complex." *Isis* 96, no. 1 (2005): 52–55.

Schiebinger, Londa, and Claudia Swan, eds. *Colonial Botany: Science, Commerce, and Politics in the Early Modern World*. Philadelphia: University of Pennsylvania Press, 2004.

Schmidt-Biggemann, Wilhelm. *Philosophia perennis: Historical Outlines of Western Spirituality in Ancient, Medieval, and Early Modern Thought*. Dordrecht: Springer, 2004.

Schroeder, H. J. *Canons and Decrees of the Council of Trent: Original Text with English Translation*. London: Herder, 1941.

Scott, Heidi V. *Contested Territory: Mapping Peru in the Sixteenth and Seventeenth Centuries*. Notre Dame: University of Notre Dame Press, 2009.

Scribner, Robert. *For the Sake of Simple Folk: Popular Propaganda for the German Reformation*. Cambridge: Cambridge University Press, 1981.

Segev, Ran. "'For the Sciences Migrate, Just Like People': The Case of Botanical Knowledge in the Early Modern Iberian Empires." *Perspectives on Science* 30, no. 4 (2022): 732–56.

———. "The Problem Solver: Colonial Knowledge, Authority, and the Compilation of Natural Marvels in Juan de Cárdenas' *Problemas y secretos* (1591)." In *Between Encyclopedia and Chorography: Defining the Agency of "Cultural Encyclopedias" from a Transcultural Perspective*, edited by Anna Boroffka, 339–61. Berlin: De Gruyter, 2022.

———. "The Science of Faith: Religious Worldviews and the Study of Nature in the Spanish World, 1530s–1640s." PhD diss., University of Texas, 2015.

———. "Sephardic Conquistadores in a New World: Menashe ben Israel on the 'Rediscovery' of the Lost Tribes." *Journal for Early Modern Cultural Studies* 18, no. 4 (2018): 124–50.

———. "Spatial Evidence in a New World: Fray Antonio Vázquez de Espinosa's Geography." In *Evidence in the Age of the New Sciences*, edited by James A. T. Lancaster and Richard Raiswell, 209–27. Dordrecht: Springer, 2018.

Serrano Espinosa, Teresa Eleazar. "Las cofradías del Carmelo Descalzo en la Nueva España." *Fronteras de la historia: Revista de historia colonial latinoamericana* 18, no. 1 (2013): 69–103.

Serrano y Sanz, Manuel. *Apunes para una biblioteca de escritoras españolas*. Madrid: Ediciones Atlas, 1975.

Shalev, Zur. *Sacred Words and Worlds: Geography, Religion, and Scholarship, 1550–1700*. Leiden: Brill, 2012.

Shea, William R. "Galileo and the Church." In *God and Nature: Historical Essays on the Encounter Between Christianity and Science*, edited by David Lindberg and Ronald L. Numbers, 114–35. Berkeley: University of California Press, 1986.

Short, John Rennie. *Making Space: Revisioning the World, 1475–1600*. Syracuse: Syracuse University Press, 2004.

Slater, John. *Todos son hojas: Literatura e historia natural en el barroco español*. Madrid: CSIC, 2010.

Smet, Joachim. "Some Unpublished Documents Concerning Fray Antonio." *Carmelus* 1, no. 1 (1954): 151–58.

Smith, Jonathan Z. *Map Is Not Territory: Studies in the History of Religions*. Leiden: Brill, 1978.

Smith, Pamela H. "Alchemy as a Language of Mediation at the Habsburg Court." *Isis* 85, no. 1 (1994): 1–25.

———. "Science on the Move: Recent Trends in the History of Early Modern Science." *Renaissance Quarterly* 62 (2009): 345–75.

Smith, Pamela H., and Paula Findlen, eds. *Merchants and Marvels: Commerce, Science, and Art in Early Modern Europe*. London: Routledge, 2001.

Soergel, Philip M. *Wondrous in His Saints: Counter-Reformation Propaganda in Bavaria*. Berkeley: University of California Press, 1993.

Sola, Diego. *El cronista de China: Juan González de Mendoza, entre la misión, el imperio y la historia*. Barcelona: Universitat de Barcelona Edicions, 2018.

Solano, Francisco de, ed. *Cuestionarios para la formación de las relaciones geográficas de Indias, siglos XVI–XIX*. Madrid: CSIC, 1988.

Sorrell, Roger D. *St. Francis of Assisi and Nature: Tradition and Innovation in Western Christian Attitudes Toward the Environment*. Oxford: Oxford University Press, 1988.

Spate, Oskar Hermann Khristian. *The Spanish Lake*. Minneapolis: University of Minnesota Press, 1979.

Spinks, Bryan D. *Early and Medieval Rituals and Theologies of Baptism: From the New Testament to the Council of Trent*. Farnham, UK: Ashgate, 2006.

Stagl, Justin. *A History of Curiosity: The Theory of Travel, 1550–1800*. New York: Routledge, 1995.

Starr-LeBeau, Gretchen D. *In the Shadow of the Virgin: Inquisitors, Friars, and Conversos in Guadalupe, Spain*. Princeton: Princeton University Press, 2003.

Stolarski, Piotr. *Friars on the Frontier: Catholic Renewal and the Dominican Order in Southeastern Poland, 1594–1648*. Farnham, UK: Ashgate, 2010.

Stroumsa, Guy G. *A New Science: The Discovery of Religion in the Age of Reason*. Cambridge: Harvard University Press, 2010.

Syria, Pedro de. *Arte de la verdadera nauegacion, en que se trata de la machina del mundo*. Valencia: Juan Chrysostomo Garriz, 1602.

Tabulse, Elías. *Los origénes de la ciencia moderna en México, 1630–1680*. Mexico City: Fondo de Cultura Económica, 1994.

Talavera, Gabriel de. *Historia de Nuestra Señora de Guadalupe*. Toledo: Thomas de Guzman, 1597.

Tar, Jane D. "Flying Through the Empire: The Visionary Journeys of Early Modern Nuns." In *Women's Voices and the Politics of the Spanish Empire: From Convent Cell to Imperial Court*, edited by Jennifer Lee Eich, Jeanne L. Gillespie, and Lucia G. Harrison, 263–302. New Orleans: University Press of the South, 2008.

———. "The Literature of Franciscan Nuns in Early Modern Spain." PhD diss., University of Wisconsin–Madison, 1998.

Taylor, Larrisa Juliet. "Funeral Sermons and Orations as Religious Propaganda in Sixteenth-Century France." In *The Place of the Dead: Death and Remembrance in Late Medieval and Early Modern Europe*, edited by Bruce Gordon and

Peter Marshall, 224–39. Cambridge: Cambridge University Press, 2000.

Taylor, René. *Arquitectura y magia: Consideraciones sobre la idea de El Escorial*. Madrid: Siruela, 2006.

Teresa de Ávila. *Obras de Santa Teresa de Jesús*. Edited by Silverio de Santa Teresa. 9 vols. Burgos: El Monte Carmelo, 1915–24.

Thevet, André. *La cosmographie vniuerselle*. Paris: Chez Pierre L'Huillier, rue Sainct Iaques, à l'Oliuier, 1575.

Toft, Evelyn. "Tomás de Jesús." In *Renaissance and Reformation, 1500–1620: A Biographical Dictionary*, edited by Jo Eldridge Carney, 351. Westport, CT: Greenwood Press, 2001.

Tomás de Jesús. *De procuranda salute omnium gentium, schismaticorum, haereticorum, Iudaeorum*. Antwerp: Sumptibus Viduae & Haeredum Petri Belleri, 1613.

Topham, Jonathan R. "Natural Theology and the Sciences." In *The Cambridge Companion to Science and Religion*, edited by Peter Harrison, 59–79. Cambridge: Cambridge University Press, 2010.

Torquemada, Antonio de. *Jardin de flores curiosas, en que se tratan algunas materias de la humanidad, philosophia, theologia y geographia, con otras cosas curiosas [. . .]*. Antwerp: Iuan Corderio, 1575.

Torquemada, Juan de. *De los veynte y un libros rituales y monarchia yndiana con el origen y guerras de los Yndios Occidentales*. Seville: Matthias Clauijo, 1615.

Turley, Steven. *Franciscan Spirituality and the Mission in New Spain*. Surrey, UK: Ashgate, 2014.

Tweed, Thomas A. *Crossing and Dwelling: A Theory of Religion*. Cambridge: Harvard University Press, 2006.

Twomey, Lesley K. *The Sacred Space of the Virgin Mary in Medieval Hispanic Literature from Gonzalo de Berceo to Ambrosio Montesino*. Cambridge: Cambridge University Press, 2019.

Tyler, Peter. *Teresa of Avila: Doctor of the Soul*. London: Bloomsbury, 2014.

Valadés, Diego. *Retórica cristiana*. 1579. Facsimile edition with Spanish translation. Edited by Esteban J. Palomera, Alfonso Castro Pallares, and Tarsicio Herrera Zapién. Mexico City: UNAM, Fondo de Cultura Económica, 1989.

———. *Rhetorica christiana*. Perugia: Petrumiacobum Petrutium, 1579.

Valle, Ivonne del. "From José de Acosta to the Enlightenment: Barbarians, Climate Change, and (Colonial) Technology as the End of History." *Eighteenth Century* 54, no. 4 (2013): 435–59.

Van Deusen, Nancy E. *Between the Sacred and the Worldly: The Institutional and Cultural Practice of Recogimiento in Colonial Lima*. Stanford: Stanford University Press, 2001.

Van Duzer, Chet. "*Hic sunt dracones*: The Geography and Cartography of Monsters." In *The Ashgate Research Companion to Monsters and the Monstrous*, edited by Asa Simon Mittman and Peter J. Dendle, 387–436. London: Routledge, 2012.

Vanzo, Alberto. "From Empirics to Empiricists." *Intellectual History Review* 24, no. 4 (2014): 517–38.

Varey, Simon, Rafael Chabrán, and Dora B. Weiner, eds. *Searching for the Secrets of Nature: The Life and Works of Dr. Francisco Hernández*. Stanford: Stanford University Press, 2000.

Vargas Machuca, Bernardo de. *Milicia y descripción de las Indias*. Madrid: Pedro Madrigal, 1599.

Vargas Ugarte, Rubén. *Biblioteca Peruna I*. Lima: Tall. Tip. de la Empresa Periodística La Prensa, 1935.

Vázquez de Espinosa, Antonio. *Compendio y descripción de las Indias Occidentales*. Edited by Balbino Velasco Bayón. Madrid: Historia 16, 1992.

———. *Confessionario general, luz y guía del cielo para poderse confesar*. Madrid: Juan Goncales Impressor, 1623.

———. *Tratado verdadero del viaje y navegación*. 1623. Translated by Sara L. Lehman. Newark, DE: Juan de la Cuesta, 2008.

Velasco, Bartolomé. "El P. Antonio Vázquez de Espinosa en América." *Missionalia hispánica* 15 (1958): 169–217.

Velasco Bayon, Balbino. "Obispos Carmelitas en América." *Boletín de la Real Academia de la Historia* 195, no. 3 (1998): 415–50.

Venegas, Alejo. *Primera parte de las diferencias de libros que ay en el vniuerso.* Madrid: Alonso Gomez Impressor de Corte, 1569.

———. *Primera parte de las diferencias de libros que ay en el universo.* Toledo, 1546. Facsimile edition. Edited by Daniel Eisenberg. Barcelona: Puvill Libros, 1983.

Verástique, Bernardino. *Michoacán and Eden: Vasco de Quiroga and the Evangelization of Western Mexico.* Austin: University of Texas Press, 2000.

Vermij, Rienk. "Subterranean Fire: Changing Theories of the Earth During the Renaissance." *Early Science and Medicine* 3, no. 4 (1998): 323–47.

Vermuelen, Hans F. *Before Boas: The Genesis of Ethnography and Ethnology in the German Enlightenment.* Lincoln: University of Nebraska Press, 2015.

Verner, Lisa. *The Epistemology of the Monstrous in the Middle Ages.* New York: Routledge, 2005.

Vespucci, Amerigo. *Cartas de viaje.* Edited by Luciano Formisano. Translated by Ana María R. de Aznar. Madrid: Alianza Editorial, 1986.

———. *Der Mundus Novus des Amerigo Vespucci: Text, Übersetzung und Kommentar.* Translated by Robert Wallisch. Vienna: Austrian Academy of Sciences Press, 2012.

———. *Mundus Novus: Letter to Lorenzo Pietro di Medici.* 1503. Translated by George Tyler Northup. Princeton: Princeton University Press, 1916.

Vetancurt, Agustín de. *Teatro mexicano: Descripción breve de los sucesos ejemlares, historicos, politicos, militares, y religiosas del nuevo mundo.* Mexico City: M. de Benavides, Viuda de J. de Ribera, 1698.

Von Henneberg, Josephine. "Saint Francesca Romana and Guardian Angels in Baroque Art." *Religion and the Arts* 2 (1998): 467–87.

Walsham, Alexandra. "Catholic Reformation and the Cult of Angels in Early Modern England." In *Conversations with Angels: Essays Towards a History of Spiritual Communication, 1100–1700,* edited by Joad Raymond, 273–94. New York: Palgrave Macmillan, 2011.

———. "The Reformation and the 'Disenchantment of the World' Reassessed." *Historical Journal* 51, no. 2 (2008): 497–528.

Wandel, Lee Palmer. *The Eucharist in the Reformation: Incarnation and Liturgy.* Cambridge: Cambridge University Press, 2006.

Warner, Marina. *Alone of All Her Sex: The Myth and the Cult of the Virgin Mary.* 2nd ed. Oxford: Oxford University Press, 2013.

Waters, David. *The Iberian Bases of the English Art of Navigation in the Sixteenth Century.* Coimbra: Junta de Investigações do Ultramar-Lisboa, 1970.

Waterworth, J., ed. and trans. *The Canons and Decrees of the Sacred and Ecumenical Council of Trent.* London: Dolman, 1848.

Weber, Alison. "Literature by Women Religious in Early Modern Catholic Europe and the New World." In *The Ashgate Research Companion to Women and Gender in Early Modern Europe,* edited by Allyson M. Poska, Jane Couchman, and Katherine A. McIver, 33–51. Abingdon: Routledge, 2013.

———. *Teresa of Avila and the Rhetoric of Femininity.* Princeton: Princeton University Press, 1996.

Wey Gómez, Nicolás. *The Tropics of Empire: Why Columbus Sailed South to the Indies.* Cambridge: MIT Press, 2008.

Williams, Glyndwr. *Voyages of Delusion: The Quest for the Northwest Passage.* New Haven: Yale University Press, 2003.

Withers, Charles W. J. "Reporting, Mapping, Trusting: Making Geographical Knowledge in the Late Seventeenth Century." *Isis* 90, no. 3 (1999): 497–521.

Worster, Donald. *Shrinking the Earth: The Rise and Decline of American Abundance*. Oxford: Oxford University Press, 2016.

Xavier, Ângela Barreto, and Ines G. Županov. *Catholic Orientalism: Portuguese Empire, Indian Knowledge (16th–18th Centuries)*. Oxford: Oxford University Press, 2014.

Xavier, Francis. *The Letters and Instructions of Francis Xavier*. Translated by Joseph Costelloe. St. Louis, MO: Institute of Jesuit Sources, 1992.

Ximénez, Francisco. *Quatro libros de la naturaleza y virtudes de las plantas y animales que estan receuidos en el uso de la medicina en la Nueva España*. Mexico City: Casa de la Viuda de Diego Lopez Davalos, 1615.

Ximénez Samaniego, José. *Relación de la vida de la V. Madre Sor María de Jesús*. Madrid: Imprenta de la Causa de la V. Madre, 1762.

Yates, Frances. *The Occult Philosophy in the Elizabethan Age*. London: Routledge, 2001.

Zamorano, Rodrigo. *Compendio del arte de navegar*. Seville: Casa de Ioan de Leon, 1588.

Zárate Salmerón, Gerónimo. "*Relaciones de todas las cosas que en el Nuevo-Mexico se han visto y sabido [. . .] desde el año de 1538 hasta el de 1626 por padre Gerónimo Zárate Salmerón*." In *Documentos para la historia de Mexico*, 3–55. Mexico City: Vicente García Torres, 1856.

Županov, Ines G. *Missionary Tropics: The Catholic Frontier in India (16th–17th Centuries)*. Ann Arbor: University of Michigan Press, 2005.

Index

Acosta, José de, 24, 60, 87, 119, 123, 132–33
  on flood zoology 123–24, 132–37
  Historia natural y moral de las Indias, 119, 131, 133–34
Adam
  knowledge and the Fall, 16, 67, 79–80, 139, 144–45, 164n25
  naming the animals, 79–80, 145, 150, 153–54
alchemy, 9, 50
alumbrados, 61
Ambrose of Milan, 120, 164n25, 174n56
America, 6–8, 59–60
  conquest of, 96, 127, 144
  discovery of, 2–4, 7, 104, 126
  invention of, 23, 83–84
  as terrestrial paradise, 106–7, 114–15, 121
  study of, 94–94, 123, 133 (*see also* expeditions; questionnaires)
Amerindians
  animism, 15, 111
  characteristics and perceptions of, 60–61, 96, 127
  the humanity of, 122–24 (*see also* Sublimis Deus)
  origin of, 108, 124, 142–45
Ana María de San José, 76
Angels, 47–78

angelology, 68, 76
  communication and knowledge, 67–9
  devotion to, 68
  transportation of humans and animals, 76, 135–40, 149–54
  See also Michael (Archangel)
Animals, 119–57
  extinction, 136–37, 145, 156
  geographical distribution, 138
  migration, 123, 135–37
  mutation, 155
  in the New World, 125–29 (*see also* Armadillo; Bison; Lizard; Llama)
  species, 119 (*see also* classification, biological, and of humans)
anthropocentrism, Christian, 31–35, 162
Antonio de la Ascensión, 90–91, 107, 116
Apian, Peter, 55
  Cosmographicus Liber, 55
Apostles, in the New World
  Santiago (Saint James), 73, 112
  Thomas the Apostle, 100
  Twelve Apostles of New Spain, 59, 72
  See also evangelization; spiritual conquest
Aquinas, Thomas, 132, 138, 142, 143
  on astrology and the occult, 42
  authority of scripture, 140–42

Aquinas, Thomas (*continued*)
  on the fifth argument for God's existence, 138, 165n50
  influence on the Catholic Church, 29, 123
  Summa Theologiae, 42, 138
Araucanian wars, 96–97
Aristotle, 22, 32–33, 133, 166n86
Armadillo, 119, *131*, 155
Asia, 81–82, 121
astrology, 9, 41–43
astronomy, 29, 42–44
Atlantic World, 5–6, 9–10
Augustine, 11, 93, 174n56
  on angels, 135–37
  curiositas, 8
  geographic distribution of animals, 135
  on monsters, 148

Bacon, Francis, 5
baptism, 38–39
Bartolomé de las Casas, 122
Black Legend, the, 9, 82–83, 160, 164n30
Bellarmino, Roberto, 40, 111
  De ascensione mentis in Deum per scalas rerum creatorum, 57
Benavides, Alonso de, 49, 53, 69, 70–77, 90, 116
  Memorial, 53, 75, 91, 169n28
Bernardino de Sahagún, 62, 164n19
bilocation, 49, 52, 69–75
Bireley, Robert, 44, 103
Bison, *127*
book of nature, 11–19, 33, 62
Botero, Giovanni, 44, 87
  Relationi universali, 44, 87
Buffon, Georges-Louis Leclerc, Comte de., 151, 155–56

Cañizares-Esguerra, Jorge, 160, 164n30
Cárdenas, Juan de, 138
Carmelites, 100–115
  discalced carmelites, 100, 103, 107–14
Casa de la Contratación, 5, 35–36, 90
Castañega, Martín de, 60
Catholic mission, 14–15, 48, 76–78, 102, 107, 122, 152
  and global science, 7–8, 162
Catholic Reformation, 9–10, 19–20, 29–31, 161–62
celestial bodies, 41–43, 55

Cervantes, Fernando, 60
Chile, 90–97, 107
Christian neopythagoreanism, 31, 57
Cieza de León, Pedro de, 121, *122*
Cisneros, Francisco Jiménez de, 10
classical traditions. *See* Aristotle; climate; Mela, Pomponio
classification, biological, and of humans, 123, 125, 148, 151
climate
  theory of climate zones, 121, 128, 137
Cobo, Barnabé, 119, 151
Colleges, 132–33, 122, 144
  Colegio de Santa Cruz, 62
colonialism, and creation of knowledge 5, 20, 82, 90, 161–62
Congregatio de Auxiliis, 140–41
Consejo de las Indias, 5, 90–91, 94–95, 130
Cortés, Hernán, 99, 144
cosmography, 6, 22–23 28–30, 50, 62–63
Council of Trent, 9–10, 14, 19, 32, 35, 41–43
  See also sacraments; transubstantiation
creation, 28, 57, 64–66
cross, sacred, 59, 100

Darwin, Charles, 21, 120, 137
Dee, John, 48, 67
demonology, 60
  See also Devil
descriptive geography (descripción), 79–117
desert, 98, 111–13
  spiritual retreat, 113–14
devil, 42, 60–61
discalced reforms, 10, 102, 113–14
Ditchfield, Simon, 9–10, 112
Diversity, in nature, 7, 24, 28, 47, 58, 134–57
  See also America: as terrestrial paradise
Dominicans, 123, 139–44

Eden, Garden of, 7, 16, 39–40, 80, 107–14
Eliade, Mircea, 84, 116
Elijah (biblical prophet), 101, 109–13, 115
Empiricism, 5, 8, 11–12, 83
Enciso, Martín Fernández de, 85, 94
enthusiasm, religious, 12
eschatology, 59–60
Espinosa, Antonio Vázquez de, 24, 80–81, 100–106
  Compendio y descripción de las Indias Occidentales, 100–101

ethnography, 86, 173n33
Eucharist, 34–38
evangelization, 14–15, 20, 25, 53, 72
exegesis, 24, 119–46
expeditions, 2, 65, 90–91, 129–30
experience (scientific authority), 11, 22, 64–65, 82, 86–87, 140–42

Fernández de Enciso, Martín, 85, 94
　Suma de geographía, 85, 94
Ferrer de Valdecebro, Andrés, 121
　Gobierno general, moral y político, 121
Ferrer Maldonado, Lorenzo, 39
　Imagen del mundo, 39
flood zoology, 119–57
foreknowledge, God's 141–53
four elements, 33–34
　water, 38–39
　earth, 40
Franciscans, 14–15, 49–54, 58–60, 72–73
　and secular knowledge, 62–63
　See also Francis of Assisi
Francis of Assisi, 62, 76
free will, in Christianity, 40–44, 152

Galileo Affair, 9, 153–54
García, Gregorio, 2, 24, 119, 139, 141, 143
　Origen de los Indios, 124, 142
Gaukroger, Stephen, 8, 83
Geographia sacra, 7, 84
geography, 79–92
Ginés Rocamora y Torrano, 31–34
　Esphera del universo, 33
Giorgio, Francesco, 57, 68
Girava, Gerónimo, 87
Godínez, Miguel, 12
Gómara, Francisco López de, 55, 127, 127–28
González de Salas, José Antonio, 79–80, 145
　Compendio geográphico i histórico, 79–80
Granada, Luis de, 16, 65, 67, 152, 166n70
Guadalupe (monastery), 93, 98–99

Habsburg Monarchy, 5, 10, 20, 29, 82, 107
Hale, Matthew, 155
Harkness, Deborah, 67
Harley, John, 89, 96
Harrison, Peter, 11, 179n19
heaven and hell, 39–41, 56
heavens (celestial spheres), 55–57

heresy, 10, 60–62, 73, 102
Hernández, Francisco, 2, 128, 130
Heylyn, Peter, 45, 173n27
Hieronymites, 92–93, 97–99
Hispaniola, 108, 178n9

Immaculate Conception, 23, 48, 52
Index of Prohibited Books, 14, 16, 42–43
　Quiroga's Index, 9, 42
　Valdéz's Index, 16
indigenous peoples. *See* Amerindians
Ingoli, Francesco, 40, 91, 103
Inquisition, 9, 53, 61, 71, 104
Isidoro de Seville, 36, 55, 148
　Etymologies, 36, 55, 148
itinerary (geographical method), 89, 95, 100n90, 116
　See also descriptive geography (descripción)

Japan, 76, 81, 174n37
Jesuits, 8, 16, 72, 82, 132–41
Jesús María, Juana de, 74

Kamen, Henry, 9
Kircher, Athanasius, 69, 154–55
　Arca Noe, 155
knowledge, 21–22
　and Catholicism, 1–11
　See also science

Ladder, to God, 1, 19, 57–58, 68, 159
Libellus de Medicinalibus Indorum Herbis (botanical codex), 8
Lizard, 128, 129
Llama, 122, 145, 147
Long, Charles, 84, 161
López de Velasco, Juan, 95, 130
　Geografía y descripción universal de las Indias, 95
Loyola, Ignacio de, 10, 16, 131–32
Luther, Martin (Reformation), 10, 12, 61

Machiavelli, Niccolò, 43–44
　Il Principe, 43
MacLean, Katie, 72
Mancall, Peter, 6
maps, 28, 59, 64, 81–97
Martínez, Enrico, 42–45
　Reportorio de los tiempos y historia natural desta Nueua España, 42–45

Martyr d'Anghera, Peter, 121, 126–27, 178n9
   De orbe novo decades, 126–27
marvels and curiosities, 47, 60, 128, 148
Mary, 35–38, 54, 66, 89–101
   Black Madonna, 98–99
   Marian devotion, 23, 29, 31, 35
   Stella Maris, 36
medicine, 2, 4–5
Medina, Pedro de, 27–28, 30, 40
   Arte de navegar, 27
   Libro de la verdad, 27
Mela, Pomponio, 28, 79–80
Mendoza, Juan González de, 81–82, 174n49
Merton, Robert K (Merton Thesis), 11, 165n39
metals and minerals, 15, 56, 96, 134
   gold, 60, 96
Michael (Archangel), 76–77
Mills, Kenneth, 93
monogemism 91–92, 103, 108, 117, 121–22, 142
monsters, 147–49
   Mount Carmel, 101
   in the New World 109–15
Moya, Juan Pérez de, 66
   Varia historia de sanctas e ilustres mujeres, 66
mysticism, 12, 23, 47–78, 65–67, 78

natural history 86, 120, 124–25, 138
   in America, 128–30, 157
natural theology, 12–15
navigation, 28, 35–39, 56, 139
New France, 177n142
New Mexico, 48, 53, 69–77
New Spain, Viceroyalty, 62, 72, 77, 100, 103
New World. *See* America
Nicaragua, 60, 106
Nicholas Gallicus, of France, 113
Nieremberg, Juan Eusebio, 7, 16, 48, 68, 151, 154
   Curiosa y oculta filosofía, 16
   Historia naturae, 16
Noah's Ark, 24, 121–22, 126–27, 131–36, 145, 153–56

Ocaña, Diego de, 24, 92–95, 97, 100–107
   Relación del viaje de Fray Diego de Ocaña por el Nuevo Mundo, 92, 97
occult, 22, 42, 48, 67, 166n87

O'Gorman, Edmundo, 23
Omnímoda (bull of 1552), 103
omnipotence, 141, 152–53
Oré, Luis Jerónimo de, 14–15, 166n70
   Símbolo católico indiano, 14–15
Ortelius, Abraham, 64, 65, 81
   Theatrum orbis terrarum, 64, 65, 81
Ottoman Empire, 35, 74
Ovando y Godoy, Juan de, 94, 130
Oviedo y Valdés, Gonzalo Fernández de, 128–29
   Historia general y natural de las Indias, 128–29
   De la natural historia de las Indias, 128–29

Padrón Real, 85
Padrón, Ricardo, 6, 85, 89, 174n52
Pallas, Gerónymo, 109
Paul V (pope), 68, 141
Peru, Viceroyalty, 93
Philip II (king), 10, 64, 85, 93
Philip IV (king), 48, 52, 74
Philippines, 15, 90
Pius V (pope), 35
plants, 86, 123, 131–47, 166n87, 179n42
Poor Clares, 52
Portuondo, María, 6, 81, 133
predestination, 29, 40, 141, 155
   Prieto, Andrés, 8, 133
production of space, the, 83
   Henri Lefebvre, 173n20
Propaganda Fide, 40, 91, 103–5
propaganda, religious, 29–31, 38, 45, 99–100, 117, 161
Protestantism, 9–11, 40, 61, 73, 91
   sola scriptura, 41
   scriptural literalism, 11
   See also Luther, Martin
providence, in Christianity 137–39
Ptolemy, 54, 85–86, 91, 173n28

Questionnaires, 62, 85, 94–95, 129–30

Rada, Martín de, 90
Relaciones geográficas de Indias, 85, 94–95, 130
Rodríguez de León, Juan, 4
   El predicador de las gentes, 4
Román y Zamora, Hieronymo, 120
Rowe, Erin, 73

Sabunde, Ramón, 13–14
  Theologia naturalis, 13–14
sacralization, of places, 23, 79–157, 111
sacraments, 19–31, 38–41, 60, 161
Sacrobosco, Johannes (John) de, 31, 54
  De sphaera, 31, 54
Santiago (Saint James), 73, 112
Satan. *See* devil
scholasticism, 12, 54, 141–42, 156–57
science, 22, 166n86
  early modern, 2–4, 86–87, 132, 160
  empirical practices, 5–25, 62, 85–87, 130–33, 151–52, 159
  and empire, 4–5, 82, 89, 163n8
  and religion, 8–9, 20, 81, 164n25
  as state secret, 81
Scientific Revolution, 5, 6, 9, 125, 164n30
scripture, 13–17, 15, 32–33, 108–9, 124–25, 134, 164n25
  See also Adam; flood zoology; Noah's Ark
Smith, Jonathan Z., 21
Smith, Pamela, 50
Solomon's temple, 58–59
Sor María de Jesús de Ágreda, 47–78
  La mística ciudad de Dios, 49, 53–54, 65–66
  Tratado sobre la redondez de la tierra, 23, 48–50, 54–60
  Lady in Blue (*Dama Azul*), 49, 52–53, 71–77
soul
  the human soul, 19, 43–47
  three essential functions, 32
Spaniards, 58
  compared with classic civilizations, 2–3
  new 'chosen people', 110–12
Spanish imperialism, 5, 10, 29, 84–85, 161
spiritual conquest, 15, 52, 73–76, 107–8
  See also evangelization
stones, 111–12
Stroumsa, Guy, 7
Suárez, Francisco de, 68
Sublimis Deus (papal bull of 1537), 61, 142

symbolic vocabulary, 21
Syria, Pedro de, 38
  Arte de la verdadera nauegacion, 38

Teixeira, Luis, 81–82
Tenochtitlan, 60
Teresa de Ávila, 10, 12, 50–51, 72–73, 75, 102, 113–14
Thevet, André, 62
typology, biblical 59–60, 108–13, 115
Tomás de Jesús, 104, 114
  De procuranda salute omnium gentium, 104
Torquemada, Juan de, 59–60
  Monarquía indiana, 59–60
transubstantiation, 34
trinity, 19, 31–32
Turner, Victor, 21
Tweed, Thomas, 84, 162

Urban VIII (pope), 74, 91

Valadés, Diego, 63
  Rhetorica christiana, 63
Valladolid debate, 122, 134
Vargas Machuca, Bernardo de, 88, 89
  Milicia y descripción de las Indias, 88, 89
Venegas, Alejo, 11, 17, 18, 32, 87, 144
Vespucci, Amerigo, 125–26, 178n7

Weber, Alison, 50
West Indies. *See* America
Women, in Spain, 50–52, 66, 72–76
world machine (*machina mundi*), 4, 47, 133–34
Xavier, Francis, 61

Ximénez, Francisco, 1–2
  Quatro libros de la naturaleza, 1

Zamorano, Rodrigo, 56, 36
  Compendio del arte de navegar, 56, 36
Zoology, 124–30

www.ingramcontent.com/pod-product-compliance
Lightning Source LLC
Chambersburg PA
CBHW032337300426
44109CB00041B/1082